Organizations and te

What is distinctive about new technology? How has it come to be used in particular ways in organizations? What objectives are set by managers and other employees? Which strategies guide its adoption? These are the kinds of issues this book examines. David Preece looks at the social and managerial processes underpinning the adoption of new technology. Expanding on *Managing the Adoption of New Technology*, David Preece has thoroughly updated his study to examine the key issues of choice, flexibility and change both within and without the organization.

Four detailed case studies illustrate the main stages of initiation, progression and feasibility, investment decision, and planning and systems design, as well as the central issues of strategy, objectives and employee participation. Changes which have occurred since the earlier stage of adoption in the 1980s are highlighted.

This text will be of interest to students and researchers in management, organization analysis, information systems and related fields.

David Preece is Co-Director of the Management and Decision Support Research Unit and Senior Lecturer in Organization Analysis at the University of Portsmouth Business School. He is author of *Managing the Adoption of New Technology* (Routledge, 1989).

The Routledge Series in the Management of Technology

Series editors: David Preece, *Portsmouth Business School* and John Bessant, *Brighton Business School*

This series offers groundings in the central elements of the Management of Technology syllabus. Designed specifically to introduce students to the area, they present stimulating approaches to a range of technology issues, placing them in the context of management problems and solutions. Using case studies to illustrate the topics together with summaries on the key points, these texts can build together to cover a management of technology course.

The series will be an excellent resource for advanced undergraduates, postgraduates and MBA students.

Forthcoming title:

Technology and Quality
Patrick Dawson, University of Adelaide

Creative Technological Change
Ian McLoughlin, Brunel University

New Perspectives on Management and Innovation
Ian McLoughlin and Martin Harris (eds), Brunel University

Organizations and technical change

Strategy, objectives and involvement

David Preece

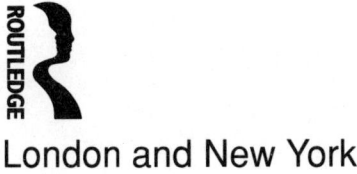

London and New York

First published 1995
by Routledge
11 New Fetter Lane, London EC4P 4EE

Simultaneously published in the USA and Canada
by Routledge
29 West 35th Street, New York, NY 10001

© 1995 David Preece

Typeset in Times by
Ponting–Green Publishing Services, Chesham, Bucks
Printed and bound in Great Britain by
T.J. Press (Padstow) Ltd, Padstow, Cornwall

All rights reserved. No part of this book may be
reprinted or reproduced or utilized in any form or by
any electronic, mechanical, or other means, now known
or hereafter invented, including photocopying and
recording, or in any information storage and retrieval
system, without permission in writing from the
publishers.

Every attempt has been made to seek copyright permission
for the figures and tables used in this book.
Copyright holders should contact Patrick Proctor at
Routledge, London, with any queries.

British Library Cataloguing in Publication Data
A catalogue record for this book is available from the
British Library

Library of Congress Cataloging in Publication Data
Preece, David, A.
    Organizations and technical change: strategy, objectives,
and involvement / David Preece.
        p.   cm. – (The Routledge series in the management
of technology)
    Includes bibliographical references and index.
    ISBN 0–415–12514–6. – ISBN 0–415–10186–7 (pbk.)
    1. Technology–Management. 2. Technology–
Management–Case studies. 3. Technological innovations–
Management. 4. Technological innovations–Management–
Case studies. I. Title. II. Series.
    T49.5.P74   1995
    658.4'062–dc20   94–34917
                                                                 CIP

ISBN 0–415–12514–6 (hbk)
ISBN 0–415–10186–7 (pbk)

For Mo, Jamie and Laura

Contents

List of figures	x
List of tables	xi
Preface	xii
Acknowledgements	xiv

1 Introduction 1
   Outline of the book 12
   A note on methodology 12

Part I Adopting new technology

2 Adopting new technology: managerial strategies 17
   Definitions and problems 18
   Why should managers have a strategy for new technology adoption? 19
   Do managers have strategies for new technology adoption? 23
   Where does that leave us? 25
   New technology and organizational strategy 26
   Strategies at the technology level 29
   Labour strategies 33
   Conclusion 37

3 Why is new technology introduced? 39
   Financial and economic objectives 40
   Business and technical objectives 52
   Social and organizational objectives 60
   Why studying objectives is not a straightforward matter 74

Conclusion	83
4 Adopting new technology: processes of involvement	**85**
Managers and staff specialists	86
Employees	91
Conclusion	119

Part II Case studies in new technology adoption

5 Bramley Building Society	**123**
The organization and its context	123
The technological changes	130
New technology objectives	131
The process of adoption of new technology	133
Managing the social and organizational aspects of adoption	136
Key developments since 1986/7	140
6 Park Hill Building Society	**150**
The organization	150
The technological changes	158
New technology objectives	162
The process of adoption of new technology	164
Managing the social and organizational aspects of adoption	166
Key developments since 1986/7	168
7 Don Ltd	**172**
The organization and its context	172
The technological changes	180
New technology objectives	181
The process of adoption of new technology	182
Managing the social and organizational aspects of adoption	186
Key developments since 1986/7	190
8 Meadows & Butler	**195**
The organization and its context	195
The technological changes	198
New technology objectives	199
The process of adoption of new technology	203
Managing the social and organizational aspects of adoption	209

Key developments since 1986/7	210
9 Conclusion	218
Issues raised by the case studies	218
Adopting new technology: social, managerial and organizational processes	226
Notes	236
Bibliography	258
Index	274

Figures

1	The concept of an engineering system	6
2	Stages in new technology adoption and introduction	7
3	Whipp and Clark's framework of innovation	27
4	Worker reactions to technical change	101
5	The emerging bank culture?	142
6	Park Hill Building Society: part organization chart	152
7	Park Hill Building Society: branch network management hierarchy	157
8	Don Ltd: old grading scheme for shop-floor workers	175
9	Don Ltd: old grading scheme for staff	175
10	Don Ltd: new grading scheme for staff and workers	175
11	Don Ltd: part organization chart, 1973–81	178
12	Don Ltd: part organization chart, January 1982 to date	179
13	Meadows & Butler: part organization chart	197

Tables

1	Examples of new technology	3
2	Framework for manufacturing strategy development	30
3	New technology objectives: research findings	39
4	Basis of cost justification of CAD	45
5	Factors affecting employee participation in technological change	97
6	Country-specific factors and their influence on participation levels in particular member states	98
7	Theoretical perspectives on participative job redesign in the office	114
8	Bramley Building Society: branch office numbers, 1975–86	124
9	Bramley Building Society: staff numbers, 1975–85	124
10	Building Societies, 1975–91	126
11	Park Hill Building Society: branch office numbers, 1980–7	151
12	Park Hill Building Society: staff numbers, 1975–87	151
13	Park Hill Building Society: staff employed at Head Office and in branch offices, 1975–87	152
14	Meadows & Butler: CAD cost justification	206

Preface

This book is a study of the adoption of new technology by business organizations. The adoption phase precedes introduction, and provides the main opportunity for the actors involved to design and shape the purposes for which, and the strategies through which, the technology will be utilized. There is, then, a degree of choice in these matters (in part connected with the distinctive characteristics of new technology) and one of the major objectives of the book is to see whether, and, if so, to what extent and in what ways, this choice has in practice been exercised by the people involved. It is equally of interest to discover who does not get involved, and why certain people are excluded.

The focus is upon managing new technology adoption; 'managing' is interpreted broadly to refer not just to what people who are called managers do and say, but to refer also to other employees, such as engineers, technical specialists, personnel specialists, computer specialists and staff association representatives. It is a key premise of the book that in order to understand the process of new technology adoption it is necessary to locate that process within the relevant social, political and economic contexts (both internal and external to the organization). A slightly different way to put this would be to observe that one can expect to find organizational change which does not involve technological change, but that the reverse is highly unlikely to hold true. Four main stages of new technology adoption are identified, and these provide junctures at which there is the possibility for organizational actors to become involved and to shape outcomes.

The analysis and literature informing the book are drawn from a variety of subjects, but a sociological orientation has the strongest influence and provides the 'glue' which binds the argument together.

The first section of the book, consisting of three chapters, critically reviews the existing literature on new technology objectives, strategies and employee involvement; the second section of four chapters incorporates four case studies conducted by the author in manufacturing and financial services organizations. The key findings are brought together in a concluding chapter.

The book began life as an updated version of an earlier book of mine – *Managing the Adoption of New Technology* – but fairly quickly turned out to be much more than that, so much so that hardly a single sentence has been left unaltered from the previous book, a good deal of new material has been added and a lot of the earlier material omitted. The case study chapters have also been substantially rewritten, and a new section has been added on pertinent events since the earlier period of research.

The book will be of interest to a wide-ranging readership, including undergraduate and postgraduate students of engineering, IT/IS, Personnel Management, Computer Science, Organization Analysis, Business Administration, Technology Management and Organization Development/Change, as well as managers, trade unionists and other practitioners interested in the social, economic and organizational processes connected with new technology adoption.

Acknowledgements

My major debt is to my wife, Maureen, for her patience and support whilst I shut myself away in the loft with my papers, books and notes, and she was elsewhere, inside or outside the house, with Laura and Jamie (and, indeed, other children on many occasions!). Without her understanding the book simply would not have emerged. I am also indebted to my colleagues at the University of Portsmouth, in the Business School and the Management and Decision Support Unit in particular, and to my MBA and Business Studies students for their observations and feedback on the earlier book. Francesca Weaver of Routledge provided valuable editorial advice and Jane Bower's comments at an early stage were most helpful. Michael Wood, Jill Rockensuss and Pat Mays played key technical roles: Michael through helping me to overcome my deficiencies in word-processing, and Jill and Pat through typing some parts of the early drafts. Finally I would like to thank the staff at the four case study organizations who so freely gave of their time for my interviews and who commented on the relevant draft chapters.

Acknowledgement is due to the undermentioned sources for permission to reproduce the following figures and tables: Cambridge University Press for Figure 1; Pinter Publishers for Figure 3; Sage Publications for Figure 4; the European Foundation for the Improvement of Living and Working Conditions for Figure 5; Macmillan Publishers for Table 2; Sage Publications for Tables 5 and 6; Martin Beirne for Table 7.

D.P.

Chapter 1
Introduction

Why does new technology come to be used in organizations in particular ways, influenced by the particular objectives and strategies developed by certain people? The central thesis of the book is that the key to understanding this is to study what happens *before* the new technology comes to have a physical presence within the organization. This adoption phase, as I have termed it, presents a range of choices for the actors involved with respect to a number of matters relating to the form of new technology utilization which occurs after implementation. As has been implied here, however, this choice is not so obviously available to those organizational actors who, for one reason or another, are not involved. (Of course, their wishes may be taken into account by those who are involved, but that is another matter, and is certainly at best an indirect form of involvement.)

The book explores these issues through two main routes. Part I, consisting of three chapters, provides an overview and commentary upon what the recent research record tells us has been happening when new technology has been adopted in organizations in the areas of, respectively, strategy, objectives and employee involvement. Part II consists of four case study chapters which provide a detailed examination of new technology adoption in two building societies and two engineering companies. Each chapter considers these organizations' early experience of new technology adoption during the 1980s, as well as subsequent adoptions during the 1990s. The concluding chapter attempts to draw together the main findings and issues identified by the primary and secondary data collection processes, and presents some pointers for further research into, and the management of, new technology adoption.

Before we move on to these considerations in the following chapters, however, it is necessary first of all to offer an explanation of our understanding of the nature of new technology, of the adoption phase, and of the contexts within which new technology adoption occurs. The chapter concludes with a section on methodology.

In using the term 'new technology' we refer to microelectronics and microprocessors as computing technologies, defining the latter as a 'miniature integrated electrical circuit on a wafer of semi-conducting silicon or gallium arsenide which performs functions of a computer's central processing unit'.[1] To date they have found their main applications in the following areas:

1 Production/engineering/design machinery or processes (sometimes termed 'Advanced Manufacturing Technology', or AMT).
2 Information capture, storage, transmission, analysis and retrieval ('Information Technology', or IT), whether allied to AMT or used separately in the office environment in manufacturing companies, or used in non-manufacturing organizations, or, indeed, the home.
3 The provision of services to customers, clients or patients.
4 Products themselves, that is, the new technology is the product.

See Table 1 for an illustration of the varieties of new technology captured by the above.

Of course, there is some overlap between a number of the above categories, and the list is by no means exhaustive, but it is sufficient to illustrate the varieties of new technology available. In the chapters which follow we will be looking at applications of the first three categories, that is to say, new technology as applied in design and production processes, in communication and administration, and in service provision; we will not be examining new technology as a product, however.

A few points of clarification are necessary. The first one is that we will be studying only the social, economic and political processes surrounding new technology adoption *into* organizations; there is no consideration here of the processes connected with the invention, design and development of the new technology in the first place. (The closest we will get to this is where software is amended or developed internally within the organization.) Putting it another way, to all intents and purposes the computer hardware and software are taken as given and as being generally available to any organization which can afford it – this is one of our starting points.[2] Secondly, it should be borne in mind that there may be ways other than new technology through which managers can achieve their objectives: a 'magical waving of the new technology wand' at a problem or challenge is by

Table 1 Examples of new technology

Advanced manufacturing technology
Computer numerical control (CNC) machine tools
Robotics
Computer-aided design/draughting (CAD)
Flexible manufacturing systems (FMS)
Computer-integrated manufacturing (CIM)
Computer-aided production planning and control
Materials requirements planning (MRP I)
Manufacturing resource planning (MRP II)

Information technology
Word-processing/personal computers
Intelligent knowledge-based systems
Mainframe, mini, microcomputers, used in a stand-alone mode or networked
Tele-conferencing
Video-conferencing

Service provision
Cash dispensers (or automated teller machines, ATMs)
Electronic funds transfer (EFT)
Electronic data interchange (EDI)
Electronic point of sale (EPOS)
Teletext
Patient monitoring systems

Products
Pocket calculators
Electronic games
Digital watches
Programmes for washing machines, television sets, etc.

no means always going to be the best solution: organizational changes *per se* may be sufficient in themselves, albeit an investigation into the possibility of introducing new technology (that is, the beginnings of an adoption process) could have been the spark which led to that conclusion.

It will be apparent that the 'new' in new technology does not mean 'recent or very recent in time', for, clearly, on this definition some 'new' technology would be quite old; NC and CNC machines, for example, having been around since the 1940s and '50s. The reference is to microelectronics and microprocesses, but in practice it is also to the fact that new applications are being developed all the time, and the take-up rate of various forms of new technology is expanding continuously as more organizations become aware of new technology's potential.[3] It has been argued by Friedman and Cornford, for example, that computer systems have undergone three main phases of development: from their beginnings in universities and defence industries in the 1940s, dominated by hardware problems, and lasting until the mid-1960s, through the second phase, which lasted from then until the early 1980s, and was dominated by software development, to the third phase, which is centred upon user relations. The coming fourth phase, they argue, is likely to be focused upon exploiting the strategic potential of new technology, which will be realized through installing computer networks, i.e. telecommunications between different people, offices, organizations and locations.[4]

On the basis of the above clarification of the meaning of new technology, let us now explain why our focus in the book is upon the adoption as against the introduction phase. There are two main reasons. First, the adoption phase has been neglected and under-researched by scholars of technology management and deployment; the great majority of writers interested in the social, economic, political and managerial issues and consequences associated with new technology utilization in organizations have concentrated upon what happens after the new technology has been introduced into the organization. In many respects they have been correct to do so, for if one wishes to understand the consequences or 'outputs' of the process, that is where one must look. However, it is to neglect the formative (and, in some cases at least, constraining) influence of what has happened before that phase is reached: this is where the present book comes in, and provides the second main reason for the focus which it takes.

The starting point is the observation that new technology is inherently flexible, and therefore potentially allows of a wider range of choice with regard to how, and for what purposes, it is employed in the organization. This flexibility is a result of four main characteristics:

1 Its compactness or very small size. Compare an old, non-new technology mainframe computer of 1960s vintage, which took up the space of a large room yet had a processing power considerably less than that of a modern microcomputer.

Introduction 5

2 Its low energy use, and hence low per-unit running costs.
3 The decreasing cost of new technology in relation to processing power – a trend which has continued for a number of years.
4 Its software, or programs, which are, of course, reprogrammable.

In addition, in an environment where a number of organizations are moving to open systems and away from an environment where they are 'locked into' the product(s) of a particular computer manufacturer, flexibility is also coming from this ability to interlink different makes and models of computers, both within and across the same and different organizations via telecommunications and area networks.

The upshot of this flexibility is that the actual way in which the new technology is utilized in the organization has much to do with social (e.g. decision-making) processes within (and, occasionally, outside, as we shall see in the case study chapters) that organization. In other words, social choice is important, and this immediately alerts us to the observation that it is important to know *who* is making that choice: who gets involved in the 'design space' which is opened up by the new technology? At the same time, I do not wish to imply that 'anything goes' – that is, that new technology has no constraining influence upon matters such as working practices and skill requirements. I am not able to discuss here the variety of ways in which technology has been conceptualized over the years – the reader is referred to the literature for that purpose. Suffice it to say that, on the basis of my own and other people's work, I have found it helpful to employ a rather narrow definition, but one which is sensitive to the immediate people and job-related implications. This perspective on technology has been put most forcibly and effectively by Clark *et al.* through their concept of an *engineering system*, which sees all technologies as 'not just pieces of hardware and software, but systems based on certain engineering principles and composed of elements which are functionally arranged in certain ways' (see Figure 1).[5]

It will be seen that an engineering system has two primary and two secondary elements. The former is composed of an *architecture*, that is, the design principles and their functional arrangement, and the *technology*, i.e. hardware and software. The latter consists of the *dimensioning*, or the ways in which the system is adapted for a particular organization, and the *appearance* to the user of the engineering system. In a book on new technology *adoption* we shall not, of course, be looking at the relative impacts of the technology

6 Introduction

> **Primary elements**
>
> | Architecture | Technology |
> |---|---|
> | System principles | Hardware |
> | Overall system configuration | Software |
>
> **Secondary elements**
>
> Dimensioning
> Detailed design for a particular
> organizational setting
>
> Appearance
> Audible and visual characteristics
> Ergonomics
> Aesthetics

Figure 1 The concept of an engineering system
Source: J. Clark, I. McLoughlin, H. Rose and R. King (1988) *The Process of Technological Change*, Cambridge: Cambridge University Press, p. 14

per se (and the wider engineering system of which it forms a part) as against the influence of social choice, with respect to the 'technology-in-use', that is, post-introduction: Clark *et al.*'s work provides ample data on this. On the other hand, it will be possible, particularly in the case study chapters, to obtain a sense of whether technology is treated as an immutable, deterministic artefact (at one extreme), as having unrestrained plasticity (at the other), or whether it is seen as being located somewhere along this continuum (perhaps approximating to Clark *et al.*'s engineering system) by the actors involved in adopting the new technology. This, therefore, is to raise questions about the effects upon social processes and outcomes of the particular conceptualizations of technology held by particular actors within organizations – those who, for one reason or another, get involved in a meaningful way in new technology adoption.

In order to facilitate analysis, I have found it helpful to employ a framework which identifies seven stages in the two phases of new technology adoption and introduction: these are summarized in Figure 2.

Introduction 7

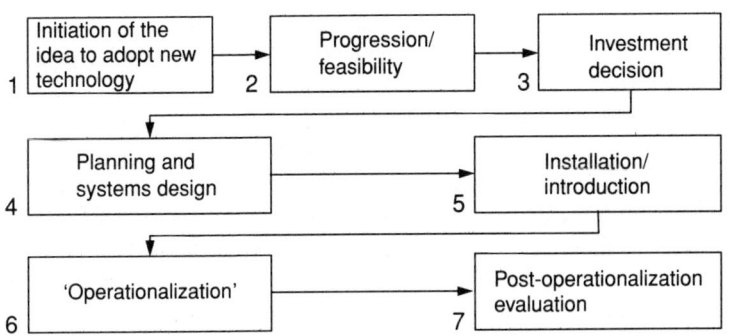

Figure 2 Stages in new technology adoption and introduction:
Key: Stages 1–4 = adoption phase
　　　Stages 5–7 = introduction phase
Note: A number of the stages may be iterative, and involve going back to an earlier stage before further progression ensues

The adoption phase consists, it will be noted, of four stages: initiation, progression/feasibility, the investment decision, and planning and systems design. It is only after events approximating to these stages have occurred that one can talk about the new technology being introduced into the organization, and we then, therefore, move on to the second phase, stages 5–7. I will briefly outline the adoption stages; the reader is referred to an earlier publication for details of the introduction phase.[6]

Initiation is concerned to identify whose idea it was to introduce some form of new technology into the organization, what that person's job is, where the idea came from (magazine, conference, competitors, technology supplier, etc.?), who else was involved (and why) at this early stage, etc. The premise is that people's different backgrounds, expertise and orientations will have a differential impact upon the way in which the new technology adoption is shaped from this point on, for example in terms of the objectives which are first tentatively set for the new technology introduction, and the type of strategy (assuming a strategy does develop) which is pursued. There are a range of possibilities with regard to the strategies and objectives which can and have been pursued, and, indeed, the concepts of strategy and objectives themselves require explication. These issues will be considered in detail in Chapters 2 and 3, and primary material will be presented in the four case study chapters. It is possible that the initiators will go on to become 'change agents', if they follow their idea through and help to manage the change process in organizational and social, as well as technological, terms.[7] I have been particularly interested to tease out the role of personnel/human resource specialists in the new technology adoption process: have they been initiators, for example, or have they had only marginal, if any, involvement after other people have already made the key decisions? Personnel specialists possess certain attributes which would appear to put them in a favourable position for acting as 'new technology change agents': their across-the-organization brief (i.e. not confined to a functional role within just one department) and their expertise and skill in people issues.[8]

The progression/feasibility stage involves the more detailed work which follows, assuming that the initial idea 'struck a chord' with other members of the organization who are in a position to influence events and take decisions. It can include, for example, searching for further information inside and outside the organization, perhaps drawing on software and hardware suppliers. It may also involve looking in more detail at what competitors are doing (even, perhaps, 'benchmarking' best practice, to borrow a term from the quality management literature).[9]

Stage 3, the investment decision, is an area which has been extensively discussed by finance specialists, and a range of techniques are available for assessing whether an organization should invest in technology or capital equipment. Many of the techniques, however, relate to technology of the non-new technology variety, and there is continuing debate about whether they are appropriate to new technology: some discussion of these matters will be found in Chapters 3 and 8. In any event, the focus in the present book is upon the social and political issues and processes which surround and impinge upon the 'supposedly rational' financial and economic decision. There appears, however, to be no getting away from the fact that, for the great majority of 'sponsors' of new technology introduction, a formal proposal has to be put before the senior management team or board: this key contingency creates its own problematics, as we shall see. It may be at this stage also that the new technology's objectives (or 'benefits') and costs are formally articulated for the first time – if for no other reason than that they have to be in order to be presented to the board. I certainly found these documents a rich source of data in some of my case study companies.

Finally, in terms of the adoption stages, planning and systems design, given that the go-ahead has been obtained to invest in some form of new technology, involve detailed work preparing for the now impending introduction. They could involve, for example, narrowing the range of possible suppliers to one or two, user training, communication with the parties affected, changing operating procedures in readiness, wiring and other physical changes. To 'jump the gun' somewhat, it may be the first time that the people who are going to use the technology (or their representatives) have been involved in the adoption process, clearly pretty late in the day in relation to what has gone before and the decisions which have already been taken. A good deal of evidence on, and discussion of, this key consideration of user involvement is presented in Chapter 4 and in the case study chapters.

It is important to emphasize that this framework is a heuristic device – one derived, however, from the findings of my own and other people's empirical research. There is no implication intended that all organizations have to go through all these stages, and in a linear, sequential order. What happens in practice can be expected to vary from one organization to another and over time: practice (as always) can be expected to be much more messy and uneven than the framework, and could involve iteration from one 'later' stage back to an earlier one (and this may recur a number of times, such that the new technology adoption process gets 'stuck' and does not proceed to introduction). The stages can be viewed as critical junctures at which there is at least the possibility of various actors becoming involved in the process, and perhaps shaping it and the 'outcome'/introduction which follows in particular ways – outcomes which may serve their own and/or the organization's (senior management's?) interests. Whipp and Clark capture the issue as follows:

> At which stages in the process of strategic innovation do particular members of the enterprise gain access to decision arenas; in short, who occupies the design space? Which members are absent, and does their absence also mean that their position is ignored? The degree of representation of labour is of interest, particularly with respect to the earlier stages. . . . Labour [in the UK] is usually approached at the commissioning stage, and offers of participation by management are usually highly qualified . . . the translation stage of selecting specific technologies . . . is one in which equipment suppliers, internal engineers and external advisers may have the most direct impact on choices. A related issue concerns the ways in which those choices are legitimated and the explanations offered for choices which were ignored.[10]

To summarize and recap, then, the process of new technology

adoption is seen as possessing elements of rationality, but also as being imbued with political and other wider social motives, objectives and strategies; the new technology allows a degree of flexibility here, but not completely open-ended flexibility. There is a danger that the focus of the discussion so far will give the impression that the book is concerned only to present and analyse findings on new technology adoption from an intra-organizational perspective. Whilst the orientation is certainly upon events as they have unfolded in my case study organizations, and in organizations studied by other authors, these events and processes are theorized through a model of change which places them in the wider contexts of the organization itself and its external contexts. It is to a consideration of the contexts of new technology adoption that we now turn.

The key distinction is between external and internal (or 'outer' and 'inner', to use Pettigrew's terminology)[11] contexts, that is, the social, economic and political environment in which an organization is located, on the one hand, and the structure and culture(s) to be found within the organization, on the other. Descriptions and discussions of external contexts are well rehearsed, so I shall comment here on the internal context only. It consists of such aspects as the structure of the organization (for example, bureaucratic/mechanistic, decentralized/divisionalized, matrix/organic/ad-hocracy), the predominant form of work and job design and of working practices (Tayloristic? Flexible? Semi-autonomous work groups?), the 'softer' but equally important elements such as culture (or cultures, for one should not assume that there is one overarching culture), attitudes and orientations towards work, jobs, the organization itself, etc., managerial style/strategy, and the nature and climate of employee relations and personnel management. Also, it should be remembered, organizations are always undergoing a process of change (to a greater or lesser degree) along or between these dimensions such that the norm is change, not stability. One of the major services rendered by the work of Pettigrew *et al.*, indeed, is to show not only how external contextual change can generate an internal response in terms of change, but also how that external change can be used by actors within the organization to legitimize the need for the change. Putting this another way, drawing upon Pettigrew *et al.*'s conceptualization of strategic change processes, external contextual change is often linked with internal processual change in specific change episodes, and is created within and through the structural and cultural properties of organizations. There is another side to this, however, for, far from external change being used to help legitimize an internal process of change through communication, training, etc., it may actually be used to 'justify' the non-involvement of employees in the change process. As Marchington and Loveridge have observed:

> The major consequence of unstable, competitive and fashion-orientated markets lies in the potential impossibility for prior involvement of the shop floor if quick decisions are to be made ... some of this non-involvement is certainly due to management themselves; to some extent, management legitimates non-involvement by reference to the external environment.[12]

This is a difficult and complex business, and there is no pretence here that it is simply a matter of identifying the correct 'recipes' and then applying them. But that does not negate the usefulness of having an explicit conceptual schema which helps us to focus upon the key social, managerial and organizational issues. We shall be employing these contextual dimensions in the case study chapters in order to understand better the social and other processes associated with new technology adoption. A word of caution: it is not always easy to decide whether a particular factor should be seen as an element of an organization's external or of its internal context. Over the years writers have found technology, for example, difficult to so categorize. Sometimes it has been conceptualized as a 'free-floating', autonomous force outside the organization, creating the need for change within, sometimes it is seen as an element of an organization's internal context (certain writers in the past seeing it as *determining* social outcomes), and sometimes as a mixture of the two – that is, as both 'in here' and 'out there' simultaneously. A simple example would be a particular form of software which has been designed, developed and produced by a software house, is sold to an organization, and then amended and added to by the organization. In addition, all the foregoing says nothing about the possibility that certain organizations (perhaps the larger or dominant ones in a given sector) help to create their external contexts by 'enacting' the environment, either on their own or through some form of alliance or venture with other organizations.

All the case study chapters which follow have sections on the external and internal contexts of the four organizations which were studied, and contextual issues are often referred to in discussions of substantive aspects of new technology adoption in the preceding chapters.

OUTLINE OF THE BOOK

The book is divided into two main sections. The first comprises three chapters. Chapter 2 involves a discussion of managerial strategies for new technology adoption, along with a consideration of related organizational and human resource issues. Chapter 3 reviews empirical findings on new technology objectives, and discusses some of the key issues raised by these findings. Chapter 4 looks at who gets involved in new technology adoption, the nature and quality of that involvement, and the impact of external and internal contexts; involvement through trade unions, consultation, and job redesign are particular areas of interest.

Part II comprises four case studies of new technology adoption. Two are based in building societies and centre on the adoption of branch office computer terminal systems. The other two are from manufacturing companies, one involving the adoption of Computer Numerical Control (CNC) machine tools and Computer Aided Design and Draughting (CAD), and the other involving CAD and a computerized order processing, inventory control, accounting and payroll system.

The concluding chapter compares and contrasts the case study findings, discusses them in respect of the secondary material presented in Chapters 2-4, and draws out some key conclusions.

A NOTE ON METHODOLOGY

The case studies are based in the main on semi-structured interviews conducted by the author with a range of people from each organization, including administrative managers, computer managers, personnel specialists, training specialists, deputy general managers, O&M specialists, branch managers and staff, engineering managers, manufacturing managers and engineers, process engineers, design engineers, a factory manager, building society staff association chairmen, and trade union officers. The interviews lasted for between one and three-and-a-half hours; some people were seen on a number of occasions through repeated visits over a period of time (in one case, for instance, involving a total of eighteen hours). The original interviews were conducted during 1983-7; follow-up interviews took place in November and December 1993 (in two of the organizations – Bramley Building Society and Meadows & Butler – involving some of the same people from the earlier period). For some of the applications, this longitudinal field research allowed me to study new technology adoption as it unfolded, and the range of people interviewed facilitated the comparison and checking of accounts of the same events or processes.

I was allowed access to company documents, and a limited amount of participant observation took place whilst I was in the organizations – for example, whilst waiting for interviews to begin, during tours of the factory or offices, or over lunch.

For reasons of confidentiality the names of the case study organizations are fictitious; whilst I have lost the advantage, therefore, of using the proper names, I have gained in terms of the willingness of interviewees to be more open with me as a result. At the request of my interviewees, in order to conceal organization identities further, I have been rather unspecific at certain points about what the companies produce, where they are located, their financial performance, etc. I believe, however, that none of this has detracted from the substantive points made and the interpretations offered. Drafts of each of the case study chapters were presented to members of the organizations for comment and correction before the final versions were written up.

Part I
Adopting new technology

Chapter 2
Adopting new technology
Managerial strategies

The central concerns of the book can be expressed as to do with the why, how, when and who of the new technology adoption process. That is to say, respectively, why is the technology being adopted? What is to be the process of its adoption? Over what time period, and in what sequence, will it be adopted? And which members of the organization will be involved in the adoption process? The present chapter will examine the 'how' question. Chapter 3 concentrates upon the 'why' of new technology adoption. Of course, there are strong links between the two, for objectives are part and parcel of strategies, whether they are formally articulated or not.

We shall consider in the present chapter the ways in which managers have gone about adopting and introducing new technology into organizations. This implies, of course, that managers actually have a strategy for new technology adoption: the assumption can be challenged, so we shall also review whether it is acceptable to talk about strategies at all in this area.

The 'when' question was addressed in chapter 1, through a discussion of stages in the new technology adoption process.

Chapter 4 focuses upon the 'who' question. That is to say, which people are involved in the various stages of adoption and introduction, and what is the nature and impact of their involvement.

The emphasis throughout is on empirical findings; the interest is in what has happened, rather than what might or should happen. This means that publications are cited for their capacity to shed light on practice; most of the texts, therefore, draw on case studies or surveys of new technology adoption. Of course, it is also necessary, in order to make sense of the findings, to draw on theoretical perspectives as well as on the statements of interested parties.

Below we consider some problems of definition relating to

managerial strategy. The rest of the chapter is devoted to a consideration of strategies at three levels: organizational, technological and people.[1] There are connections, of course, between these levels.

DEFINITIONS AND PROBLEMS

It is important to begin by looking at new technology strategy in its wider organizational context. There is a voluminous literature on organizational strategies, covering matters such as corporate strategy, business strategy, industrial/employee strategy, human resource strategy and manufacturing strategy. It is not possible to consider these issues in detail here, although there will be some discussion of a few of these varieties of strategy later in the chapter. The interested reader is referred to the literature.[2] Let us draw on the broader conceptualization of strategy and provide a definition by reference to Thurley and Wood on business strategy and industrial relations strategy. They observe that the term 'strategy' has been used to describe:

> a particular set of choices taken over a period of time for a given objective. In an organisational setting, this implies that there is a hierarchy of decision choices, so that one decision will result in memoranda or guidelines laying down 'policy', to steer the more specific decisions taken by operational managers, who have to deal with a myriad of short-term problems and issues. A 'strategy' therefore means a consistent approach over time which is intended to yield results in the medium and long term for specific problems. A strategic approach assumes it is possible to review the overall situation facing decision-makers in the way that a general reviews a battle situation before actual hostilities break out. When they do break out, tactical decisions will have to be made for temporary advantage, but it is hoped that the decision on overall strategy will help to prevent short-term decisions, taken in the heat of battle, from cancelling each other out. It follows that the term 'strategy' can be applied to any set of business decisions regardless of content.[3]

Given the present book's orientation around social and political issues associated with new technology adoption, it is appropriate to provide a second definition of organizational strategy, one which takes an explicit people focus:

Strategies are developed as corporate steering devices, which are likely to inform decisions to invest in new technology. While it cannot be assumed that corporate strategies express an explicit view about the organization of the labour process, they will at least establish certain parameters within which implementation and actual changes to jobs and employment relations take place.[4]

These definitions will serve as benchmarks against which we can consider the ways in which the term has been used in the relevant literature. The rest of this section is organized around an examination of the following questions:

1 Why should managers have a strategy for new technology adoption?
2 Do managers appear in practice to have such strategies?
3 If the answer to (2) is no, where does that leave us?

WHY SHOULD MANAGERS HAVE A STRATEGY FOR NEW TECHNOLOGY ADOPTION?

Earl has put forward nine reasons why IT should be managed strategically:

1 It is a high-expenditure activity.
2 It is critical to many organizations.
3 It has the potential to be a strategic weapon in four main respects:
   (a) To gain competitive advantage.
   (b) To improve productivity and performance.
   (c) To facilitate new ways of managing and organizing.
   (d) To develop new businesses.
4 Because of major shifts in the economic context, that is, from mass markets and economies of scale to niche markets and economies of scope.
5 It affects all levels and functions of management.
6 It has led to a 'revolution' in management information systems.
7 It has many stakeholders.
8 The technology *per se* can have major implications – positive and negative – for the organization.
9 Management makes the difference.[5]

A number of these issues are taken up in this and other chapters of the present book, but I wish to focus for the moment on three particular reasons why it can be argued that managers should have a strategy for new technology adoption:

1 Because of its *integrative* potential. (There is some overlap here with Earl's point 7.)
2 Because of its wide-ranging implications for the people who work for the organization. (This is similar to Earl's point 5.)
3 It is potentially subversive, that is, it is imbued with political implications and possibilities.

Let us take each in turn:

The integrative potential of new technology

New technology has the potential to integrate across and within the various functions, departments, divisions and control and operating procedures of the organization, both in a social sense and at the level of the various types of new technologies themselves (for example, CAD/CAM; CIM, linking manufacturing operations with business functions such as accounts and purchasing). Jones and Webb have observed that:

> CIM systems are strategic production weapons which require production managers to control their operations in an entirely different way. . . . Their strategic nature brings potential benefits which, to be realised, require different control and organisational systems. . . . The whole logic of information flow is integrative rather than subdivided and function-based.[6]

This integrative potential can also go outside the organization, connecting, for example, into customers' and/or suppliers' new technology and procedures. To illustrate, through CAD/CAM some companies have linked the designs and related databases of parts, materials, tools, etc., directly into their own CAD/CAM facilities.

Kimberly has observed that 'Successful introduction and effective use of advanced manufacturing technology are heavily dependent on the fit between the new technology and the system in which it is being used'. This requires, *inter alia*, shaping employee expectations, the provision of appropriate training, flexible reward systems, and communication.[7]

New technology has wide-ranging people implications

A second main reason for having a strategy for new technology concerns the potentially wide-ranging implications of new technology from a people and organizational point of view – for example, skill and training implications, number of people employed and their location, task structures and ranges, terms and conditions of employment, organizational structuring, recruitment and selection.

This is an argument against 'ad-hocery' and in favour of trying to anticipate and plan for the people implications of new technology introduction. But it is much more than that, for new technology's potential should be seen in terms of the contribution it can make to the achievement of objectives and strategies in the marketing, quality, human resource, manufacturing and business/corporate strategy areas. These changes need to be interrelated and integrated in order to achieve many of the benefits which can come from adopting new technology. For reasons such as this, a number of writers have argued for an IT strategy, which addresses these matters, and explicitly relates to the business strategy. As Currie has put it:

> Decision-making on new technology involves a variety of issues and is not merely an exercise in finding solutions to specific organizational problems. Instead it should be perceived as a strategic management activity, although strategic choices regarding new technology may vary considerably within the management hierarchy.[8]

This latter point needs highlighting. As we saw earlier, much of the organizational research into new technology has focused on post-implementation, and has often *assumed*, implicitly or explicitly, that its introduction was linked to a wider managerial strategy, imposed from above.[9] In so far as managerial strategies *have* been addressed, the interest has been in differentiating different types of organizational decisions (such as Buchanan and Boddy's strategic, operating and control) or between different types of decision processes (such as Hickson *et al.*'s sporadic, fluid and constricted).[10] The political strategies and sub-strategies used by the actors involved, especially during the adoption phase, have been neglected. One of the strengths of Currie's study of managerial decision-making associated with the adoption and introduction of CAD in twenty UK organizations is that she examines the formal and informal strategies deployed by engineering managers, with a particular focus upon unveiling the 'informal circumventions of the formal budgetary control system by engineering managers'.[11]

One of the salutary findings of Currie's analysis of these matters is that, whilst senior engineering managers in the large companies/units in her sample:

> were generally aware of the strategic possibilities of CAD ... organizational strategy for new technology appeared to be developed on a piecemeal basis, often becoming more clearly formulated once the technology had been implemented. Moreover, strategies for new technology were not necessarily developed at the apex of the organization, as the majority of our case studies showed that ... 'strategy' was usually formulated and refined at grassroots level.[12]

New technology is imbued with political implications

Thirdly, one can point to the potentially subversive character of new technology. Given that organizations are inherently political structures, conflicts and in-fighting can be expected to occur when things change – people may be anxious about whether they will have a job any more, or about the nature of that job, and may resist or at least not co-operate in the changes. This is to take an 'incremental-processual' perspective on strategy development, which attempts to integrate content, context and process, informed by an interpretivist view of strategy where certain dominant ideas become embedded in an organization, and help shape the ways in which employees interpret the changing environment. Here 'strategies emerge from the politicized battles between conflicting interest groups and perspectives within the firm. Their unintentional consequences can be at least as important, if not more so, as their intentional ones.'[13] If management has a strategy which can take account of these possibilities it may be able to avoid them, or at least reduce their impact before positions become entrenched.[14]

Whilst, clearly, one could spend a good deal of time discussing managerial strategies for new technology (to say nothing of managerial strategies in general!) in this normative way, it is important to move on to a review of the empirical evidence relating to practice in this area. A note of caution, however, needs to be sounded first of all. We saw above the argument for the new technology strategy being articulated with the corporate/business strategy (indeed, for it being an integral part of that wider strategy). It follows that it is difficult, and indeed in a sense unjustifiable, to talk about a 'new technology strategy' as if it were somehow separate from other organizational strategies. It has been necessary to do so below, on occasion, for the purposes of exposition.

DO MANAGERS HAVE STRATEGIES FOR NEW TECHNOLOGY ADOPTION?

Whether one is talking about technology strategy or any other kind of strategy, it would be unwise to assume or impute its existence. As Kelly and Wood have argued, 'we cannot assume all firms have strategies, and certainly not in all areas and in any integrated fashion'.[15] Rothwell, in a survey of employment policies and new technology in twenty-three organizations from both the service and the manufacturing sectors, found some evidence of planning, but no explicit strategy. This, she argued, could be due to lack of ability or experience, or the reverse – that is, 'the experience of the futility of employment planning in the past', reinforced by 'unproven technology and volatile markets'. The most common reason she found, however, was:

> lack of awareness, or lack of responsibility, resulting partly from organisational structures and functional roles: there was no clearcut responsibility for devising and implementing organisationwide employment policies; line managers had responsibility only for their own departments, while personnel managers may have had a wider remit but no powers of implementation.[16]

On the basis of a study of six manufacturing organizations over a two-year period, Rose and Jones, whilst appearing to accept that managers employ strategies in the financial, sales and marketing, and production areas, argue that, in the work organization and industrial relations areas, management policy and practice 'lacks the detailed "strategic" character so often attributed to it'. They also observe that 'the current usages of the terms "strategy" and "control" are somewhat misleading guides both to actual management conduct and to the causes of particular outcomes in work organisation and industrial relations'.[17]

In a study of motor manufacturing in the United Kingdom, Marsden et al. would appear to concur with Rose and Jones's argument. In a discussion of management strategy in the industry they argue that:

> even on a very modest definition of labour relations strategy, such

as a set of related policies directed at problems which managements recognise as interrelated, the companies' industrial relations and manpower policies did not *always* constitute a strategy. Industrial relations objectives were frequently sacrificed in order to meet product market demands. This is not to deny that the companies have long-term objectives in the industrial relations area, but rather that strategy can be overridden by other demands and degenerates into fire-fighting.[18] [My emphasis.]

Notice that the objectives remain intact and unproblematic, and the implication that a strategy can be present. 'Always' may imply that there was sometimes a strategy in the employee relations and human resource areas, even if it could be overridden by the demands of other functions, such as production or sales. This appears to be a rather less emphatic rejection of the utility of the concept of managerial strategy *vis-à-vis* labour and employment than that put forward by Rose and Jones. Let us now focus specifically on new technology strategies.

Clegg and Kemp have argued that 'often, organisations drift into a way of managing more or less by default and without explicitly identifying the anticipated costs and benefits of the alternatives'.[19] Presumably it is legitimate to substitute 'managers' for 'organizations' here. Love and Walker, in a study of the adoption of new technology in the mechanical engineering and printing industries, found that 'Despite the fact that many of the companies in the study regarded the deployment of new technology as an on-going process rather than a one-off experience, clear strategies for dealing with it were by no means always evident'.[20] Shaw *et al.* report, on the basis of a longitudinal study of computer application in a batch production engineering company, 'the main criticism of management is that their approach, until recently, apart from being mainly reactive, had been piecemeal and without a coherent strategy'.[21] 'Until recently' because, they argue, following the appointment of a new production director and the employment of external consultants, management's approach did become much more strategic and systematic. Rothwell found that it was, in the main, in the process of implementing new technology that 'employment policies could be said to have become more closely linked to business policy, if only by having to react to it more directly than before'.[22]

We have seen, then, that there is evidence to support both the argument that managers do not have strategies for new technology adoption, and the argument that they do have such strategies, at least in some 'modified' form. Where, then, does that leave us?

WHERE DOES THAT LEAVE US?

We saw earlier that Thurley and Wood draw a distinction between strategy and tactics, arguing that the latter is to do with short-term decisions 'for temporary advantage', whereas the former is closely connected with particular objectives which are seen as realizable only during a longer time period (if, *inter alia*, the strategy is maintained, and short-term tactical decisions are not allowed to cancel each other out). Bessant has also made a distinction between strategy and tactics, in this in case the investment decision-making process. 'Tactical decision-making' is seen as a recurring, structured process which is linked with annual investment budgets, and is often the responsibility of line managers and supervisors, whereas 'strategic decision-making' is associated with 'major process innovation'. Much new technology adoption falls into the tactical category, for:

> despite the novelty and technological sophistication often associated with such equipment, there is little basic change in the production process involved. For example, using a robot in the car industry to weld bodies or spray paint . . . [still involves] the basic process of making cars by welding metal and painting it . . . [Thus] from the point of view of the engineers and designers involved, IT often represents little more than a sophisticated new set of tools for carrying out the same tasks.[23]

Another way in which the integrity of the longer-term strategy is preserved, yet allowance made for localized, short-term adjustments, is through talking about 'sub-strategies'.[24] Thompson and Bannon, in a study of new technology and changing patterns of work and employment at Plessey's plants in Liverpool, use such an approach to examine the shifting 'frontier of control' between management and work force. They observe that 'Managerial strategies are seldom a coherent derivation from the "objectives of capital". To secure effective control of labour and other resources and markets, management has to utilise a variety of practices and sub-strategies.'[25] Despite this lack of coherence, Plessey management strengthened its control over the work force during the fifteen-year period covered by the research. This 'was facilitated by a restructuring of technology and markets, which created opportunities to subordinate a militant work force'.[26]

Despite the problems involved, I also wish to preserve and use this notion of a longer-term, drawn out, yet shaped and targeted managerial strategy. Friedman has expressed the matter colourfully and effectively:

> There is nothing in the definition that suggests that strategy can only be thought of as a coherent, rational and consistent activity. It would be a pity if we could not analyse a general's behaviour as guided by a strategy simply because the general occasionally lost sight of his own strategies or because some of his lieutenants were incompetent or had ideas of their own. It is also unduly restrictive to disallow inference of a strategy from an examination of the general's actions without a copy of his memoirs. This is not to imply that the general's consciousness does not matter, merely that describing the general's initiatives in terms of a general strategy is useful, quite independent of the general's degree of consciousness of his strategy.[27]

NEW TECHNOLOGY AND ORGANIZATIONAL STRATEGY

The first question which needs to be addressed is 'What is organizational strategy?'. As with all definitions, it is unrealistic to expect to be able to provide one which will be acceptable to everyone; however, we will work with the influential definition of Chandler. Strategy is: 'the determination of the basic long-term goals and objectives of an enterprise and the adoption of courses of action and the allocation of resources necessary for carrying out those goals'.[28]

Let us now broaden the discussion by looking at the connections between strategy, structure, work organization and technology. Whipp and Clark employ the notion of 'strategic innovation', which:

> refers to changes in technology and forms of work organisation at all levels, which includes boards of directors or the various interfaces between a company and its suppliers or potential customers. Strategic innovation also embraces the technologies and forms of work organisation adopted in the design and planning of an innovation and its execution, from the commissioning of new production facilities through to its operational form.[29]

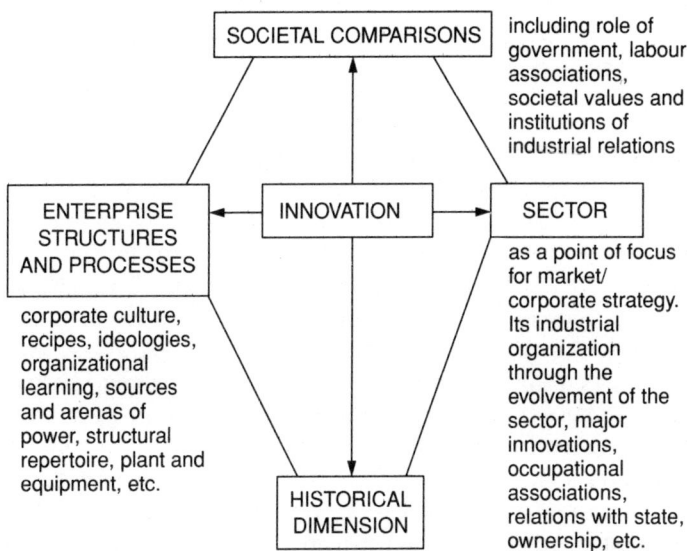

Figure 3 Whipp and Clark's framework of innovation
Source: R. Whipp and P. Clark (1986) Innovation and the Auto Industry, London: Pinter, p. 15, reproduced by permission of Pinter Publishers Ltd, London; all rights reserved

They use this framework in a detailed longitudinal analysis of the design, development and manufacture of the Rover car code-named SD1.[30] Figure 3 summarizes their model.

The adoption and introduction of new technology, then, is only one – albeit sometimes a key – element of strategic innovation. Thus, for example, it would be unduly restrictive to confine one's attention to the technical aspects of new technology adoption (from both a managerial and an academic perspective).

Political processes can also play an important part in affecting the outcomes of technological change. Scarbrough's work is illustrative:

> Even at the most detailed level, the process of technological change is inextricably intertwined with the politics of workplace industrial relations, and in particular with the pursuit of efficiency targets, the determination of work practices, and the distribution of skills in the production process. Moreover, the political conflict surrounding technological change is seen to occur upon several

different planes; not at the workplace alone, but also on the level of corporate strategy where important decisions are taken regarding the investment in new technologies and the distribution of costs and benefits arising from their introduction.[31]

The above analysis is grounded in a study of British Leyland, where industrial relations issues had been particularly prominent in the 1970s and early 1980s. Willman and Winch also employed a broadly based approach in their analysis of the development and introduction of the Metro line at BL's Longbridge, Birmingham, plant. Their book examines the 'broad links between the corporate strategy for recovery, the development of new products, the consequent choice of new processes and the emerging labour relations strategy, and the consequences of this set of linkages for trade union organisation, the organisation of work and industrial conflict at BL'.[32] Scarbrough comments that 'Much the greater part of the increase in productivity seems to have been attributable not to the introduction of new technology but to the imposition of the new managerial regime at the plant.'[33]

Notice that the process of change is driven by management imposition. This is hardly likely to gain the full commitment of the affected employees to the changes – compliance would seem more likely in a situation where the power balance has shifted in management's favour. Employees can be expected to harbour underlying conflicts and discontent. Scarbrough has argued elsewhere for the need to link a firm's IT strategy to its corporate strategy, and for the importance of achieving the active involvement of the people who possess the requisite technical knowledge, be they systems analysts, line managers or whoever.[34] This is not necessarily just because of the value placed on participation for its own sake, for there can also be instrumental reasons. Ettlie, for example, has argued that in many organizations where advanced manufacturing technology is introduced, production managers do not strongly influence the strategy formulation process, and, as a result, not all the possible benefits are obtained.[35] The involvement of managers with technical knowledge and experience in the strategy formulation and implementation process is also predicated in Earl's outline of how IT can be aligned with the organization's business strategy, and how strategic opportunities can be sought for IT.[36]

Ettlie's and Earl's arguments, note, are for the fuller involvement of certain types of managers. This is some way from arguing for the involvement of the eventual users of the new technology. Employee involvement in new technology adoption is discussed in detail in Chapter 4.

STRATEGIES AT THE TECHNOLOGY LEVEL

This section will look at how the technology can itself be used strategically, in the sense of enabling the organization to do things that it could not do otherwise, or help it to do things in a more effective and efficient way. To illustrate, new technology can be used strategically to create (or enter) a particular product market, to diversify, to provide a new service, to communicate more effectively with suppliers or customers, and to reduce set-up times and order-to-delivery cycles. Technology, as we have seen, should be integrated into the wider business and corporate strategies. Porter has argued that managers need to identify all the actual and potential technologies in the organization's value chain, and then determine which will have the most significance for reinforcing competitive advantage.[37]

It has been argued, however, that technologies are not always chosen at random, but rather from a restricted spectrum of opportunities. Researchers at the Science Policy Research Unit, for example, use the notion of 'technological trajectories' to capture the sense in which the technological directions of organizations have unique qualities, influenced by their particular histories and activities. This means that technological emulation by another ('follower') company is necessarily subject to its ability to unravel the innovating company's tacit knowledge, resources and skills as encapsulated in the technological trajectory.[38]

The strategic use of new technology can be further illustrated by taking the example of applications in the manufacturing sector. Voss sees manufacturing strategy as involving the choice of process in the context of supporting the company's corporate strategy in the market place: this is the 'strategic element in manufacturing technology planning, selection and implementation'.[39] Voss uses Hill's model of manufacturing strategy, reproduced in summary form in Table 2.

Further illustration of the strategic use of manufacturing technology is provided by Skinner, who has stated that it can:

> produce superior quality, shorten delivery cycles, reduce inventories, minimise investment in plant and equipment, cut down the

Table 2 Framework for manufacturing strategy development

Corporate objectives	Marketing strategy	How do products win orders in the market place?	Manufacturing strategy	
			Process choice	Infra-structure
Growth	Products	Price	Choice of	Function
Profit	Market	Quality	alternative	supports
Return on	segments	Delivery,	processes	Manufac-
investment	Range	speed,	Trade-offs	turing
Other	Mix	reliability	embodied	systems
financial	Volumes	Colour	in the	Controls
measures	Standard-	range	process	and
	ization or	Product	choice	procedures
	customiza-	range	Role of	Work
	tion	Design	inventory	structuring
	Level of	leadership	in the	Organiz-
	innovation		process	ational
	Leader or		configur-	structure
	follower		ation	

Source: T. J. Hill (1985) *Manufacturing Strategy*, London: Macmillan, p. 40

new product development cycle, make possible entirely new products, shift economies of scale so that short production runs are feasible, and create new production economics, allowing for a richer product mix, more product proliferation, and more customer specials.[40]

Skinner was commenting on US practice, but Buchanan and Boddy, in their UK studies, also found that managers 'do not explore the strategic opportunities of the new technology'; rather 'emphasis was on the use of information technology to perform existing functions more effectively, and to reduce dependence on human intervention and control in their operations'.[41] This may in part be because new technology is often introduced on a piecemeal or incremental basis, with some of the 'old' technology still in place. Boddy and Buchanan take up a position very much towards the end (managerial) choice-end of the choice–determinist continuum relating to the potentialities and possibilities of new technology in the organization. They argue that:

> It is [more] accurate and appropriate to view technical change as a *trigger* to processes of organizational decision making in which

critical *strategic choices* emerge. Technical change is accompanied by a series of organizational decisions which emerge in the process of change and which influence the outcomes.[42] [Emphasis in original]

They see the key strategic choices as being to do with equipment design and layout; objectives; job, systems and organization design; and the change process itself. They draw a distinction between strategic *choices* and strategic *objectives*. (See p. 43 for an overview of their distinction between the latter and operation and control objectives.) It will be recalled that strategic objectives are focused upon *future* market opportunities, and hence are concerned with the external contexts of the organization, for example meeting/getting ahead of the competition. Objectives can be outward or inward-looking, therefore, and notice that Boddy and Buchanan imply that choices are to be made here also, in terms of what to use the new technology for, how to use it, and the social processes of use. This is a strong managerial choice position.

The integrative potential of new technology has sometimes been put forward as an argument for manufacturing strategy. Indeed, many analysts have argued that the full potential of the technology will be realized only when this integrative potential has been tapped.[43] The *raison d'être* of CIM is its integrative organization-wide potential. Goldhar and Jelinek, in putting the case for a strategic approach to achieving the benefits of flexibility and CIM, have observed that 'the strategic importance of manufacturing capabilities will demand much closer integration of manufacturing expertise with the perspectives of marketing, R&D and design'.[44] In their view, 'manufacturing competence' will be moved 'into the front line as a competitive weapon'.[45] This also means that 'senior management must see the evaluation and implementation of advanced manufacturing technology as a fundamental part of corporate strategy and therefore as one of their own major responsibilities'.[46]

Recognition in itself is, of course, not sufficient. It is also necessary to develop a technical and organizational infrastructure which can support the strategy's implementation. The lack of such an infrastructure may be an important impediment to the diffusion of CIMs.[47]

The particular strategies which are chosen will, of course, depend in part upon the objectives which are identified for new technology adoption. (New technology objectives are the subject of Chapter 3.)

A preliminary indication, however, of the articulation between strategies and objectives can be gleaned from a comparative study by Gerwin and Tarondeau of the introduction of flexible manufacturing systems in four companies, one in each of the following countries: the United States, the United Kingdom, western Germany and France. The authors observe:

> The criteria used in making adoption choices were relatively diverse, reflecting each company's attempt to seize upon different CIM advantages. Both the US and French companies selected CIMs because of their flexibility in dealing with market uncertainties. In Great Britain, uncertainty reduction was reflected in desiring a centralised source of production information and wanting to avoid the vagaries of the skilled labour market.[48]

The discussion above has focused on technology strategies in a manufacturing context, where AMT and CIM have provided the main illustrations. It is important to turn now to IT strategy, and hence to encompass both manufacturing and non-manufacturing organizations. We can draw upon the recent work of Hochstrasser and Griffiths for the purpose. On the basis of primary and secondary data collection and analysis they have argued that:

> It must be concluded that IT is best treated not as a technical but as a managerial issue... The weight of evidence strongly suggests that only a comprehensive IT strategy can unify and direct efforts on all levels and across all boundaries... having an IT strategy in place has now become a prerequisite for successful business practice.[49]

They distinguish between three main types of IT applications which had been successfully developed by the companies they studied:

1 Improving internal efficiency (document processing, desk-top publishing, spreadsheets, electronic mail, skills database, electronic data interchange, etc.).
2 Enhancing external effectiveness (customer databases, help desks, point-of-sale systems, communication links with customers, etc.).
3 Capturing and creating new markets (smart cards, econometric modelling, expert systems, dealer support systems, etc.).

Fifty-seven per cent of the companies sampled rated the role of IT as on a par with other business functions, yet only 34 per cent of them had a corporate IT strategy. Of the 66 per cent of companies with no IT strategy, three out of four managers said the lack of a strategy was a serious constraint on effective operations. Hochstrasser and Griffiths found that the IT strategy was often formulated by the technology division, where there was sometimes little understanding of the broader organizational issues. At the same time, however, 25 per cent of managers complained that the board was not sufficiently interested in contributing to the generation of an IT strategy. Therefore a corporate initiative needs to be taken to 'integrate technology development within a business context so that *all* the issues involved in generating a comprehensive IT strategy can be explicitly addressed *before* any implementations are planned'[50] [emphasis in original]. Hochstrasser and Griffiths conclude:

> Although IT is seen as an investment issue by most of the companies taking part in this study, case studies have revealed that there is often a strong and sometimes counter-productive reluctance to free resources to work on an IT strategy and to convince management to address these issues explicitly. This attitude needs to be replaced by a more constructive approach regarding IT as an investment with measurable and positive returns. It must be stressed that the resources allocated and the effort spent in generating a corporate IT strategy are not considered to be overheads, but will actually save a company money by ensuring a better return on what is already being spent.[51]

Back to people again, and their attitudes and dispositions!

LABOUR STRATEGIES

Distinctions can be drawn under this heading between managerial strategies aimed at the organization and control of work and jobs; strategies focused primarily upon employment relations, and strategies aimed at regulating the management–worker relationship.[52] Following Gospel, these strategies are to do with work, employment and industrial relations, respectively, and can be defined as follows:

1 *Work relations*, 'the way technology and social processes are organised at work'.
2 *Employment relations*, 'the form of job structure and job tenure and the package of benefits, pecuniary and non-pecuniary, attached to jobs within an organization'.
3 *Industrial relations*, 'management–union relations and the institution of collective bargaining'.[53]

Gospel's work is particularly helpful because of his strong empirical orientation. He examines, over an extended time period, whether (and, if so, in what respects) British managers can be said to have had such strategies. His conclusion is in the affirmative:

> It might be objected that . . . British employers and managers have not had strategies in industrial relations, but have merely reacted, within a very limited planning horizon, to market and other conditions and pressure from workers. This may seem to be the case when looking at employers over a short time period. It is true that most British firms in the period under consideration did not have written formal policies in the labour area. In addition, much was handed over to employers' organisations and lower-level line management. However, this in itself could be said to constitute a strategy, if only one of delegation or indirect control. But when examined more closely, over a longer historical perspective, strands and patterns of strategies may be discerned.[54]

If, then, we accept that it is legitimate to work on the assumption that managers do have labour strategies, albeit they are sometimes far from the rationalistic models used in the corporate and business strategy literature (and bearing in mind our discussion of this matter earlier in the chapter), we can move on to consider the forms of labour strategy adopted for new technology.

One strand in the literature on this matter draws a basic distinction between 'direct control' and 'responsible autonomy' strategies. With the latter, 'managers try to accentuate the positive peculiar aspect of labour capacity, its malleability. Workers are given responsibility, status, light supervision, and their loyalty towards the firm is solicited' in various ways. With the former, on the other hand, managers 'try to reduce the amount of responsibility of each individual worker by close supervision, and by setting out in advance and in great detail the specific tasks individual workers are to do'.[55] Also 'there is a wide range of possible solutions between extreme forms of responsible autonomy and direct control, as well as different paths leading in each direction'.[56]

Marsden *et al.* have utilized this framework to inform their study of motor manufacture in Europe, the United States and Japan. They argue that two broad strategies are available to managers and unions for dealing with the restructuring of the industry:

1 A co-operative strategy, which involves increased labour flexibility

and the acceptance of new technology, in return for enhanced job security for the workers remaining, and consultation and participation.

2 A reassertion of managerial control over day-to-day matters, involving the removal of labour market rigidities, especially those concerned with the protection of working practices and established wage structures.[57]

It is possible, of course, for management to move from one strategy to the other. This, however, takes time, involves costs, and is by no means unproblematic. It is also possible to have one strategy for one group of workers – say a responsible autonomy strategy for senior managers, technical staff and skilled workers, and a direct control strategy for office staff, semi- and unskilled workers and contract staff. There are affinities here with dual labour markets and so-called 'core'–'peripheral' and labour flexibility strategies. (See pp. 54–5 for more detail.)

A problem with the control v. commitment/responsible autonomy model is the difficulty of differentiating between some types of work, especially where managers want to achieve both control and commitment (that is, the 'best of both worlds'). Is this theoretically and/or practically possible, or is it not internally contradictory? The question also needs to be asked, 'Commitment to what?' The organization? If so, then commitment strategies are surely about attempting to increase profits/reduce costs by increasing employees' efficiency and productivity. Perhaps, then, they are about trying to increase management control over employees, and employee cooperation through, as Sewell and Wilkinson put it in a different context, 'minimizing negative divergences from expected behaviour and management-defined norms whilst identifying positive divergences and maximizing their creative potential'.[58]

The way in which the two strategies can, in practice, be used in combination by senior management for the same group of employees over the same time period can be illustrated by drawing upon the UK motor industry studies of Willman and Winch and of Marsden *et al*.[59] Speaking of the early 1980s, Willman and Winch observe that a 'reassertion of management control on the shop floor' had taken place. At the same time Marsden *et al*. found that consultation and direct communication with the work force had increased at all the main car manufacturers. Thus 'The strategy behind industrial relations reform [can be seen] as an attempt to minimise the extent to which employees and their representatives could interfere with production efficiency while maximising their commitment to efficiency as a desirable goal.'[60] Also, 'all managements stress that their strategy is not so much to avoid bargaining, or an outright rejection of it, but rather is aimed at changing the scope of bargaining in management's favour'.[61] What is more, this labour strategy was directly linked with the corporate strategy:

> Many of the labour relations changes in the UK car industry have been the result of strategic decisions . . . [they] resulted from board-level decisions about the development of personnel and industrial relations matters in the medium term . . . [the] changes . . . were decided at the highest level as part of a broader competitive strategy upon which they were premised.[62]

Evidence that similar strategies have been adopted outside the motor industry is provided by Northcott *et al.* in a study of the extent of, and the factors affecting, new technology adoption. They observe that, since 1980, there has been a 'dominant trend' towards a 'new management strategy having two main features: greater confidence and determination on the part of managers and more sophisticated use of a variety of procedures to carry the work force along with change'.[63] They note the continuance of union recognition and collective bargaining, and the growth of consultation and direct involvement, and embrace schemes for employee participation, whether of a 'direct' nature or based upon representative machinery. At the same time, many managers want, as has been argued, commitment as well as control, and try to achieve both via 'packages of motivation and control', with 'effective, firm and "inapprehensive" leadership from management'.[64] Thus, by the mid-1980s, it was possible to talk about 'a new management strategy for handling changes such as those implied by new technology'.[65] In a study of the utilization of new technology in three major UK insurance companies Storey found that management had failed to fully 'exploit the control potential of the technology. In large measure these companies have "soft-pedalled". This is so, in so far as the full control rigour made possible by the adopted technology had not been pursued.'[66] Storey puts forward a number of possible reasons for this, including: managers protecting their own interests; organizational culture; the fact that the new technology was still at an early stage of implementation, where the need for staff co-operation was at a premium; and that it may represent a '"phoney war" preceding a more decisive campaign'.[67]

The above reminds us again of the central role played by managerial and employee interests, objectives, attitudes and strategies in shaping the utilization of new technology in organizations, and in contributing to the 'outcomes' of that deployment. Whilst, as discussed in Chapter 1, I have no doubt that the technology itself makes a difference, it is important to reassert that there is a degree of choice for managers. IT, *technically,* as in the insurance industry example cited above, can certainly be used in a centralized and/or decentralized mode, and different companies have taken up different strategic positions on this key structural issue over various time periods.

Social control aspects of new technology adoption will be discussed in some detail in the next chapter, but we can conclude here by illustrating one of the fundamental paradoxes thrown up by the introduction of new technology into an organization when its technical capabilities and potentialities do not sit readily or easily with the organization's socio-political regime. Flexible manufacturing systems offer major strategic and operating benefits, yet, as Loveridge and Pitt, drawing on Jones's work, have observed, 'to secure these, managers must cede much more control to lower levels of management and staff than often they feel able to do'. What is more, 'instead of using *inherent* flexibility to secure strategic advantages commensurate with new organizational competence, most firms operate with the conventional Fordist paradigm, ignoring many possible benefits of a flexible response'[68] [my emphasis].

CONCLUSION

We have seen that defining managerial strategies, including strategies for new technology, is by no means a straightforward matter, whether we are talking about strategies in the broader or in the narrower sense. The question why it is considered important that strategies for new technology should be developed was then considered, followed by an examination of the empirical evidence relating to the existence of such strategies. The data were found to be inconclusive; some supported the existence of strategies, others did not. We therefore moved on to see whether the strategy notion could be preserved in amended form through employing the notions of strategies and tactics, and through talking about sub-strategies. In essence, we came down in favour of retaining the strategy concept, albeit in a form which is much more politically and organizationally oriented than the models put forward in the corporate strategy literature.

Three levels of new technology strategy were distinguished: organizational, technical and people. It was argued that the choices around the new technology (in addition to those relating to the technology itself) can be central to the outcomes of the adoption process; for example, achievement of the flexibility benefits which new technology offers can be prevented by an inflexible/Taylorist/Fordist form of management control and work organization. But much of this depends upon the objectives which managers (and other organizational actors) are pursuing when they adopt new technology: it is to a consideration of these matters that we now turn.

Chapter 3
Why is new technology introduced?

This chapter is divided into two main parts. The first and longer part reviews the empirical evidence relating to the objectives which have been pursued through the introduction of new technology into organizations. The second considers the range of objectives which might be and have been pursued, and the issues of rationality and implementation.

The empirical evidence on new technology objectives is summarized in Table 3. It is important to add here the caveat that the classification is somewhat arbitrary in terms of the particular objectives which are delineated, and the headings under which they are placed. There is a good deal of overlap across many of the objectives with regard to what they imply in terms of practice, and some of them could equally well have been discussed under a

Table 3 New technology objectives: research findings

Financial and economic objectives	*Business and technical objectives*	*Social and organizational objectives*
To increase profitability To meet competition To save on non-labour costs To save on labour costs	To achieve improvements in the capture, processing, storage, transmission, and analysis of information To increase flexibility To improve control and consistency To achieve improvements in the product or service	Control Skill

different heading. A number of them have financial and economic, business and technical, and social and organizational elements and implications. For example, 'To increase flexibility' could have been listed under either the 'financial and economic' or the 'social and organizational', rather than under the 'business and technical' heading where I have placed it.

It is also important to emphasize that the focus throughout is on empirical findings for new technology objectives: only that material is drawn upon which is based upon some form of direct communication with organizational members who have been involved in new technology adoption. This means in practice that the researchers have used a case study/interview or survey research methodology.

Let us examine, then, the empirical findings relating to new technology objectives.

FINANCIAL AND ECONOMIC OBJECTIVES

To increase profitability

Hill has argued that:

> Managers introduce new production techniques in order to maintain or increase profitability, and their assessments of new methods may contain no conscious evaluation of the control potential. What are important are the internalised design values and unconscious assumptions about what constitutes 'progress' which managers and engineers bring to bear when they apply scientific and technical knowledge to industry. These embody a central feature of conventional capitalist production, that control is one condition of profitability.[1]

This quotation encompasses a number of the issues relating to the social and organizational aspects and implications of technological change, issues which recur throughout this book. Some of these will be taken up in more detail later. Let us here note the point that new methods of production are introduced in order to maintain or increase profitability. This would presumably be taken as uncontroversially true by just about everyone reading the present text. However, it is worth while pausing for a moment to note that it would not necessarily hold true of non-capitalist societies, where profit generation and maximization may not form a central axis of the economic infrastructure. The production and distribution of goods and services, for example, may rely, in a much more basic way, on state planning and directives.

The present book is centred on a study of the adoption of new technology in organizations in capitalist societies, with particular reference to the United Kingdom. It is generally taken as given, by researchers and organizational members alike, that in such societies a primary organizing principle and objective of organizations within the market sector of such societies (and, increasingly, in many of these societies, the non-market and state sectors) is the attempt to maintain or increase profits. Given that this is taken as axiomatic, it is not perhaps surprising that when objectives for the adoption of new technology are discussed, this most basic of objectives is not even mentioned. The objectives which are mentioned can in fact be viewed as the means by which the attempt is made to achieve the profitability objective (improved productivity, enhanced management control, quality improvements, increased flexibility, etc.). However, whilst this objective is usually taken as given, there are important differences in the literature in the extent to which the pursuit of profit by managers/organizations is taken as influencing practice. To illustrate, some analysts explicitly begin from the position of examining the adoption of new technology in capitalist societies, with concomitant implications for the analysis of work and labour in such societies. This position is encapsulated in the Marxist tradition, where the concepts used include surplus value, valorization, exploitation, ownership and non-ownership of the means of production, class structure and class conflict.

A modern form of this Marxist tradition ('labour process' theory and research) can be traced to the publication in 1974 of Harry Braverman's *Labor and Monopoly Capital*.[2] As with all major traditions (indeed, as a key element of the defining features of such a tradition), it has had an impact upon subsequent work, both from within the tradition and from outside it. Here the organizational search for profitability is accorded a central place in the analysis, and is seen as influencing or determining much else that goes on in organizations, including events related to the introduction of new technology.

Many other analyses of the adoption and introduction of new technology into organizations in capitalist societies are not informed by reference to, or the utilization of, an understanding of the social, economic and political contexts of capitalism. There is, in some cases, an affinity with the Marxist analysis, for example in the sense that is taken for granted that the major objective is the attempt to maintain or increase profits, but often one does not know *what* is being taken for granted, because matters such as these, including the conceptualization of context, are left unexplicated. Examples include descriptive and normative approaches which treat what happens or should happen when new technology is introduced in a 'matter-of-fact' way, paying little, if any, attention to human agency, politics or social conflict. The consequences of the introduction of new technology are seen as following from the decisions of managers and the objectives they have pursued.

Hill, as we saw above, argues that managers' 'assessments of new methods may contain no *conscious* evaluation of the control potential' [my emphasis]. Control criteria are built into managerial orientations and practices in capitalist society, and underpin the design/redesign of work and organizations. It is taken as given by managers, he appears to be arguing, that they need to maintain or increase their control over work and employees in order that profitability may be achieved. We shall examine the question of control and new technology below. Reference to the design of jobs alerts us to matters such as the educational and training systems to be found in different countries, and the effect they can have on knowledge and skills relating to work and occupations. To illustrate, Sorge *et al.*, in explaining why there is greater use of operator, as against planning/production engineering, programming for CNC machine tools in West Germany, compared with Great Britain, argue that the difference is connected, *inter alia*, with the different qualification structures to be found in the two countries. In Britain there has been differentiation of technician from worker apprenticeships, whereas in West Germany technician training is usually subsequent to craft training.[3]

To meet competition

The research of three groups of authors can be drawn upon to illustrate the objective of 'meeting the competition'. In a study of the introduction of new technology into six organizations in Scotland, Buchanan and Boddy found the objective of meeting the competition to be *one* of the explicit objectives of the introduction of new technology at Caterpillar Tractor. The fact that it did not appear as an objective for the other five companies is presumably to be explained essentially in terms of the different external and internal

Why is new technology introduced? 43

contexts of those organizations. In summarizing the reasons given for the introduction of new technology in the six companies, the desire to 'meet changing market conditions' at Caterpillar Tractor is referred to under 'strategic objectives'.[4] They distinguish between three possible broad types of objective for new technology: strategic, operating, and control. Strategic objectives are 'external, economic, market and customer-orientated'; operating objectives are 'internal, technical, performance-orientated, related to the achievement of strategic objectives'; control objectives are 'orientated towards reducing human intervention, reducing dependence on operator control, increasing the amount of production performance information, increasing the speed at which information becomes available'.[5]

Carrie and Banerjee have referred to one of the benefits of new technology in manufacturing as its integrative potential in relation to product design, production planning, and process control systems. This integrative potential, they argue, is likely to enable companies to 'respond more effectively to the challenges of international competition'.[6]

On the basis of a survey of the implications of CAD interactive graphics for employment and skills in the British engineering industry, Arnold and Senker comment that:

> large sections of the United Kingdom motor vehicle and aerospace industries are under serious competitive threat from overseas firms. In order to be successful in staving off this competition, firms in these industries need to be able to design new product ranges, and to modify them rapidly in order to forestall competitors; or, where this is impossible, to meet the competition from new product ranges as soon as possible.[7]

To save on non-labour costs

Possibilities under this heading include capital, energy, material and space savings. These possibilities can be illustrated by drawing on Bessant's survey of the organizational and economic effects of investment in new production technology.[8]

With regard to capital saving, 'investment in microprocessor based machinery can contribute significant savings because the improved performance and flexibility which it offers may make it possible to replace several single purpose dedicated machines. For example, many firms buying CNC machine tools report that one of them can typically replace three conventional machines'. On energy saving, the 'use of microprocessor controllers provides tighter overall control and can be linked to self-optimizing routines within the system. This gives the advantage of reducing energy costs on a continuous basis, adapting to ambient conditions and producing consistent "best" performance.' On material saving, Bessant provides the example of the use of microprocessor-controlled cutters in the clothing industry which can scan material with sensors and calculate the optimum number of patterns to be cut, in order to produce the maximum output with the minimum waste. In a comparison of UK and US government policy towards CAD, Arnold argues that material savings can be made through the creation of databases containing standards information. This enables users to achieve greater volumes with bought-in components by maximizing parts commonality.[9]

On space saving, microprocessor controls are much more compact than the conventional technology. The major advantage, however, is the possibility of remote control – the control system can be located away from the machine, connected via an electronic data link. (This technical control possibility, incidentally, has labour control implications; for example, having the control panel located in a separate room from the machine, with only certain managers and supervisors, and not machinists, having access. Wilkinson found management had done exactly this in one of his case study organizations.[10] More will be said about this matter in a later section on social and organizational objectives in the adoption of new technology.) Additionally, on space saving, the greater flexibility of CNC machine tools can mean that fewer of them are needed than would have been the case with conventional machine tools, with the consequent savings in space.[11]

A note of caution must be entered here regarding the basis of the identification of costs *per se*, along with the attribution of specific figures to particular cost headings. Many promoters of new technology adoption will be required to conduct a form of cost–benefit analysis at stage 3 (investment decision). The analysis will inform senior management's deliberations regarding whether to give the proposal the go-ahead. What do we know about the costing process in practice? Arnold and Senker studied the cost justification(s) given for CAD in thirty-four establishments (see Table 4). Their findings point to an overwhelming emphasis on saving labour costs. Addi-

Why is new technology introduced? 45

Table 4 Basis of cost justification of CAD

Cost justification basis	No. of establishments
Savings in drawing labour	21
Savings in drawing and design labour	3
Savings in estimators' labour	1
No cost justification	5
No reason given	4
Total	34

Source: E. Arnold and P. Senker (1982) *Designing the Future: the Implications of CAD Interactive Graphics for Employment and Skills in the British Engineering Industry*, EITB Occasional Paper, Watford: Engineering Industry Training Board, p. 6

tionally, it is not clear whether 'No reason given' means that there was a cost justification exercise in these establishments but the respondents were not willing to reveal details, or whether they simply refused to answer this particular question. With regard to 'No cost justification' given, perhaps an indication as to why this was so is provided in the following observation:

> Managers had little experience upon which to base any accurate cost-benefit analysis of CAD prior to installation. Forecasts of the potential benefits of CAD included in potential users' investment appraisals were generally based on information provided by CAD systems suppliers hoping to sell their equipment. In general, respondents treated the issue with cynicism, and a number felt that they had produced spurious justifications. It was not clear whether this was because of mistrust between engineering and financial personnel, a feeling that the type of justification demanded by the accountants could not be based *a priori* on any 'hard' evidence, or a sense that the real benefits of CAD were not quantifiable and therefore that any quantitative justification for firms' accountants must necessarily be spurious.[12]

This extract raises some key issues:

1 Managers' and staffs' lack of experience and/or knowledge as a basis for making cost–benefit forecasts.
2 The role of technology suppliers in facilitating the provision and use of figures which will help to justify the purchase of their equipment.
3 The tendency to produce cost justifications because it is expected

or demanded, not because the figures are regarded as accurate or informative (a form of 'ritualistic' behaviour).

4 The possibility that some of the benefits of new technology are not quantifiable anyway.

The danger of overemphasis on the figures is that it drives the analysis rather than strategic considerations having primacy, and that measurements may be seen as supportive. Discussing the costs and benefits of IT in the office, Nahapiet has argued that the result of an emphasis on economic and quantifiable factors is:

> to produce conservatism in the implementation of change. The logic of the approach applies only to well understood, routine problems in an environment with stable conditions so that predictions about the future can be made with a high level of confidence. Attention is therefore mainly concentrated in those activities that are tangible enough to suit these methods of measurement.[13]

Internal politics and public displays of rationality may also play a part (the latter, for example, for the benefit of auditors):

> The decision style of the enterprise may be such that it requires a detailed, economic justification of capital investments ... even when many of those involved recognize its limitations. In such circumstances, it may be politic to present a decision as if it had been adopted primarily as the result of conventional cost benefit analysis, although it is accepted in private that this is not the primary justification for the development. Similarly, an assessment may be used to signal to important outside groups that appropriate processes have been followed, even if, in reality, they have not determined the actual action taken.[14]

To save on labour costs

If organizations are to save on labour costs through the introduction of new technology, there would appear to be five main possibilities, which may be taken up either singly or in combination:

1 An absolute reduction in the number of employees.
2 A reduction in the hours worked by some, at least, of the employees (remuneration rates remaining the same).
3 A reduction in payment for hours worked.
4 A redistribution of work and skills such that there are fewer workers on the higher levels of pay and more on the lower levels.

5 Intensification of work or, to express the matter differently, an increase in labour productivity.

We simply do not possess the data which would allow us to make statements about the extent to which these possibilities have been taken up in practice when new technology has been introduced. The most extensive evidence we have, however, about the social and organizational effects of technological change in the United Kingdom comes from the Workplace Industrial Relations Surveys (WIRS) of 1980, 1984 and 1990.[15] For present purposes it is the 1984 survey which is of especial interest. The 1980 survey is too early, and the 1990 survey, unfortunately, did not carry many questions on new technology (or 'advanced technical change', as it is termed in the WIRS studies). The great advantage of the 1984 survey, however, is that Daniel produced a separate volume based on detailed analysis of responses to those questions which had relevance to technical change, that is, 'advanced' and 'conventional' (the latter not incorporating new technology).[16] The 1984 survey was based upon 2,019 establishments in the United Kingdom employing more than twenty-four people.

Daniel summarized the findings for the employment effects of new technology as follows:

> in a substantial majority of cases the introduction of advanced technical procedures had no short-term impact upon the number of people employed in the sections directly affected. Where, however, it did make an impact, jobs tended, on balance, to be lost ... So far as applications affecting manual workers were concerned, it appeared that the introduction of advanced technology led to increases in manning in about one case in every ten but to decreases in about one case in every five.[17]

Where labour requirements were reduced in a particular part of an organization as a result of new technology introduction, it was rare for employees to be dismissed. More usually they were redeployed, for example to other parts of the organization, or not replaced when they left, or took voluntary early retirement or redundancy. This meant, among other things, that there was often a time lag in labour supply adjustments. It was much more likely that people would lose their job as a result of other changes, such as a downturn in business activity. Indeed, another key finding of both the 1984 and the 1990 surveys was that, generally speaking, workers were likely to support technical change both absolutely and relative to organizational change.[18]

Clearly, much more could be said on the matter of the quantitative effects of new technology. The reader is referred to the literature for a much fuller presentation and discussion of findings than I can offer here.[19] Suffice it to say that, however extensive the survey, it is difficult to disentangle the employment effects of technological change from other changes which have taken place in the organization over a similar period, and from what has been happening in the organization's external contexts. It is yet another matter to evaluate attributions made by managers and others about what has caused any change in job numbers. At the same time it should be borne in mind that, whilst management may have intended to reduce labour numbers, the aim may not have been achieved in full, for a variety of reasons. These are likely to be both organizational and technical, and this is why it is so important to try to tease out what actually happens in practice – that is, outcomes.

A sense of the difficulty of isolating the labour-saving (however that may be defined – see the beginning of this section) intentions and effects of new technology introduction from effects attributable to other causes can be gleaned from the following extracts.

In Arnold and Senker's survey of CAD cost justification, it was seen that all the justifications mentioned referred to savings in labour costs (see Table 4, p. 45). Contrast this with Bessant *et al.*'s finding that:

> In a majority of cases potential labour savings were not a prime motive for innovating: of far more importance were such factors as the need to expand output; to increase the quality of output or the consistency of production; to improve safety by the elimination of hazardous or physically strenuous operations...[20]

This is despite the fact that in their view all the technological innovations they examined were potentially labour-saving.

Bessant *et al.* argue that the crucial factor here is the particular strategy adopted by management and labour towards innovation. To what extent, and in what respects, for example, do managers try to impose changes without taking into account – say, through negotiation – potential labour responses? An 'imposition' strategy, they argue, may well lead to hostility and resistance. This does not altogether explain why labour savings were not found to be a major objective of management in the organizations they studied, unless

Why is new technology introduced? 49

Bessant *et al.* are implying that managers *as part of their strategy* preferred to play this aspect down, given the employee reaction it could provoke. It may be the case, however, that cost centres are switched from labour to machinery, especially where a lot of new technology has been introduced into a given organization. The primary objective may now be to obtain high levels of machine utilization. Labour costs may have become insignificant in relation to machinery and materials. Attention may therefore switch to controlling or reducing the latter, and labour may be treated as an overhead cost. Motteram and Sizer have documented an instance of this type of change at Rolls-Royce, Derby.[21] However, when considering labour costs on a broad front (here subsuming under 'labour' managers, supervisors, machinists, professional engineers, etc.), the switch from emphasizing direct labour costs in production to emphasizing machine utilization and material costs may switch the labour control and cost emphasis from direct to indirect labour.

A later survey of 130 companies by Bessant found labour savings very much on the agenda. (As always, this must be put in context. By the early 1980s UK manufacturing was in the midst of a major recession.) Bessant notes that:

> In economic terms, investment in microprocessor technology offers significant advantages in terms of savings in factor inputs (labour, energy, materials, and so on) which can be achieved through better control and in improved product quality, consistency and differentiation . . . in many cases microprocessor technology can be both labour *and* capital saving.[22]

He found that 'the most important factors were improvements in process control/machine operation, savings in factor inputs (particularly labour and capital), improvements in quality and product range, and improvements in reliability and ease of maintenance'.[23] Labour saving included savings in direct labour costs (through, for example, making workers responsible for more machines); savings in skilled labour (for example, through the replacement of manual lathes with CNC machine tools); savings in indirect labour (for example, through a reduced requirement for maintenance staff because of the increased reliability of equipment and modular design); savings in supervisory labour (via, for example, monitoring and communication systems incorporated into the technology).[24]

Leaving aside outer contextual changes, how might we account internally (i.e. within the organization) for these differences in the attention given to labour costs? One answer may be found in the link which is made between improved control, product quality, consistency, and differentiation, on the one hand, and savings in factor inputs, including labour, on the other. In the extract above, savings in factor inputs appear to be the objective, whereas improved control, etc., appear to be the means. Other findings have pointed to improved product quality and consistency and enhanced control over operations as objectives in their own right. Perhaps what is pointed up here is the difficulty of distinguishing ends from means, and also in deciding which objective(s) are to have primacy.

Another possible explanation relates to the tendency of different managers and technical specialists to allude to or emphasize different potentialities of the new technology. Davies, for example, has argued that different objectives for new technology will be found across different groups of people in the organization: 'The objectives adopted will depend on who participates in the process, and on what assumptions, in terms of human needs and organizational goals, lie behind the design solutions.'[25] It may, therefore, be helpful to talk about 'constellations of motives' for new technology adoption. Methodological problems should also be recognized; for example, it can be difficult to tease out of production engineers preparing the investment justification why they are doing certain things; in any event, their views can differ, even in the same firm. Currie, in a study of managerial decision-making relating to CAD adoption and introduction in twenty UK organizations, found a gap between what engineering managers were espousing in respect of potential costs and benefits and their actual objectives. Note that the existence of this gap had much to do with formal methods of (budgetary) control:

> Whilst engineering managers formally justify CAD in cost-benefit terms by emphasizing those benefits which are amenable to quantification, it appears that informally their priorities are geared to maximizing the qualitative advantages of the technology. Since the existing formal budgetary system acts as a control mechanism of top management, engineering managers have little alternative but to comply with this approach, although many admit that information becomes contrived for the purpose of acquiring resources.[26]

The objectives given for the adoption and introduction of new technology, then, may well depend upon who is actually being interviewed. This could lead the researcher into an analysis of the 'vocabularies of motive' of different occupational groups over time, related to their location in the organization in terms of power, specialism and centrality, and to the changing contexts of their work. It could also lead to a study of the claims to and base(s) of inter-occupational control over certain 'spheres of interest' in the organization related to new technology.

In a study of design engineers at a British Aerospace factory in Bristol, Smith found that equipment suppliers, design engineers and technical managers all emphasized different aspects of the potential of the new technology:

> NC and CAD are usually sold on the strength of their capacity to reduce lead time, save on labour and cheapen labour costs, increase work tempo, and replace skilled operators or draughtsmen by unskilled or less qualified staff. However, designers seeking to buy in such equipment may have to emphasize the opposite features, i.e. how the machinery enhances skill, gives the draughtsmen greater freedom, etc., in order to justify to management that such machinery will not upset industrial relations. If a technical manager was dealing with the board, then labour saving may also appear as a rationale.[27]

Support for savings in labour costs as an important management objective for new technology is to be found in the work of Buchanan and Boddy, White, and Fleck. The latter has argued that 'The elimination of labour, or labour saving, provides the prime economic motivation for introducing robots'. He found 'that the average net effects were in the region of 2·5 people per robot, taking into account patterns of shift working and increases in indirect labour requirements due to the management, engineering and maintenance effort demanded', although these 'indirect' effects were, in the main, concentrated in the early installation phase.[28]

Likewise, in the service sector, Storey, in a study of new technology adoption in insurance companies, found that management's main objective was to reduce unit costs through

> staff reductions locally and at head office, branch mergers and a consequent reduction in the number of highly-paid branch managers and deputy branch managers. The key appears to be one of 'efficiency' judged in terms of cost control, rather than

technological innovation in pursuit of new products or even improved service.[29]

Of course, one of the objectives of new technology adoption may be to increase labour productivity. This clearly has implications for labour cost reduction, either through the displacement of labour and/or through an intensification of work.

Evidence is provided by a number of studies that management's expectation of increased labour productivity is a new technology objective in many organizations. Arnold has argued that one of the two major benefits of CAD is increased draughtsman productivity (the other is increased control over the design process): 'increased productivity reduces design costs, speeds documentation and reduces lead times. High productivity allows a firm to tender for more jobs, increasing its chances of getting work'.[30]

Referring to the formal criteria used to choose between different makes of machinery, Wilkinson observes, 'Reference was made in great detail to costs, suitability to production needs, payback periods, productivity gains and so on' but 'choices among alternative options were frequently coloured by considerations of the type of work they implied and, relatedly, the control issues involved.'[31] He illustrates the control issues through a discussion of the preferences of some interest groups for operator programming on CNC machine tools, as against others who preferred the machines to be programmed separately. In essence, the argument was about whether skill and control were to be retained on the shop floor or transferred to the office.[32] Strategic, control and skill issues relating to new technology adoption are taken up in more detail later in the chapter.

BUSINESS AND TECHNICAL OBJECTIVES

We focus in this section on four main objectives:

1 To improve the capture, processing, storage, transmission and analysis of information.
2 To increase flexibility.
3 To improve control and consistency in production.
4 To achieve improvements in the product.

With the exception of the third, it should be noted that all these objectives are just as likely in principle to be pursued in service and other types of organizations as they are in manufacturing companies.

To achieve improvements in the capture, processing, storage, transmission and analysis of information

These objectives should be familiar to the great majority of readers, for, at the simplest level, they can be achieved through the use of word-processing software on a microcomputer. Such new technology is known to be widely diffused across organizations, whatever their size or the sector in which they are located (to say nothing of use in the home).[33] Given this, it will suffice to provide just a few examples from less well known applications.

Clark et al., in a study of industrial relations issues associated with the introduction of electronic news-gathering equipment into an independent television company, argue that the new technology has major potential advantages over conventional film for the gathering of television news, 'both in the speed with which the news can be brought from the scene to the viewer and in the elimination of film processing'.[34] Arnold and Senker, in their CAD survey, found that a number of organizations had installed this new technology in order to reduce lead times.[35] White draws attention to a number of advantages of new technology: better and more timely information about the state of a process (leading, among other things, to reduced levels of work in progress); faster response time in dealing with errors; the communication of information in marketing, buying and process control becomes more direct, accessible and rapid.[36] Bessant found that better information availability (linked with improved production control) was a common motive for the adoption of advanced manufacturing technology.[37] Direct numerical control can lead to improvements in the capture, processing, monitoring and analysis of information about manufacturing. Computer numerical control machine tools can monitor and respond to tool wear, heat, torque, and various other operating conditions.[38] A control objective of United Biscuits in the introduction of new technology in biscuit manufacture was to obtain rapid management information on key aspects of production. Ciba-Geigy adopted new technology in order to improve the recording and analysis of process performance information.[39]

To increase flexibility

Organizational flexibility can take various forms:

1 Labour.

2 Structural.
3 Manufacturing.
4 Technical.[40]

In turn, each of the above forms of flexibility can be divided into a range of sub-forms. Take labour flexibility as an example. It can take one or more forms: functional/task, numerical, financial and time. It is not possible to explore these possibilities in any detail here.[41] Suffice it to say that they are often closely interlinked in practice, and that the discussion of flexibility, particularly the labour variety, has generated a good deal of debate and controversy in the literature. From the perspective of the organization in its context, the essence of flexibility is the ease with which the organization can respond to changes and developments in its product markets; also the ability to be proactive *vis-à-vis* those markets, that is, to initiate changes before competitors. Much of the debate has centred on whether and, if so, the extend to which managers have explicitly formulated strategies and pursued them, with the aim of making an organization more flexible in one or more of the above ways. Some writers have argued that during the last twelve years or so there has been a significant increase in the number of organizations pursuing flexibility.[42] Others have argued that flexibility is really nothing new, and that its incidence has been overstated.[43] The debate on labour flexibility has polarized around those 'for' its enhanced significance (essentially, Atkinson and his colleagues at the Institute of Manpower Studies, although they have since amended their position somewhat) and those 'against'.[44]

Whilst we cannot enter into the debates here, an indication of the meaning of the terms being used is necessary. *Functional labour flexibility* refers to the process of employees learning and taking on additional job skills and knowledge over time; *numerical flexibility* refers to quantitative adjustments in labour supply, for example not renewing short-term contracts when business conditions worsen. *Financial flexibility* relates to the ways in which pay and grading structures reflect and support the two former types of flexibility. *Time flexibility* focuses upon alternatives to the traditional full-time, forty-two to forty-five weeks in a year contract – for example, an 'annual hours' contract where employees work more hours in the winter months than in the summer, all at the same rate of pay.

Structural flexibility, as the second main form referred to above, is essentially to do with alternatives to the inflexible bureaucratic structure as exemplified in the writings of Max Weber. Examples include matrix and decentralized/divisionalized structures. Manufacturing flexibility has to do with the development of manufacturing organization so as to make the production of goods more responsive to changes in product markets and consumer preferences. Technical flexibility, of course, is very much to do with the nature of new technology *per se*, that is, the inherent flexibility which stems from the programmability of the software, but also its compactness, low energy use and decreasing cost in relation to processing power. We are now in a position to provide some examples from the literature of attempts by managers to increase the flexibility of their organization by the adoption of new technology.

Sorge *et al.*, on the basis of their Anglo-German comparison of CNC machine tool use, have argued that 'it is possible to summarize challenges in production engineering as pointing towards more flexible production, geared to more exacting requirements with regard to design and precision, and subject to tighter control. CNC development and application has responded to such challenges and has helped to bring them forth.'[45] They link the need for more flexible manufacture to the switch many firms made during the 1980s, in a context of low economic growth, away from producing standard products for mass markets and towards a focus on smaller, segmented markets and customized products. This refocusing has resulted in a requirement for a larger number and greater variety of parts, and hence more and different metal cutting, bending, shaping, etc., operations. They argue that the satisfaction of these requirements is both dependent upon, and a causal factor in, the wider diffusion of CNC machinery. The implications for flexibility requirements are that:

> This increased variability of batches is not one which can be handled bureaucratically, through an increased division of labour. On the contrary, it implies increased variability right at the level of the machine and the operator; every CNC operator is likely to have to deal with a greater and more frequently changing range of jobs. Part of this logic then is the increased flexibility and decentralisation of electronic control, by which more flexible changeovers and improvements of programmes can be achieved.[46]

Further evidence of how increasing product differentiation has fuelled the need for manufacturing, technical and labour flexibility is to be found in Bessant, Buchanan and Boddy (where strategic objectives included reduced pre-production lead times and enhanced product quality and consistency), Arnold and Senker, and White, who found that CAD was being used to increase the 'versatility of design processes, enabling alternatives to be systematically and rapidly explored and tested'.[47]

To improve control and consistency

There is some overlap between this objective and the one we discussed earlier relating to improvements in the capture, processing, storage, transmission and analysis of information. However, whilst the latter objective can equally well apply in an office/IT or in a manufacturing context, this one tends to be confined to the latter. Examples include applications of new technology in the control of machine operations, in monitoring machine status, compensating for changing conditions and providing procedural and diagnostic information for operators. This, in turn, facilitates working to finer tolerances and extended machine and tool life as a result of compensation for wear, reduced downtime and self-optimization. A Policy Studies Institute survey of 1,200 UK establishments found 75 per cent rated 'better control of production' to be 'very important' (the most commonly mentioned objective in this category).[48] Sell found the advantages of new technology included enhanced machine control and consistency, more timely and better information, and faster response times.[49]

In the design/draughting area, Arnold found that CAD can bring two main benefits: greater control over the design process and increased draughtsman productivity. The former is achieved by establishing a database of standard component drawings which is then treated as the 'master' version, helping to ensure that any amendments and documentation are consistent throughout.[50] With respect to robotics, Fleck, in a survey of thirty-two cases of industrial robot introduction, found that 'the outstanding advantage of robots is that managerial and technical control is enhanced. An improvement in process control was found in more than half of the successful cases of robot adoption, and was less in evidence among unsuccessful users.'[51]

To achieve improvements in the product or service

The present book has as its focus managerial, social, technical and economic factors associated with the adoption of new technology by organizations; it is not concerned with examining how new products and technology are invented and developed in the first place, whether this happens within the organization or outside it. That is, it takes as given the availability of the technology in the first place. It is not, therefore, appropriate to discuss the product development process. However, I do want to illustrate briefly how new technology can be used in production and service processes to help achieve improvements in the products offered to customers. Common objectives under this heading have been found to be improving product quality and consistency, and reducing the product price.[52] New technology is, of course, only one element in this – other organizational changes would also need to take place, such as in working practices and the training employees receive. And then, also, all these changes may in turn be the means of enhancing the competitiveness and profitability of the organization (back to, among others, the very first objective we considered above). There is a real sense in which it is not just that senior managers may decide to aim for particular objectives, but that they actually have them *imposed* upon them in certain circumstances. The quality objective can be used here to illustrate, drawing on Smith's research in aerospace manufacture:

> The cost-plus funding of the industry lifts it, to some extent, out of the commercial pressures of the market place. Therefore there are more experiments, a greater degree of choice in materials, techniques and machines, and the criteria of cheapness in materials and machines is not always applicable to government contracts. Moreover, the requirements of flight and military considerations frequently meant that quality rather than cheapness of parts was usually a major purchasing principle.[53]

In the service sector new technology has also been used to improve service quality in an attempt to enhance competitiveness and profitability. Examples can be drawn from the banking sector. Home banking through telecommunication links, cash dispensers and itemized account statements are just some of the innovations which have been made in service provision in recent years. In a very real sense, however, these 'innovations' are now taken for granted and allow an organization merely to compete, not to gain 'competitive advantage'. Putting it another way, if they haven't got the technology they are not even in the race, never mind getting ahead of competitors. This means, of course, that if an organization wishes to compete in certain sectors it has to have the technology – it is not an 'option' any more. How the organization uses the technology is another matter, and this has much to do with the process of its adoption and introduction. Hence we are back to managerial and social issues and considerations.

The imprint of social and political phenomena

It is helpful, in concluding this section, to return to the points made earlier about there being constellations of objectives for new technology adoption, and the political nature of the social processes involved. Let us draw on Wilkinson's research. During the adoption phase of CNC technology in the Machine Tool Manufacturer company a capital justification was drawn up, and it appeared as if cost/financial criteria predominated in the decision-making process. However, the observations of a production engineer seemed to indicate some wider concerns:

> With justifications, we look at machines against the type of work anticipated, then justify them solely on the grounds of costs–payback periods and so on . . . It's very important to get the right man for the job, otherwise production suffers. But we get the machine first, *then* the operator . . . If we don't have the right one we'll go outside to find him.[54]

Given the considerable amount of informal discussion which went on before the capital justifications were drawn up, Wilkinson is of the opinion that 'formal justifications could be "*post hoc*" technical rationalisations which tend to play down the social and political considerations which go into them'.[55] Common yardsticks, such as efficiency, product quality and productivity were 'difficult to measure with any degree of accuracy, and in any case are rarely measured in sufficient detail to determine the exact economic advantages over any alternatives'. Formal justifications of capital expenditure included detailed financial and economic comparisons, and formed the basis of decisions, 'But it is probably safe to say that in no instance could it be demonstrated that *in practice* the new technology met the measured expectations of the production engineer who "justified" the technology, or of the machine supplier who advertised it.'[56] Where engineers and managers referred only to financial/economic and production/technical criteria, 'one must remain suspicious and expect to find additional motives'. Given that measurement is necessarily subjective, that there is always more than 'one best way', and that it cannot be taken as given that the employees affected will readily go along with management's plans, 'one must question the real role of "efficiency" arguments in technical change ... arguments about the efficiency of new production technologies can serve as scientific glosses which conceal or obscure the political considerations which have gone into decisions on technical change and work organisation'.[57]

Support for Wilkinson's arguments on the indeterminacy of new technology investment appraisals is to be found in Sorge et al.'s study of CNC introduction: 'A general appreciation of economical [sic] justification methods and values for CNC equipment is very difficult. Formal assessments before acquisition and ex-post evaluations were to be found, but they often had strong elements of hunch and guesswork, and predictions often turned out to be wrong.'[58] Further, 'The justification of CNC ex-ante was in rather general terms often intuitive through lack of information about manning requirements, down time ... equipment reliability, organisational implications and so on.' The emphasis appears, however, to have been on technical advantages/objectives, for 'Ex-ante and ex-post, CNC use in general was justified on the basis of the complexity of the geometric design of the components and the required cutting cycles and sequences. Economic justifications were also discussed by respondents but were often presented as secondary considerations.'[59]

One can also move away from a narrow focus on, say, just the financial implications of new technology by placing it in its wider organizational contexts. For example, it may be unsatisfactory to treat individual departments as profit centres, and attempt to justify new technology on the basis of pay-back or discounted cash flow (DCF) criteria purely within those departments. New technologies 'offer systems gains, potentially improving the performance of the firm as a whole ... DCF and similar methods cannot take account of investment in the long-term technological future'. Putting the matter another way, the new technology should be viewed strategically, in all the senses we discussed in Chapter 2. Arnold has observed:

> DCF and related approaches to 'management by numbers' have displaced engineering competence from corporate strategy formation, and caused concentration on short-term investments ... with managers making financially 'safe' investment decisions at the expense of more risky projects with larger but longer-term payoffs.[60]

Primrose *et al.* have made the point forcefully through their research on CAD investment appraisal practice, and have developed a method for explicitly taking the wider, 'non-quantifiable' benefits into account in the analysis.[61]

SOCIAL AND ORGANIZATIONAL OBJECTIVES

We focus in this section on qualitative issues associated with new technology adoption and introduction. The more strictly quantitative implications were, of course, discussed in the earlier section on labour cost saving. Although an extensive range of issues could be discussed, the concentration here will be on control and skill. As will be seen, there is much overlap and there are many interconnections between these two areas.

Managerial control and new technology

Let us begin by looking at the question of managerial control and, in particular, whether managers use new technology in order to attempt to increase their control over employees. The second main question is, of course: if they do use new technology in this way, are they successful? The emphasis on control over people is to be contrasted with other ways in which the control issue could be addressed; for example, as a means of achieving enhanced control over production (see the discussion on p. 56). This could imply enhanced control over employees as a corollary or result, but, again, much depends on management's objectives and strategies.

Carlo de Benedetti, the Managing Director of Olivetti, has been quite unequivocal about the essence of IT: it 'is basically a technology of co-ordination and control of the labour force'.[62] Benedetti appears to believe that IT is the main means of managerial control over office workers. Downing has also argued that IT, in the form of word-processors, will de-skill staff and, at the same time, increase management control.[63] In a study of the introduction of new technology in the brewing sector, Davies found management's main objectives to be increased control over employees, improved cost efficiency and work-force contraction. She did not find evidence of de-skilling, however, as many of the workers were already semi- or unskilled.[64] Buchanan and Bessant, in an analysis of the introduction of computer integrated manufacturing (CIM) at a process plant, found increased control over production and energy to be key objectives; a production manager observed that 'the computer gives management a greater feeling of control and security: management is no longer dependent on a man patrolling the plant'.[65]

One could continue to provide examples of the control potential of new technology, but at this point it is helpful to pause for a moment in order to review the argument of perhaps the most influential post-war analyst of the labour process, Harry Braverman, for he had much to say about control and skill issues. Braverman observes that:

> Machinery comes into the world not as the servant of 'humanity', but as the instrument of those to whom the accumulation of capital gives the ownership of the machines. The capacity of humans to control the labour process through machinery is seized upon by management from the beginning of capitalism as the prime means whereby production may be controlled, not by the direct producer but by the owners and representatives of capital ... machinery [also] has in the capitalist system the function of divesting the mass of workers of their control over their own labour.[66]

No equivocation there! And much agreement with Benedetti's position. Technology in capitalist societies has always been used by managers as a means of control. Braverman is even more explicit in the following passage:

> Machinery offers to management the opportunity to do by wholly mechanical means that which it had previously attempted to do by organizational and disciplinary means. The fact that many machines may be paced and controlled according to centralized decisions, and that these controls may thus be in the hands of management, removed from the site of production to the office – these technical possibilities are of just as great interest to management as the fact that the machine multiplies the productivity of labour.[67]

At one point in the above extract Braverman may appear to attach some significance to management decisions. This would be to misread him, however, in terms of his basic analysis, because, for Braverman, technology of whatever nature is always going to be tainted by capitalism – in particular, the pursuit of increased profits through the exploitation of workers, ever tightening management control and de-skilling. (Braverman attaches a key role in all this to Taylorism, or 'scientific management'.)

How does one break out of this (assuming one wants to)? Essentially, by arguing that capitalism does not have to mean that management is always going to win and workers lose, or, to put the matter another way, employees can make some 'local' gains whilst still leaving overall managerial control intact. Those 'gains', further, may be won through worker action, but they may also result from managers recognizing that there is 'more than one way to skin a cat', that is, it may be more effective in terms of achieving their objectives for them to be rather more subtle in the exercise of control and, therefore, for example, for them to exercise control from a distance through the devolution of some autonomy to workers. Managers might even thereby 'increase their control by sharing it'. (Friedman argues for the location of managers' control strategies on a continuum ranging from 'direct control' to 'responsible autonomy' according to the nature of the particular external and internal organizational contexts at a given point in time.)[68]

Theorists and researchers of new technology since Braverman have tended to fall into one of three camps:

1 Essentially agreeing with Braverman.
2 The 'managerial choice' perspective, that is, the purposes for which and the ways in which new technology is actually used are down to management's decisions, and the possibilities are open-ended.
3 A sort of 'half-way house' between the two former positions, where there is a certain amount of scope for managerial choice, but where this choice is seen as subject to certain important constraints, such as product markets (a proxy, in a sense, for capitalism) and, not least, the particular type of technology concerned.[69]

It should be apparent that my own position falls into this third camp, that is to say, where certain technologies provide more opportunity for the control and monitoring of work than others. Contrast direct numerical control (DNC) with stand-alone CNC machine tools, for example. With CNC it has been shown that it is perfectly possible for programming and editing work to be done at the machine itself and, what is more, this may also be the most effective option from an organizational point of view. (It seems, however, that many managers fear it would take away their control over production.[70]) The change from stand-alone CNC to DNC, it has been argued, however, results in an erosion of the machinist's discretion: 'Because the machine tool is linked to a central computer that guides and monitors the machine operation, it allows greater control of the machinist's activity.'[71]

An influential post-Braverman analysis of the control question has been offered by Edwards, who sees sequential periods of different forms of managerial control developing over time in parallel with the development of organizations and capitalism. 'Technical control' is one type of control strategy. It:

> involves designing machinery and planning the flow of work to minimise the problem of transforming labour power into labour as well as to maximise the purely physically based possibilities for achieving efficiencies.... Technical control is structural in the sense that it is embedded in the technological structure or organisation of production. It can be distinguished from simple mechanisation, which merely increases the productivity of labour without altering the elements of control.[72]

This may be to understate the role of human agency in new technology deployment and utilization. However, there can be little doubt that in many organizations new technology has transformed the control system.[73] Whilst it follows from my perspective on the control question that managers are not necessarily always going to have things their own way (there will, for example, always be some constraints affecting their choices and room for manoeuvre, and there may on occasions be opposition from affected employees), there are particular problems associated with trying to resist technical control, for:

> Whilst it is a relatively simple matter to defy time and motion technicians ... it is much more difficult to resist the introduction of new technology. The time and motion study person stands before the worker as a blatant symbol of worker oppression by capital. The machine, however, is a mystified oppressor, often taken to be a neutral artifact of technological society.[74]

Let us now look at the research evidence on the control issue. Wilkinson found that an underlying objective of managers in 'at least' two of the companies he studied was to take control over production away from workers.[75] In the plating company, increased management control was sought through de-skilling, and

> the equipment was chosen with this end unambiguously in mind. In fact the firm was even able to instruct the machine control system

suppliers to install the system with this end in mind. The control panels for the plating process were located in a separate room so that only managers could alter them, and thus direct management control over quantity and quality of production could be secured. Thus control was sought through isolation and separation.[76]

However, the picture was rather more complex than this would imply, for there were differences in orientation within management. In the machine tool manufacturer, for example, superintendents and foremen were in favour of shop-floor control of production, whereas some engineers and top managers wanted to take control away from operators to the office.[77] This may be expected to provoke a reaction from the work force, particularly if the introduction stage has been reached. It should be remembered that it is at this stage that 'people on the receiving end of technological advance can most seriously attempt to impose their own interests'.[78] At Wilkinson's machine tool manufacturer the operators had, over the years, developed a certain amount of control over their working practices, aided by some managers. Therefore 'The support of operators by foremen and superintendents meant that programmers would find the appropriation of the editing function extremely difficult unless there was a significant change of policy implemented by higher management.'[79] In the plating and rubber moulding firms management had expressed a preference for shifting control to the office. However, the 'workers succeeded in imposing their own interests, and the working practices which evolved were not to management's designs'.[80]

Whilst it may well be true that it is at the new technology introduction stage that employees have their best opportunity to exercise some influence over events, it is important to recall that it is precisely the new technology itself which can make worker resistance more difficult.[81] Managers also have other means at their disposal for achieving their objectives; for example, they can threaten to shift the work elsewhere if the new technology and new working practices are not accepted. A second possibility is that they can attempt to increase their control over employees through a strategy of de-skilling. Let us now consider the skill question in more detail.

Skill and new technology

Thompson is quite unequivocal about the potential provided by new technology for de-skilling work and, thereby, employees: 'New technologies and work organisations have always provided the opportunities to impose greater control over the workforce and to lower costs through dividing and reducing skills. Current developments centred upon computer technology, radically increase those possibilities.'[82]

Before we develop our discussion of new technology and skill, however, it is necessary to look briefly at the main ways in which skill has been conceptualized. I will draw on Littler's work for this purpose.[83] He has identified three possibilities:

1 On the basis of task range. More highly skilled jobs involve more tasks.
2 On the basis of discretionary content. More highly skilled jobs have more autonomy or discretion. The concept is taken from Fox: 'the behaviours called for by the role may be either specifically defined, thereby offering little choice, or diffusely defined, thereby requiring the exercise of discretion'.[84]

These conceptualizations see skill as having objective characteristics which can be identified and 'added up', as it were. The third version relaxes this requirement:

3 Skill as social status. 'It is theoretically possible for skill to be socially constructed through the artificial delimitation of certain work as skilled.'[85] There are two varieties of this concept of skill:
   (a) A 'strong version', which asserts that certain work can be labelled as skilled whatever the technical content.
   (b) A 'weak version', which accepts that skilled jobs usually have some objective skill content, but 'that it is strategic position within the production process combined with collective organization which gains the occupation a skill label'.[86]

In a study of the social implications of technological change in the British printing industry in the latter years of the nineteenth century, I found it helpful to utilize this 'weak' version to help explain the response of compositors to the introduction of the first composing machines. Despite this major technological innovation, which heightened the division of labour and tied compositors to machines for the first time:

> Many printing workers still viewed their occupation as a highly skilled one, as being part of the labour aristocracy, and therefore as being distinct from many other working-class occupations in

terms of status considerations which flowed from its high skill and historical element . . . It might be added that it no doubt suited the printers, and the union of which they were members, to use status/skill arguments in their efforts to preserve their occupational identity, control and influence.[87]

Conceptualizations of skill have sometimes been idealized in a model of 'craftsmanship', not least, it has been argued, by Braverman. But take Wright Mills as an illustration:

> There is no ulterior motive in work other than the product being made and the processes of its creation. The details of daily work are meaningful because they are not detached in the worker's mind from the product of the work. The worker is free to control his own working action. The craftsman is thus able to learn from his work and to use and deliver his capacities and skills in its prosecution. There is no split of work and play, or work and culture. The craftsman's very livelihood determines and infuses his entire mode of living.[88]

Whether idealized or not, the conceptualization of craftsmanship has had an important influence on writing on the (changing) nature of work. It forms the bedrock of Braverman's analysis of the deskilling and degradation of work under twentieth-century capitalism. As Littler expresses it, 'Braverman's concept of skill emphasises the unity of conception and execution, of planning and doing.'[89]

When referring to skill it is important to distinguish between the job and its requirements and the worker and his/her capabilities. Failure to draw the distinction can lead to confusion in levels of analysis. As Lee has observed:

> Braverman writes as if the 'degradation of labour' and the 'de-skilling of workers' were interchangeable terms, whereas in fact they are not. Even within the workplace the extent to which workers are affected by job changes consequent on the reshaping of production methods is not assessed. The outcome will depend on a large number of factors, including the possibility of worker resistance.

Further, account should also be taken of context, for 'workers' options are not necessarily determined solely at workplace level. Their fate will also vary according to the external availability of employment, for example, which is subject to a wide range of influences.'[90]

On the basis of the above overview, we can now turn to address the question of de-skilling. Braverman's conceptualization involves four dimensions:

> first, the process whereby the shop-floor worker loses the right to design and plan work (that is, the divorce of planning from working); second, the fragmentation of work into meaningless segments; third, the redistribution of tasks among unskilled and semi-skilled labour, associated with labour cheapening; fourth the transformation of work organization from the craft system to modern, Taylorized forms of labour control.[91]

Analysts such as Senker or Thompson and Bannon, have found support for Braverman's de-skilling thesis on the basis of their empirical research. Senker, for example, has observed that 'British managements have been too inclined to look to new technology to dispense with the need for workforce skills, rather than as providing an opportunity for developing those skills and using them more effectively'.[92]

Some researchers, on the other hand, have rejected the inevitability of de-skilling with new technology, arguing that it is in principle equally reasonable to expect to find examples of re-skilling or a redistribution of skills across different groups of workers or occupations. This does not exclude the possibility, of course, that, looking at the skill effects in aggregate across the organization, there will have been, net, a de-skilling of jobs.

Evidence of this open-endedness in terms of skill outcomes has been provided by Jones. On the basis of case studies of five firms in south-west England and south Wales, where NC machines had been introduced, he says that:

> There are, therefore, grounds for rejecting a unilateral motivation and capacity to de-skill on the part of capitalist management. It can be argued that the forces working to determine the skill composition of an enterprise's or an industry's labour force cannot be deduced from inherent tendencies to generate inferior forms of skills.[93]

The factors identified by Jones as likely to affect skill composition are:

> (a) the traditions, strengths, and strategies of the trade unions

involved, and their relationship with the relevant labour markets;
(b) the relevant product market and the physical characteristics of the product;
(c) the occupational structure and production organization within the firms.

Jones concludes as follows:

> There is nothing 'inherent' in the hardware of NC or its concept that would allow for the de-skilling and control and surveillance assumed by both theorists of the labour process and publicists for NC installations. This is not to deny that such motivations exist among manufacturing management . . . [but] management cannot construct, *de novo*, the conditions under which labour is to function . . . no process of a general reduction of skills can be said to be taking place.[94]

Labour process theorists in basic agreement with Braverman's view have tended either to concentrate on instances where new technology *has* deskilled jobs and/or workers or, where re-skilling has been found, to argue that this is only an isolated, marginal case – the long run trend, it is argued, is still to de-skilling.

What is more, even in these 'exceptional' cases, whilst in the short run an increased level of skill may be required, in the longer run these jobs will also be subject to an inexorable process of de-skilling. (See, for example, Kraft's paper on the 'industrialization' of computer programming.)[95]

It seems, then, that what one finds is in part a result of where one looks, of which particular 'spectacles' are worn. It may also be to do with the periodization of the sample. For example, Jones's work involved intensive study of a range of occupations in a few firms over a comparatively short period of time, whereas Kraft's focused on one particular occupation over a longer period.

A variant of the argument that there is a long-term de-skilling trend is that, within this trend, a process of 'skill polarization' is taking place, with a few occupations benefiting from new technology in terms of new and enhanced skills whilst the majority of occupations are de-skilled, and the chances of the occupants of the latter jobs moving into the former occupations are severely restricted. Crompton and Jones, in a study of the changing nature of clerical and administrative work in three large white-collar bureaucracies (a local authority, a clearing bank and a life assurance company), have argued that it is the concentration of females in 'lower-level'/de-skilled jobs which 'props up' the chances males have to move into the relatively few, more highly skilled, jobs at the top of the organization.[96] Computerization plays a key role in this skill polarization:

> On our evidence, it is unquestionable that the computer does 'de-skill' much clerical work and that, as a consequence, control within the organisation is centralised. Yet at the same time, it must be recognised that some highly skilled jobs do emerge: the 'new' jobs of programming, systems analysing and so on.[97]

It should be noted that in the main Crompton and Jones are talking here of computerization via mainframe computers, typically used in a batch-processing mode. This often does not present much opportunity for the re-skilling of clerks' jobs. However, one of Crompton and Jones's organizations had introduced an on-line system of information processing, which could have given more scope. None the less, it 'did not seem to have brought "meaning" and "purpose" back into the work of the bank clerk; indeed the extent of functional specialization in the bank was the greatest of our three case studies'.[98]

Crompton and Jones's work illustrates again the close relationship that exists between skill and control, as well as the need to be aware of gender issues in the restructuring of work associated with technical change. They comment:

> We regard 'control' as essential to the definition of 'skill' . . . workers may be said to exercise 'control' in respect of their *own* labour-power, as well as 'control' in respect of organisational resources – which may include both the labour-power of others and/or material resources. The introduction of computers has both routinised and fragmented the work tasks of the clerk – that is, attenuated control in the first sense – and, by centralising control within the organisation, has removed elements of 'control' in the second sense from lower-level clerical employees.[99]

And, later, that 'The greater the level of mechanisation . . . the more likely was the work of the lower clerical grades to be rated as unskilled or semi-skilled . . . .' However, 'the potential effect of technologically induced de-skilling on the male career structure has been, up to now, significantly reduced by the presence of women who are largely excluded from promotion'.[100]

We can see clearly in the following comment that managerial objectives *vis-à-vis* control are seen as playing a crucial role in the creation of particular forms of work structuring:

> it may be in the managerial interest to maintain an organisational hierarchy (or internal labour market) which *supposedly* [my emphasis] reflects skill differences, even in situations where a 'task centred' analysis might reveal few differences, in terms of skill levels, in fact exist. It is suggested that this strategy – the 'divide and rule' principle – achieves control through compliance, as employees engage in individualistic striving within the internal labour market . . . [hence] work content may play only a minor part in the labelling of a job as 'skilled'.[101]

The above extract also illustrates the possibilities for the social construction of work as skilled, but this time by management to suit *its* purposes.

Notwithstanding our discussion above, we must guard against assuming too close an association between skill and control, for it is necessary to distinguish between the ability of workers to retain skills in, and control over, their jobs. Thompson has observed:

> There is considerable evidence that workers can exercise the power to determine elements of working conditions and rewards, *after* de-skilling has taken place . . . de-skilling can sometimes *confer* bargaining power in circumstances where mechanisation replaces craft labour with semi-skilled workers who have been previously unskilled. This enabled such workers to exercise some control over output and in general to extend workplace organisation . . . what *are* often retained are specific dexterities, which still involve levels of training . . . forms of expertise may be narrower than traditional skills, but they can still constitute effective obstacles to capitalist initiative . . . the struggle in the labour process persists through craft de-skilling . . . [and] worker resistance reconstitutes the struggle at a different level.[102]

In addition, it has been argued that craft-type skills are still required in some cases, for changes in the deployment of skills have been slow to take effect, and 'their impact, even in cases of computerisation, is to modify rather than to destroy traditional skill and to shift the locus of the manual skill requirement from production to planning and maintenance'.[103] Lee's observations are themselves open to question, for some researchers have found a continued need for production skills with the introduction of new technology.[104] Braverman, as we saw, argued that this was perfectly possible 'in principle' but rarely occurred in practice because of an in-built trend within capitalism for work to be degraded and de-skilled. Authors broadly in agreement with Braverman's views on control and de-skilling do, none the less, usually accept that he paid insufficient attention to the possibility that workers will not always readily go along with management's objectives in this area, and may even manage to maintain or reassert some degree of control over their jobs. As Manwaring and Wood have noted, managers will always have to rely on workers exercising their 'tacit' skills.[105]

Rather than managers setting out to de-skill jobs or to create the illusion that de-skilled jobs are actually skilled, it is of course perfectly possible that they do wish to create skilled jobs (or to re-skill jobs) around new technology. Take Wilkinson's optical company. Here managers introduced a system of job rotation and wanted a 'skilled and flexible workforce, rather than a set of specialised, de-skilled machine minders'. Why did management take this approach?

1 The production and general managers appeared to have a moral aversion to any de-skilling possibilities: 'there's no training needed to operate this, so it's de-skilling the job and I don't like that, I like to train somebody . . . All you need to know is about four different movements, whereas on a focimeter (of the old type) you have to know what you're doing.'[106]
2 The general manager had a 'strong philosophy of participation'.
3 Rotation means that absences can easily be covered.
4 It was believed that multi-skilling would allow a low level of shift supervision.
5 They expected it would achieve high levels of motivation and thus a low level of errors due to inattentiveness.
6 The anticipation of a more effective production unit.[107]

A classic example of managers setting out to de-skill work is provided by Noble's research in a US manufacturing plant, where NC programming was separated out from operating the machine tool. Noble asked two shop-floor managers why the operators were not allowed to do their own programming:

At first they dismissed the suggestion as ridiculous, arguing that the operators would have to know how to set feeds and speeds, that is, be industrial engineers. I pointed out that the same people probably set the feeds and speeds on conventional machinery, routinely making adjustments on the process sheet provided by the methods engineers in order to make out. They nodded. Then they said that the operators couldn't understand the programming language. This time I pointed out that the operators could often be seen reading the mylar tape – twice removed information describing the machining being done – in order to know what was coming . . . Again, they nodded. Finally they looked at each other, smiled, and one of the leaned over and confided, 'We don't want them to.' Here is the reality behind technological determinism in deployment.[108]

Despite such attempts to de-skill machinists, Noble argues, management does not usually achieve this objective. The reasons are:

(i) Problems and disputes over the assignment of grades and payment rates to the technology, which [have] not been resolved.
(ii) Problems with the reliability of the machinery: 'management has [thus] had to have people on the machines who know what they are doing simply because the machines (and programming) are not totally reliable; they do not run by themselves and produce good finished parts'.
(iii) The machinery is costly, and mistakes can be very expensive.

If this is true of NC machine tools, it is even truer of CNC, for here the technology incorporates a microcomputer at the machine tool itself, allowing, technically, programming and editing at the machine (with NC, because there is no computer at the machine tool, programming and editing have to be performed separately away from the machine). An illustration of what this can lead to, and hence perhaps of why some managers have resisted moves towards operator programming, is to be found in an electronics plant in Norway: 'Just as CNC has made automatic machining more accessible to shop-floor control, so computer-integrated production systems have made it possible to eliminate certain managerial functions by simply extending the reach of the people on the shop floor.' Noble comments:

How this technology will actually be employed in a plant depends less upon any inherent nature of the technology than upon the particular manufacturing processes involved, the political and economic setting, and the relative power and sophistication of the parties engaged in the struggle over control of production.[109]

It should not be assumed, however, that managers and supervisors are always going to oppose re-skilling, for they may realize that there are some good organizational arguments for creating/maintaining a skilled work force with technological change. As Elger has put it, whilst talking about the integrative nature of much new technology, there is a 'growing importance, for capital, of engineering an active vigilance, responsibility and initiative among workers on its behalf, as a result of the increasing integration, interdependency, and capital intensity of the production process'.[110] Gallie, on the basis of a comparative study of work and worker organization and attitudes in oil refineries in France and the United Kingdom, has argued that:

> There was clearly good reason for management to encourage people to develop skills in handling jobs on different units. It made it much easier to cover illnesses, and the manpower shortfalls due to holidays . . . the real aim of management was to create a much more general capacity for flexibility . . . [111]

Whilst Elger accepts that there may be limits on the potential for de-skilling some jobs in process industries, at the same time he finds no evidence to support a re-skilling thesis, for:

> In that sector capital has, for a period, cultivated residual forms of expertise organised in a manner which enhances their subordination to the requirements of accumulation, as well as developing a more general ideological offensive designed to engineer the forms of 'responsibility' required by capital in the context of capital-intensive production.[112]

Sorge *et al.*, in talking about the switch some of the companies in their sample were making from a functional production layout to group technology (machines of different types grouped together following the logic of a family of parts), found evidence of recognition by managers of the need to develop forms of responsibility on the shop floor, this time in a batch production environment: 'One motivation for such an organization and layout is to cope with greater machining complexity by appealing to, and developing, responsibility and independence on the shop floor.'[113]

The above discussion has brought us back to the flexibility question, for we have, in effect, been talking about aspects of labour, structural, technical and manufacturing flexibility. Let us conclude this section by taking labour flexibility and relating it to the skill and control issue. Even if managers do not have the achievement of labour flexibility as one of their initial new technology objectives, they may subsequently find, after introduction, that they need it in order to achieve wider business objectives such as reduced delivery times, reduced work in progress and stock levels, and enhanced product quality. This raises the possibility that they may recognize the advantages of changing from a de-skilling/management control to a re-skilling/redistribution of control strategy. The change may, of course, be in essence cosmetic (as Elger argues); it will certainly take time and it will have a cost. It is not easy to switch from a strategy which has been in operation for some time and represents a major investment of effort, but that does not mean that it cannot be done.[114]

WHY STUDYING OBJECTIVES IS NOT A STRAIGHTFORWARD MATTER

In the concluding part of this chapter we shall address the following matters:

1 The range of objectives which new technology allows an organization to pursue.
2 Which objectives have been pursued in practice, according to research findings.
3 The imputation of rationality to the process of adopting new technology.
4 Implementation issues.

What's possible? The variety of objectives

We have seen that new technology, because of its inherent flexibility, compactness, low energy use and decreasing cost in relation to processing power, technically allows the pursuit of a wide range of objectives. Child has emphasized the central role of choice in the adoption and introduction of new technology; Buchanan and Boddy talk about new technology having enabling (rather than determining) characteristics; Bessant talks about the central importance of 'design space', in the sense of the range of possibilities and choices that are available.[115] Tricker's schema provides a further illustration of the choices opened up by new technology and the central role of managerial decisions and control. He observes that 'the questions are fundamentally about management and organization, not about computers . . . the choices need to be driven by the business needs, not those of computer systems'.[116] In distinguishing the main issues faced by top management in the design of information systems, three main levels need to be taken into account: the technical, the operational and the organizational. The technical level provides facilities 'for the communication and processing of data for legitimate use anywhere in the organization'.[117] It includes telecommunications, computers and support systems. The operational level is concerned 'to ensure the availability of relevant data, for the enterprise to transact its business and for the decision-takers to be informed'. Consequently it includes the capture, storage, processing, retrieval and presentation of data. Facilities at the technical level will obviously affect what is feasible at the operational level, but the two levels are none the less quite distinct: 'Management at the operational level involves administration of the date resource: it is different from management of computer and communications technology. Attention is directed to the user rather than to the equipment . . . .'[118] The organizational level is the level of the management of the enterprise, concerned, for example, with setting goals, allocating resources and structuring the relationships between its parts. The connections between the levels can be illustrated as follows:

> The changes that are now feasible at the technical and the operational level provide new opportunities at the organizational level for creating the structure and adopting the management style that the executives think consistent with their strategies. They may shift towards greater central oversight of corporate affairs or devolve power to decide out towards the periphery of their organization.[119]

Objectives in practice

Our detailed overview of the three main types of objective has shown that, on the surface at least, financial, economic and technical criteria predominate. To take a few brief, additional examples here, Hopwood has argued that the objectives set for computer-based information systems are normally of a short-term technical, and quantitative economic nature, whilst the human and organizational objectives and aspects are usually ignored. Why is this the case? 'Generally, the technically-orientated approach has predominated because it is based on relatively well-developed methodologies ... and tends to reinforce the existing and well-established power structures.'[120]

Symon and Clegg, on the basis of a study of CAD/CAM implementation, have addressed the question of why the process was technology-led. They put forward four main reasons:

1 Organizational differentiation, with the resulting group loyalties, divisions of the work force and political behaviour.
2 Scarcity of organizational resources, particularly expertise with the technology and its wider implications.
3 Lack of strategic orientation.
4 The complexities and uncertainties involved.[121]

Child also appears to give primacy to financial and economic objectives, with social and organizational objectives being seen as essentially derivative, or even as not objectives at all, but rather as consequences of objectives and strategies formulated in the former area (see pp. 77–8).[122]

But let us reflect upon the nature of these objectives and strategies. Are they as rational as some commentators and managers would have us believe?

Rationality and new technology adoption

The nature of one's response to the above question very much depends, of course, upon how rationality is defined. I have no intention of entering into that debate here, but will provide some indication as to its use in the new technology adoption area. Hopwood has argued that:

> Information system requirements are closely related to organisational power and emerge from essentially political processes which characterise organisational life. Although official evaluations attempt to suggest that new systems are neutral technical artefacts, there is strong grassroots awareness that this 'rational' perception is a very partial representation of reality.[123]

Hopwood, an accounting specialist, recognizes, as we saw above, that the technical emphasis sits comfortably with existing power structures. Perhaps the most influential statement on this matter, however, has been made by Child.[124] He points to a number of problems with the rationality concept. 'Rational' from whose point of view, for example? Internal political processes and satisficing behaviour can be influential. In relation to implications for the labour process, it is the 'outcomes' that matter, and different strategies have different implications for employees. Indeed, one might add that different strategies and policies might be formulated for different groups of employees. (The Institute of Manpower Studies distinguishes, as we saw, between 'core' and 'peripheral' groups, and argues that different employment and development policies are applied to each group.) Furthermore, whilst it should be recognized that many managerial strategies are not formulated with labour aspects and implications centrally, if at all, in mind – for example, those directed at the financial or marketing areas – they could well none the less still have consequences for labour. Finally, it should not be taken as given that, because a strategy has been formulated, it is going to be implemented exactly as planned. One only needs to point here to the work of people like Wilkinson on the political processes involved, to make the point.

Given the above, it needs to be asked whether there is any point in talking further about 'managerial strategies' for labour. Child recognizes this. His response is as follows:

> The point of departure is the observation that in capitalist economies corporate managerial strategies will necessarily reflect a consciousness of certain general objectives which are the normal conditions for organisational survival. These objectives are orientated to accumulation and are often expressed by senior managers in terms of 'profitable growth'.[125]

Further, these strategies:

> may sometimes be unspecific and poorly understood, they may be subject to reinterpretation and opposition by functional and junior managers, and they may encounter worker resistance both informally in the workplace and through trade union action. Even in the absence of such opposition, the translation of policies and strategic decisions to the organisation of the labour process will require detailed working out by lower levels of management, by

specialists ... and possibly by shopfloor and office workers themselves.[126]

Storey's work brings into question whether even top management can be said to develop strategy. On the basis of a review of empirical research in this area, he concludes that 'there seemed little evidence here of sophisticated construction of strategy'.[127] He refers to Spencer's study of directors, where she found them willing to admit that 'boardroom decisions were reached in a fashion "like any sort of dinner party"'.[128] Despite the misgivings that writers such as Storey have about the notion of managerial objectives and strategies, there is understandable reluctance to abandon the notion altogether. One alternative is to talk about 'the imperatives of capitalism', which might jettison analysis of the complexities of this matter. Another is to adopt an anarchic analysis, where everyone's objectives, power and interests count equally, yet somehow come together via a miraculous 'guiding hand', or balancing of forces.

McLoughlin et al. accept that there have been valid criticisms of the managerial strategy concept but argue that 'some notion of strategy is inherent in managerial actions concerning processes of change in organisations, such as the introduction of new technology'.[129] They argue for:

> a more dynamic and flexible notion of strategy which seeks to avoid static or unitary conceptions, and which is sensitive to divisions and conflicts within management. What we propose is a view of managerial actions as a series of strategies or 'substrategies' which are developed over time, and in the context of changing opportunities, problems and constraints.[130]

The lack of an explicit, coherent strategy for the adoption of new technology on the part of many managers has been recognized by management consultants, who have seen a market opportunity here for their services. Keen, for example, has argued that piecemeal approaches are commonly adopted which include a technocratic orientation, vague definitions, and a lack of sensitivity to the political and organizational aspects and implications. He puts forward a recommended strategy for introduction, which emphasizes taking the 'people' element into account.[131] There is an important educational point here, for if managers are not aware of all the options they can hardly be expected to consider them.

Sorge et al.'s work would appear to indicate, however, that

clear-cut strategies are lacking, not just because of technocratic approaches and restricted perspectives, but also of the indeterminacy of the contextual and technical aspect

> With the increased variability of CNC application and organisation techniques, initial justification for CNC machines was becoming much more uncertain than for NC machines of previous types. Realistic estimates of payback increasingly depended on the kind of utilisation and organisation strategies adopted. This, on the other hand, often had to be tried out or found out. Therefore, justification for CNC machines before acquisition was becoming more and more precarious.[132]

The above recognition is not necessarily inconsistent with maintaining that managerial objectives and strategies should be of central importance in the adoption of new technology; rather, it is to accept that it is not easy to capture and conceptualize all the complex implications, aspects, interrelationships and possibilities. Perhaps in the end it has to be accepted that technological innovation involves an element of faith. However, that 'faith' should be based on a broad, contextual, awareness of the range of possibilities which new technology's flexibility allows.

Implementing objectives and strategies

There is not much point in having well researched and thought through objectives and strategies for new technology if, when it comes to implementation, managers, technical specialists and other employees take no notice of them. In other words, if there is a 'loose coupling' between the former and the latter. It is not within the remit of the present work to discuss how a 'tightness of coupling' might be achieved, but we will now look at what has been found to occur in practice. It is helpful here to draw on Buchanan and Boddy's distinction between strategic, operating and control objectives. Whilst Buchanan and Boddy saw strategic objectives as playing a crucial role in technological change on the basis of the technology's flexibility, they found that 'the strategic gains may be overlooked in the pursuit of operating and management control objectives' and that 'The impact of information technology may [thus] depend to a large extent on how managers relate its application to broader business objectives and to the roles and functions of management itself.'[133]

Bessant distinguishes between strategic and tactical decision-making, where the latter is a regular, planned process, often linked to annual investment budgets. It is employed in manufacturing innovation in a situation where the basic products or processes remain unchanged, and is often the responsibility of operational managers and supervisors. Tactical decision-making is used in 'manufacturing innovation', that is, where the basic products or manufacturing routes remain unaltered, and is often the responsibility of operational managers and supervisors. This type of innovation is 'more strongly influenced by local level issues [such as the] fit with existing patterns of production, local traditions of innovation . . . industrial relations . . . and so on'. Thus 'From the point of view of the engineers and designers involved, IT often represents little more than a sophisticated new set of tools for carrying out the same tasks.'[134] This provides another useful corrective against any tendency to see the introduction of new technology as necessarily highly innovatory and as forming part of a coherent managerial strategy.

Another reason why implementation cannot be assumed to flow smoothly from objectives and strategies is that there may be disagreements, and indeed conflicts, among the actors involved about what these are, or should be. We talked earlier about interoccupational variations here, and about the different vocabularies of motive which might be articulated (see pp. 50–1). Smith, for example, found divergences of interest and attitude between managers and design engineers over the adoption of CAD. He warns us not to assume that managers are necessarily or always in favour of making changes:

> It is often assumed in the literature on new technology and de-skilling that managers are unreservedly in favour of change, especially change that enhances their power and control at the expense of skilled labour. From my research at Filton, I found this model of management-led or inspired technical change unrealistic. Design engineers were frequently at odds with management about the necessity for changes. Managers often stood in the way of new methods and techniques in the interests of peace in their department.[135]

In their study of the introduction of NC machine tools at the Caterpillar Tractor Company, Buchanan and Boddy found some reluctance to change on the part of managers, as well as differing objectives across different occupational groups. In discussing the divergence of attitudes they found towards the introduction of NC, they report that:

> Innovation throughout the company was inhibited by [American] management conservatism and to some extent by the company policy concerning interchangeability of components. Senior manufacturing management supported the investment because they were frustrated with the old machines. Middle management not directly concerned with factory operations generally supported the investment for the productivity and cost benefits they felt would result. Senior cost accounting managers opposed the investment because the plant was at that time unprofitable and they could not justify the expenditure on a return on investment analysis. Factory management were opposed to the investment as they felt that it would weaken their control over workflow.[136]

In summarizing the findings from all their case studies, the same authors observe that:

> Different management levels and functions had different expectations about technological change and the opportunities and threats that it presented. Senior management and accountants concentrated on costs, return on investment, company image and competitiveness. Middle line management tended to concentrate on control of workflow. Supervisory management appeared to focus on reducing disruption of workflow and human frustrations. Service departments concentrated on the ability of the technology to deal with information that was previously handled manually.[137]

Not only may objectives differ across occupations, but they may actually conflict. Voss, for example, has observed that 'whereas manufacturing management often adopted [the new technology] because of the advantages of short lead times, senior management policies aimed to utilise their cost reduction possibilities and consequently loaded them so heavily that lead times were not improved'.[138]

Given the range of objectives and strategies, it is perhaps not surprising that some of them may conflict, particularly if they are pursued by different groups in the organization. Hence they will not always provide an unequivocal indication of whether to undertake the investment in new technology. The opportunities for the exercise of power, negotiation and persuasion are apparent in a context of uncertainty and competing rationalities and rationales.

One way out of this impasse, not just of differing objectives and strategies but also of lack of information upon which to base assessments, has been to turn to the suppliers of the new technology (hardware and software). However, this approach has not always resolved the problem either. The figures and the evaluation method to be used at the investment decision stage, for example, could be provided by the supplier(s). The possibility must therefore exist, to put it mildly, that the figures will be somewhat biased in favour of adopting the new technology. The strategies new technology suppliers use to try to win business are an under-researched area, and we know little about the specifics of their objectives and tactics in this matter. Certainly there is evidence that they try to get the purchaser 'locked into' their product, sometimes perhaps exploiting the latter's unfamiliarity with new technology. In his study of the introduction of IT in three UK insurance companies, Storey observes that 'many managers see themselves as locked into a certain technology' and adds that 'This may even extend itself into being committed to a particular supplier,' as Barras and Swann found with a number of major British insurance companies in their relations with IBM.[139]

Given their lack of knowledge, managers from the purchasing company may place their trust in 'successful' suppliers, as Arnold and Senker found in their CAD research:

> Until managers were conversant with CAD they were not adequately qualified to select the best system for their needs, but they could not become conversant with CAD without first making this selection and acquiring a system. Often, managers selected the market leader's product on the basis that high market share implied high product quality and because of the extensive and credible after-sales service and support offered. The ability to perform a technical evaluation of CAD was rare. One manager had used a 250 question questionnaire found in a magazine as an instrument with which to 'poke' vendors. He said that he did not understand some of the vendors' replies, and that he often did not understand the questions either.[140]

We must be careful, of course, not to assume that all managers place a high level of trust in their suppliers. There is a possibility, for instance, that the influence is the reverse of that just described, with the purchasers influencing the suppliers of the technology on the basis of *their* knowledge of its capabilities and characteristics. We can again draw on Arnold and Senker's work to illustrate:

> The subsidiaries of United States firms which market United States-designed CAD systems provide less, and less effective help to their customers in the United Kingdom than they provide to their customers at home. United States vendors' sales and support organisations in the United Kingdom are smaller than, and inferior in quality and experience to, their counterparts in the United States. It was clear from some of our interviews that many of the vendors' staff barely knew more about CAD applications in industrial practice than recent United Kingdom purchasers. On a number of occasions ... users said they had approached vendors' staff in the United Kingdom for assistance, only to find themselves in the position of advising vendors' staff, rather than the other way round.[141]

CONCLUSION

Our review of new technology objectives, then, has revealed a wide range of objectives and a good deal of associated complexity across our three broad areas: financial and economic, technical and production, social and organizational. Indeed, as we found, it is sometimes difficult to disentangle and categorize the objectives, given the close interconnections in practice. And this despite the fact that I focus throughout the book on empirical findings – either my own or those of other researchers. Analysis and 'disentanglement' can become problematic when one tries to unravel the latter, for studies are inevitably informed by particular theoretical perspectives; some, for example, interpreting the findings within a Braverman(ic) deskilling/control/real subordination of labour schema, others within a framework which accords pre-eminence to financial/economic criteria, and yet others via an interactionist/political/contingency framework. It is important to know whether the stated objectives were actually those of the people involved in the organizations studied, or whether they were what the researchers took to be, or interpreted as, those objectives (which might not necessarily be the same, of course).

There has been implicit acceptance in a number of studies that what organizational members *tell* researchers have been the objectives of the adoption of new technology corresponds with reality. To make observations like this is, of course, to raise methodological issues. That could lead into a discussion of the internal and external validities of, say, survey techniques as against longitudinal case studies. Many additional issues – such as 'Who was interviewed/questioned?' 'Did the researcher cross-check the replies of different people?' 'Did any of the respondents have an interest in presenting a particular picture to the researcher?' – could also be raised. Further, it has occasionally proved difficult to decide where the cut-off point should be between reporting empirical findings as such (and that has its own inherent problematics, as we have seen) and elaborating upon the theoretical perspectives which have informed those studies. Indeed, the former are sometimes so closely interwoven with the latter that separation becomes virtually impossible. As someone once said, 'Facts seldom speak for themselves.'

Chapter 4
Adopting new technology
Processes of involvement

The main objective of this chapter is to consider the mechanisms or processes through which employees in particular, but also managers and other staff specialists, have been involved in the adoption of new technology. Our focus in the previous two chapters on managerial strategies and objectives for new technology has meant that we have already paid a good deal of attention to the part played by managers in the adoption process; therefore we shall devote much more attention here to employees. Two further preliminary comments are in order. As always, the emphasis will be upon reporting the empirical evidence on the various forms of involvement found in practice, as against setting up a theoretical model of the possibilities for involvement as seen or desired by the researcher.[1] Secondly, the distinction between managers/staff on the one hand and employees on the other is, of course, in a formal sense a false one, for managers and staff specialists are also employees if they have no share in the ownership of the organization for which they work – as is by far and away the most usual case. The distinction is more than a matter of convenience, though, for, whether managers have ownership or not, as individuals they are in positions imbued with a greater degree of power than non-managers or staff specialists. This allows them to exercise at least some degree of control over the work of employees below them in the organizational hierarchy, and this fact of itself commonly makes for notable differences between the nature of the work performed by these people, not least in terms of issues like involvement in new technology adoption.

The chapter is divided, then, into two main sections. The first looks briefly at the involvement of managers and staff specialists in new technology adoption, whilst the second examines employee involvement in terms of three major possibilities: through trade unions, consultation and job (re)design.

MANAGERS AND STAFF SPECIALISTS

Of course, a broad range of, in many cases, very different jobs can be included under this heading, ranging, for example, from scientists working in an R&D department, process engineers and IT staff on the one hand to accountants, sales people and personnel specialists on the other. We shall of necessity here have to talk in rather general terms about a range of occupations and sub-specialisms.

Having said that, in studying the adoption of new technology it is important to know which particular managers or staff specialists have been involved, for the actual objectives set, the strategies of adoption and introduction, the processes of involvement, etc., are all likely to be a result of decisions/actions taken by some of these people. This means that their work and non-work backgrounds, qualifications, experience and orientations to work and employment will probably have had some impact upon those decisions; but the nature of the decisions themselves, their premises and expected concomitant effects, as well as their process of implementation, can be expected to vary according to who has made them. The point can be illustrated by the case of accountants and engineers in the United Kingdom, who have often had no training or education in the management of technology. They have tended to take a restricted view, therefore, of what is required to release its potential through the effective and efficient involvement, deployment and training of users (in summary terms, commonly referred to as a 'Tayloristic/ Fordist' perspective).[2] The emphasis may be upon cost saving rather than value added.[3]

Another reason why it is important to know which particular managers/staff have been involved in new technology adoption is that there can be differences of opinion and orientation *within* management, and they can lead to conflict and the exercise of power through, for example, the imposition of particular adoption strategies. Certain groups/occupations may try to further their own interests through the adoption process at the expense of other groups whose power base has been attenuated as a result of the particular type of technology concerned. Indeed, it should not be automatically assumed that all managers will be in favour of new technology adoption. There is evidence that resistance can occur, for a variety of reasons such as lack of understanding of what it can do or how to use it, fear of the unknown, satisfaction with the *status quo*, the perceived unreliability of the technology, concern about the personal consequences of any attendant organizational changes, fear of diminished authority over those lower in the hierarchy and enhanced control by those above. Issues relating to status and personal interests, in particular, then, can figure strongly. To illustrate, managers may resist using the computer keyboard, feeling that it is demeaning and attenuates their established formal relationships in the organization.[4] Blackler and Brown have criticized what they term the 'orthodox' approach to new technology adoption for its unitary concept of organization, for its antagonistic view of participation, and for taking a short-term cost-substitution approach to evaluation.[5]

What is more, some managers or staff specialists may be excluded from the process of adoption. In a case study of new technology introduction into a clearing bank, Child documents how:

> The bank's central staff department, whose main concerns include personnel matters, job content issues and union negotiation, has only recently persuaded MSD [Management Services Department] of the necessity for their involvement in the early stages of decision-making on new technology, both to introduce a social perspective into the discussions and to permit informal communication with staff and unions.[6]

This state of affairs is by no means restricted to the United Kingdom. A European Foundation study found that across all the Western European countries it surveyed, with the exception of Germany, 'middle and lower levels of supervision were often as distant from involvement in the process of change as the workforce and their representatives, brought in only on a functional basis at the implementation of subsequent phases'.[7]

The marginal or non-involvement of certain management specialisms may be linked with their absence at corporate levels of decision-making and strategy formulation. Lee has argued that whilst:

> The technical background of engineers gives them an understanding of the potential and limitations of IT which is not available to other professionals and managers within the corporate enterprise [none the less] it is debatable whether British engineers have achieved a place within corporate capital which would allow them to exert such influence.[8]

Lee draws on Whipp and Clark's study of the Rover SDI project to pose the question why CAD was not used in the design process. Their evidence

> suggests that there was no 'engineering voice' in the company at that time which could push for an innovative approach towards the potential of IT. Top management . . . were apparently not drawn from an engineering background, so they were ill equipped to recognise the potential role of CAD for the SDI project.[9]

In contrast, in more recent years, when there has been an engineering champion on the main board, corporate strategy has embraced a major commitment to the development and utilization of new technology in engineering.

An additional dimension of managerial decision-making on new technology is revealed by the (University of) Warwick survey of industrial relations in multi-establishment organizations.[10] Three main levels of decision-making are identified: corporate, divisional and enterprise. Decisions about new technology adoption may be taken at one or more of these levels and divisions, and enterprises may be given more or less room for manoeuvre. Martin found in his analysis of the data that there were differences of view about what happened according to which level of managers one talked to:

> According to corporate-level managers, the most common procedure for deciding upon new technology was for establishments to recommend action, but for corporate level to approve, specified in 43 per cent of cases; the second most common method was for the corporate level itself to decide, in 31 per cent of enterprises; establishments were able to decide for themselves without securing anyone's approval in only 7 per cent of firms.[11]

There was, however, a good deal of sectorial variation, and the corporate level was much more likely to have direct responsibility in non-diversified companies.

According to these corporate managers, divisional managers played a minor role in new technology decisions (making the decision in 3 per cent of cases and requiring the approval of corporate managers in 10 per cent). But when divisional managers were asked directly, they gave themselves a more important role: deciding in 12 per cent and giving approval in 38 per cent of cases.[12] Establishment-level managers corroborated the views of the corporate managers;

they also said they were the level most likely to decide upon the process of adoption and introduction. Of all the specialist managerial or staff functions which might be expected to have an involvement in new technology adoption and introduction, given, as we have seen, the wide-ranging nature of the people possibilities and implications, perhaps Personnel stands out because of its expertise and focus here as well as the fact that it has an organization-wide brief and is therefore not restricted, in principle at least, to just one part of the organization.[13] Whether one is talking about IT, AMT, new technology for service provision or medical applications, there are employee (and, sometimes, customer/client) implications. The survey evidence, however, points to a very different picture. One of the main sources of empirical data on this matter is the WIRS series (see Chapter 3, pp. 47–8). A certain amount of information was gathered in the 1984 and 1990 surveys through interview questioning; some of the 1984 data are reported in Daniel's 1987 technology-focused book.[14] The Warwick company-level survey also contains some data.[15] In the main, however, I draw here on a recent paper by Legge which draws together not only the WIRS data but also the case study evidence.[16]

The position may be summarized by stating that personnel specialists have been only marginally involved in new technology adoption and introduction. Even when personnel considerations have not been ignored, 'the role of personnel specialists appears to be one of late-in-the-day facilitators of implementation, constrained by technical and financial parameters over which they have little say and to which they can merely react'.[17] Legge addresses three main questions:

1 Why has there been such a low level of involvement by personnel specialists in the United Kingdom?
2 Is this marginalization likely to continue in the 1990s, given in particular the emergence of human resource management?
3 What part have personnel/HRM *considerations* played in the technical change process in the late 1980s and 1990s?

We have not the space here to capture the richness of Legge's discussion, and so will have to content ourselves with a brief overview of the major conclusions. On the first question Legge puts forward three main responses.

First, people have been secondary to other considerations in the choice and implementation of new technology, and thus personnel specialists' peripheral and reactive involvement is only to be expected. This argument sits readily with that put forward in Chapter 3, where we discussed the objectives which dominate new technology adoption in practice.

Secondly, as employees have welcomed rather than resisted new technology, personnel specialists' involvement did not take off at implementation either (i.e. they were not usually required to deal with tricky and complex issues relating to pay, gradings, employment, etc.). We shall have more to say about this matter later in the chapter when we discuss the WIRS findings in this area.

Thirdly, even on the rare occasion when resistance did occur, Personnel's role was not seen as crucial because of the weaknesses and divisions of the trade unions and of employees more generally. An additional factor which impacts upon all the previous observations is that personnel specialists simply did not exist in the great majority of organizations. (Even on a fairly broad definition of 'personnel specialist', only 15 per cent and 17 per cent of the WIRS establishments had them in 1984 and 1990 respectively.)

On the second question posed by Legge, i.e. whether this marginalization of personnel specialists in technical change is likely to continue in the 1990s, the short answer is 'Yes.' To take the WIRS data, in the great majority of workplaces in 1990, just as in 1984, employee relations issues are dealt with locally by general and line managers.[18] Sewell and Wilkinson, for example, found many of the duties of personnel specialists had been devolved in this way, whilst their remaining responsibilities had been de-skilled and subjected to external control.[19] The external context of organizations in the 1990s has much in common with that prevailing in the mid-1980s, when WIRS 2 was published. Thus:

> the explanations in relation to the early to mid-1980s not only still hold, but have been reinforced by the return of severe recession and the continuing decay of unions' power and their marginalization in industrial and social life. New realism in industrial relations has lost its novelty and become a taken-for granted fact of life after a decade of uninterrupted Conservative government ... the fact that personnel specialists may have retreated to non-interventionist roles ... or stuck with a symbiotic relationship in which the host partner (unions) continues to grow weaker, is hardly a stance for developing a proactive role *vis-à-vis* technical change.[20]

In order to answer the third question, Legge draws upon recent

case study-based evidence, particularly that emanating fr
work of Pettigrew, Hendry et al. at the Warwick Centre for Corporate
Strategy and Change, and that of Storey.[21] Whilst, as we have seen,
personnel specialists have, in the main, continued to play either no
role in technical change in most organizations because they simply
have not had a presence or a marginalized one, there is evidence that
personnel *considerations* have come to play a more important role,
but 'as an executive and line management rather than personnel
specialist concern'.[22] This, according to Storey, has been occurring
in situations where managers have sought to develop employee
commitment to and effective utilization of new technology through
consultation, team-building and training, and 'has often been in the
context of devolved management and the revitalization and legitim-
ization of line management transformed into "manufacturing" or
"business" managers eager to experiment with non-proceduralized
approaches to managing change'.[23]

Whilst personnel specialists, then, have generally played a very
limited role in technical change, and especially in its adoption, there
are certain exceptions. In an earlier paper based upon case study
work, I showed how their involvement varied widely across different
organizations, and could certainly not be described as marginal in
two of them.[24] In a later study of personnel specialists, HRM and
technical change at a green-field site company (Venture Pressings,
in Telford, Shropshire) the former were *centrally* involved in the
strategic and organizational aspects of technical change. Clark's
findings were similar at Pirelli Cables, Aberdare, and Hendry's
likewise at GKN Hardy Spicer.[25] Further evidence that personnel
specialists can sometimes play a deeper role in technical change
will be presented in certain of the case studies which follow in
Chapters 5–8. The cases will also show which particular managerial
and staff specialists become directly involved in new technology
adoption and with what effects.

EMPLOYEES

As indicated at the beginning of the chapter, the focus here is upon
the ways in which and the extent to which employees have some
input into, and perhaps influence over, the new technology adoption
process. The interest is in three main possibilities: involvement
through trade unions, consultation and job redesign.

'Involvement' here covers a number of alternatives. Let us take two situations at the opposite extremes of a continuum from 'high degree of involvement' to 'no involvement'. Employees may significantly change or amend management's objectives and/or strategies, that is 'intervene' in the decision-making process, or they may simply be told by managers or supervisors what is going to happen. (This, incidentally, rather stretching the meaning of the word 'involvement'.) There are, of course, a number of positions which could be taken up between the two extremes. As consultation and job design are dealt with separately below, the next section focuses upon trade union involvement in new technology adoption through collective bargaining.

Involvement through trade unions

In a book about *managing* the adoption of new technology it is perhaps helpful to explain why trade unions are being considered in this discrete way. There are two main reasons. First, the process of managing – in the sense understood here, at least – does not, it seems to me, rule out employees or trade unions actually being involved, both directly and indirectly; we are not just talking about *'managers and new technology'*. Secondly, and perhaps even more important, even if one were looking at new technology adoption from a managerial perspective, or exclusively in terms of the involvement of managers, it would still be necessary to take into account the policies, approaches and impact of trade unions on new technology introduction, for what is *possible* and what is *achieved* by managers with new technology adoption can have much to do with the trade union response. There are four main possibilities in a given organization with respect to the *potential* for trade union involvement:

1 No trade union members in the organization.
2 Some union members, but no union recognized by management for the purposes of collective bargaining.
3 Some union members, some of whom are in a union which is recognized by management.
4 Some or all employees are in a union and every union is recognized by management. (There may only be one union in the organization which has employee membership and at the same time is recognized by management, in which case there could be what is referred to as a 'single-union agreement'.)

Clearly, there is no possibility of trade union involvement in 1 above! What is more, there is unlikely to be much union involvement or impact in the second case. The real possibilities occur in instances 3 and 4, but it does not follow that the chances are greater in 4 than in 3, for a number of considerations come into play; for example, perhaps the union(s) which are recognized by management in case 3 can draw strength from representing a tightly knit group of workers who possess skills and knowledge which are at a premium within the organization and outside it (in external labour markets). The new technology may be coming in to this area – perhaps, indeed, a key reason for management wishing to introduce new technology may be precisely the control exercised by these employees over their work. Back to objectives and strategy again (see especially the section on control and skill objectives in Chapter 3). On the other hand, to take case 4 above, and a single-union agreement, although union membership is open to all employees – and even if it is encouraged by managers when employees join the company – not many of them may in practice join. Whether this is the case or not, the union may exercise little effective power. The reasons could include high levels of unemployment, intense competition in product markets (especially where the emphasis is on price competition, with the resultant impact upon costs), alternative mechanisms for employee communication, grievance settlement, discipline and control (perhaps with an individualist, rather than collectivist, orientation), the predominant management style. Nissan, Sunderland, have operated a single-union agreement since the plant opened several years ago and the senior management position has been that they encourage new employees to join the union. Yet membership is reported to be less than 20 per cent, and in a recent book on work and employment at the plant, Garrahan and Stewart paint a picture of Nissan management very much in control, with little, if any, impact upon managerial decisions being made by employees, through the union or any other 'channel'.[26]

Notwithstanding the reservations which readily come to mind in the social, economic and political contexts of the 1990s regarding the potential for union involvement in technological change programmes, it is still the case that unions have at least a presence in a very large number of workplaces in the United Kingdom.[27] Thus there must always be the potential for them either to play a part directly in new technology adoption – and much will depend on management's views on this as well as power to force the union's involvement – or to affect management's approach indirectly through the latter taking their possible responses into account in its decision-making. What is more, trade union involvement should not just be seen as reacting to management's proposals/intentions, for the unions may be proactive in pressing for increased payment, regrading upwards, no redundancies, etc.

Let us now turn to examine some of the evidence relating to trade union involvement in new technology adoption. We will first draw on cross-European data, then turn to more detailed UK data.

Studies commissioned by and conducted under the auspices of the European Foundation for the Improvement of Living and Working Conditions (EFILWC) have perhaps yielded the most comprehensive data on employee involvement in new technology adoption and introduction of a pan-European nature. I will draw here on two EFILWC surveys: an earlier study of practice in five European countries and a later study based on evidence from twelve countries. (The foundation is financed by the European Commission, and is controlled by trade unions, employers and state institutions under a tripartite agreement.)[28]

The first study examined worker participation in the adoption and introduction of new technology into twenty-one organizations across various sectors in the United Kingdom, Denmark, Ireland, Italy and West Germany during 1982–3. On average, the case studies lasted for one year and, as most of the organizations had already reached the operationalization stage, retrospective analysis was used to gather information on earlier stages. The study focused on the following five main possibilities for work-force and union involvement:

1 No involvement.
2 Information receiving.
3 Discussion and consultation.
4 Joint decision-taking/negotiations.
5 Active involvement/co-determination.

Four stages of new technology adoption/introduction were identified: planning, selection, implementation and evaluation. The findings are summarized as follows:

> The clear pattern is for information to be available at the planning phase, the shift in the selection phase is towards more consultation but with little negotiated involvement; information is still an important feature. It is only in the implementation phase that we see a distinct shift towards consultation and negotiation as the

method of participation . . . the latter phases of checking and post-evaluation revert to mainly consultative methods.[29]

Five reasons were put forward for notification being the most common form of involvement during the planning stage:

1 Management's specialization and functional expertise.
2 The need for certainty prior to consultation.
3 The need for long-term planning and control.
4 The perceived need on the part of managers to develop strategies (including, on occasions, labour strategies) before involving employees.
5 The corporate decision-making structure and the lack of a workforce equivalent.

Why was there such a low level of employee involvement in new technology adoption? In addition to the above, the reasons included:

1 Managers wishing to identify the details of the changes before putting them to employees.
2 The risk of 'disturbing' long-term plans.
3 At the selection stage, given that the key decisions had been taken, the argument that the room for alternatives was now tightly constrained. (See also pp. 5–6 and pp. 58–60.)

There were a few instances of deeper employee involvement at the early adoption phase, and the reasons given for this are illuminating. A key one was the perceived need for the co-operation of skilled workers throughout the technological change process. The management need for employee co-operation is, of course, at a premium at the point of, and in the early stage of, implementing the new technology, and it is hardly surprising that there is a take-off in involvement here. What is more, by that stage the effects of the changes could be more easily plotted and were thus, potentially, more amenable to some form of joint regulation. Even then, however, involvement did not usually affect management decisions to any notable extent. Thus the distinction needs to be drawn between formal involvement and having a real effect.[30]

Overall, then, the initiation, planning and selection of new technology were set firmly within management's control. There was a

> gap between involvement in the effects of change as opposed to involvement in the conception and planning of that change. This sometimes resulted in cynicism about potential workforce

influence on the part of employees as they saw the consultation and bargaining as ancillary to real decision-making.[31]

Thus 'the studies show a pessimistic picture from the point of view of employee influence in new technology'.[32] What is more, the results are particularly disappointing for anyone who would like to see more employee involvement, for the wider picture could be even less involvement, given that the sample was based upon organizations with some form of participation in technological change. There are many organizations, one can anticipate, where there is *nil* involvement.

The second European Foundation survey was conducted between February 1987 and October 1988 in all twelve member states of the European Union. A total of 7,326 interviews, split evenly between managers and employee representatives, were held in 2,807 companies spread across the following sectors: mechanical engineering, electronics, banking, insurance and retail. Only companies with some form of 'institutionalized representation of interests' were included. The research explored and evaluated the extent of participation, along with the future possibilities for participation. Involvement in new technology adoption/introduction was defined as follows:

> any participatory procedure or practice, ranging from disclosure of information to consultation, negotiation and joint decision-making, which formally or informally involves the parties concerned with the introduction of new technology in the discussion of decisions concerning the process of change.[33]

The same four stages of technological innovation, and categorization of participation possibilities, were identified as with the first study referred to above.

The managers were found to have different views from those of the employee representatives regarding the degree of participation which employees had experienced, in some cases the latter being more sceptical than the former. None the less, a distinct pattern of response was generally found within countries:

> Two countries, Denmark and Germany, clearly have the highest level of negotiation or codetermination. There is also a middle-ranking group of countries which have higher levels of negotiation or codetermination: Ireland, the Netherlands and Belgium. At the bottom of this ranking there are a large number of countries where the amount of negotiation or codetermination is minimal: the United Kingdom, France, Spain, Greece, Italy, Luxembourg and Portugal.[34]

Table 5 Factors affecting employee participation in technological change

Variable	Favourable conditions	Unfavourable conditions
Technological objectives	Performance enhancement and problem-solving skills important for success	Cost reduction with little dependence on employees
Management style	Co-operative	Conflictual and closed
Bargaining power	Highly unionized; facing common technological threats and strategically located; technically knowledgeable and skilled membership; united and cohesive union organization	Multi-unionism, low unionization, facing uncertain or variable impact of technology; lack of research resources; inexperienced officials; unions divided along political or religious lines
Legal regulation	Strong forms of law and other regulations	'Voluntaristic' 'market forces' or weak forms of legislation
Industrial relations system	Centralized	Decentralized

Source: C. Gill and H. Krieger (1992) 'The diffusion of participation in new information technology in Europe: survey results', *Economic and Industrial Democracy* 13 (3): 344

With respect to the lack of any employee involvement in the planning stage, the pattern is similar:

> Again, Denmark and Germany have the least amount of no involvement of all the countries in the survey. These are followed (in order) by a middle-ranking group of countries including the Netherlands, Ireland, Italy and Luxembourg followed by a bottom-ranking cluster of countries which include Belgium, the United Kingdom, France, Spain and Greece. At the very bottom comes Portugal.[35]

A similar pattern was found in the implementation stage, but with an overall higher level of involvement in all twelve countries.

Gill and Krieger have identified five factors which help to explain the variation in levels of participation in technological innovation across the twelve countries (see Table 5):

1 Managers' dependence on the skills and co-operation of employees in realizing their new technology objectives.

2 The style of management and its attitude towards participation.
3 The bargaining power of organized labour to force managers to negotiate or consult its representatives in the absence of any voluntary disposition on the part of managers to do so.
4 Regulations laying down participation rights for employees or their representatives.
5 The degree of centralization of the industrial relations system in the country concerned.[36]

These five factors are used to account for the country findings on levels of participation (see Table 6). It is not possible to present them

Table 6 Country-specific factors and their influence on participation levels in particular member states

Variable	Favourable	Neutral	Unfavourable
Technological objectives	Denmark Germany The Netherlands Belgium	Luxembourg France UK Ireland	Italy Portugal Greece Spain
Management style	Denmark Belgium The Netherlands	Luxembourg Ireland UK Germany	France Italy Spain Portugal Greece
Bargaining power	Denmark The Netherlands Germany Belgium	France Ireland Italy Spain UK	Portugal Greece Luxembourg
Regulation	Germany The Netherlands Denmark Belgium	Spain Italy Ireland Portugal Greece	UK France Luxembourg
Industrial relations system	Denmark The Netherlands Belgium Germany	Ireland Spain Portugal	UK Luxembourg Italy Greece France

Source: C. Gill and H. Krieger (1992) 'The diffusion of participation in new information technology in Europe: survey results', Economic and Industrial Democracy 13 (3): 345

in detail here, but a few key points relating to new technology adoption may be extracted:

1 Management determines the stage at which employees become involved (this is usually during the early part of implementation). Involvement normally takes the form of consultation rather than negotiation.
2 'Unless there is a very strong tradition of co-operation with employees' organizations, participation will be limited to employees rather than employee representatives and to involvement in task-related matters rather than strategic matters. Indeed, management may offer involvement by employees in job-related issues specifically to avoid the involvement of trade union or employee representatives.'[37]
3 'The complexity and differential impact of changes in technology will often make it difficult to forecast its precise effects on skills, job content and job security.'[38] Where a trade union's members are affected in different ways by the technical changes it is difficult to present a united front to management in the bargaining process.
4 'There are two critical points in the process of technological decision-making where organized labour needs to be represented: at the company level, where the key investment decisions are made and questions of equipment selection and design are resolved, and at the establishment or workplace level, where those decisions are implemented. An effective organizational structure, therefore is one which enables both the negotiation of broader strategic issues at the company level and more detailed and specific issues at a localized level.'[39]
5 And, as Gill and Krieger conclude, 'it is clear that the types of participation that exist in Europe are a product of the way the contours of each member state's industrial relations system have been shaped by wider political, economic, social and historical forces'.[40]

One could be forgiven at this juncture, in the light of the evidence reported above on the limited nature of employee involvement in technical change, for beginning to wonder whether any benefits are to be gained from a deeper level of involvement. Perhaps, therefore, it would be helpful here to indicate briefly the sort of benefits which can be obtained in those (few) instances where employees have some meaningful involvement. In order to do so I shall draw upon the findings of another EFILWC study, this time based upon an oral questionnaire survey in 1987 of managers and worker representatives in West Germany, France, Italy, the United Kingdom and Denmark.[41] The questionnaire was administered in five sectors, and 4,654 interviews were achieved, split approximately equally between managers and workers' representatives. (The assessments provided by each were found to be so similar that the results below draw only upon the data of the managers.) The findings were much the same in terms of levels of employee involvement as those reported above from the other European studies. But Frohlich and Krieger render a useful service in drawing attention to what they refer to as 'participation's successes'. These can be summarized as follows: In the view of two-thirds of managers worker participation in the decision-making process connected with technological change exerts neither a positive nor a negative effect on the quality of decisions, the time taken to reach a decision or the time taken to implement the decision. When effects were mentioned, the positive effects always outweighed the negative ones (i.e. participation led to an improvement in these areas). This was particularly true of the quality of the decision-making process. The most negative effect was on the time taken to reach the decision, but the negative effects (in the view of 11 per cent of managers) were more than offset by the 21 per cent who saw positive effects here.

Frohlich and Krieger conclude that worker participation in the introduction of new technology contributes to mutual understanding, receptivity to change on the part of employees, and receptivity to the problems of workers on the part of managers. They observe:

> Employees' acceptance of new technology is a critical variable for successful innovations. Workers' opposition slows down the process of introduction, and leads to losses due to friction, and to inefficiency in the application of the technology ... worker participation has an exceptionally positive effect in this problem area.[42]

As we shall see below, however, gaining employee acceptance of new technology has not been a problem for the great majority of managers. The UK survey evidence shows that instances of worker opposition to new technology are very rare; indeed, it is much more accurate to talk about employees welcoming the introduction of new technology.

Let us turn, then, to the UK survey data on worker involvement in the adoption and introduction of technical change. The major source is again the WIRS series. As we noted earlier, by far and away the most data on technical change were picked up by the 1984 survey, analysed in detail by Daniel in his 1987 book.[43] There were some questions on technical change, however, in the 1990 survey, and we will draw on the responses to these as well as to the 1984 questions below. In addition, we will draw on other data (in particular, case studies) to supplement the former.

Perhaps the first key finding of the 1984 survey which should be mentioned is that there was strong worker (manual and non manual) support for technical change (see Figure 4)[44]. On the other hand, organizational change generated more mixed reactions, being resisted, for example, more than it was supported by manual workers. This leads us on to the second key finding, which illustrates *how* strongly technical change was supported by employees. As Daniel and Millward express it:

> so favourably were workers disposed to technical change compared with organizational change, that *technical change in circumstances of job losses was supported substantially more strongly than organizational change in circumstances where the level of employment was stable or growing.* [Emphasis in original][45]

Thus new technology 'sugared the pill' of less palatable changes.

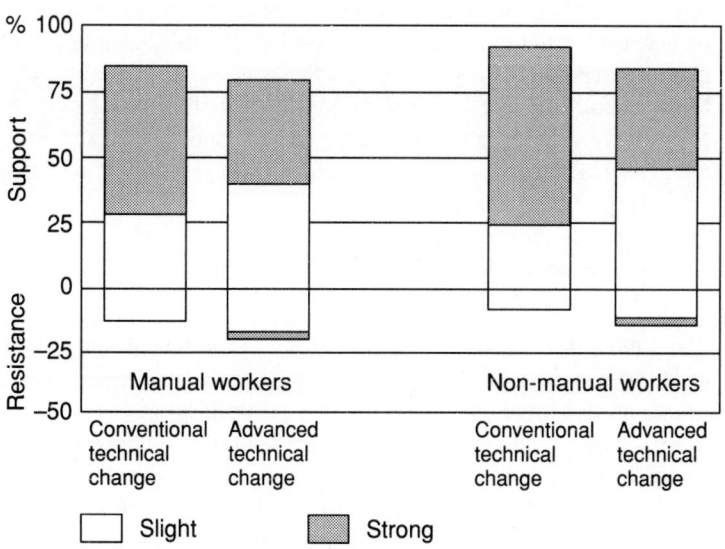

Figure 4 Worker reactions to technical change

Daniel and Millward were so surprised by this second set of findings that they conducted a number of follow-up case studies, drawing on workplaces included in the survey.[46] They found six main reasons why technical change was intrinsically more attractive to employees than organizational change:

1 Technical change is seen as progress.
2 New technology has a concrete form and identifiable outputs.
3 'The newer the technology, the better the workplace.'
4 Technical change represents investment in the future and improved job security.
5 New technology is familiar and valued in non-work contexts.
6 Technical change tends to be incremental and continuous.

What, then, of employee involvement in technical change? For ease of presentation we will draw on the WIRS data here for *all* forms of involvement, including consultation, even though the latter form is considered separately in relation to case studies in a later section. Let us draw on Daniel and Millward's own summary of the 1984 findings:

1 The general levels of discussion, consultation and negotiation were low.
2 Managers tended to consult and negotiate when they had little option, either because of initial resistance to the proposed changes or because of the existence of appropriate institutions and established procedures.
3 Discussion, consultation and negotiation, both formal and informal, were more common where trade unions were present in the organization and were recognized by management for purposes of collective bargaining.
4 A different picture emerged from the accounts of worker representatives as compared with those of managers about the level of consultation and negotiation.[47]

The 1990 WIRS survey results were broadly similar, although with certain differences. With regard to manual workers, there was a slight reduction over the period in the proportion of cases where managers reported no consultation, but it was compensated for by a reported increase in informal discussion; a reduction in discussions with shop stewards was matched by increased use of joint consultative committees. For non-manual workers the main changes were an increase in the use of joint consultative committees at the expense of a decline in consultation with shop stewards, and an increase in meetings with groups of employees at the expense of a decline in discussions with individual workers. Thus overall 'the findings do suggest that there was some increase in the levels of consultation with employees over technical change between 1984 and 1990'.[48] It should be noted, however, that Daniel and Millward add two qualifications to these conclusions:

1 Worker representatives reported a lower level of consultation than managers. (Martin reports differences in senior as against establishment-level managers' perceptions of the extent of union representatives' involvement in new technology introduction in the Warwick company-level survey of 1985, so we must not neglect the possibility that there may also be differences of view within management.[49])
2 There was an even greater decline in the amount of change introduced with union agreement, simply because fewer workplaces had union representation in 1990 than in 1984.

They summarize their key findings on employee and trade union involvement in technical change as follows:

> First, trade union organization generally provided a framework favourable to the introduction of technical change. Secondly, managers in workplaces where unions were recognized were substantially more inclined to consult and involve workers in technical change, through non-union as well as through union channels. Thirdly, although there may have been a decline in the proportion of workplaces where there were no consultations over technical change, there has also been a decline in the more substantial forms of consultation that occur when managers have to come to terms with institutions representing workers' interests.[50]

Let us now turn to examine in more detail the case study evidence for employee involvement in new technology adoption. Whilst it is not capable of picking up the broad sweep in the same way as the surveys, it has the advantage of allowing us to get much closer to the richness and detail of what has been happening. We can begin by drawing upon Davies's study of industrial relations and new technology in the brewing industry.[51] The focus is upon the potential for management–union collaboration in technological change through collective bargaining. The early part of the book includes a useful review of UK trade union approaches to technological change over the years. As Davies observes, the main concern at national level has make it an issue of collective bargaining. (See, for example, a TUC document of 1979, which argues for early, collective bargaining-based, union involvement in decision-making about technological change.[52]) Davies is well aware, however, of the disjuncture which can arise between national-level trade union policies and practices at the local level. She distinguishes between integrative and distributive bargaining and argues that, along with consultation, they are the main forms of management–union relationship likely to be found in connection with the adoption and introduction of new technology. Distributive bargaining involves the process of attempting to resolve basic conflicts of interest between the parties where one group's gain results in another's loss. Integrative bargaining refers to matters of 'common concern', that is, where objectives are not in fundamental conflict. (Consultation is defined as unilateral decision-making by management, where the union is merely informed of what has been decided.)[53]

Davies has a preference for integrative bargaining, noting with approval that 'there seems to be some interest, at least from the union side, in an integrative relationship between the sides during a technological change project'.[54] None the less, over 50 per cent of the managers said that the unions had not been involved at all in the following four matters: the initial investment decision, the cost–benefit analysis, discussions on the type of technology to adopt, and matters of redundancy. Little integrative bargaining was found in practice. The dominant management–union relationship in technological change was consultation. However, around 50 per cent of trade unionists were satisfied with their involvement in the process; at the same time, many of them were apprehensive about becoming too involved with management.[55]

When managers' and trade unionists' statements were compared it was found that, overall, the latter perceived an earlier and deeper involvement in technological change than managers perceived them as having. Thus 'a completely different impression of trade union influence during technological change would be gained from management and trade union perceptions of the situation'.[56] This, of course, makes it difficult to come to any definite conclusions on the matter. Davies finds little evidence that the TUC objective of 'change by agreement' was being achieved. In the main, technological change was simply not seen by management as a negotiable issue. Despite her predilection for an integrative bargaining approach, the evidence presented shows that distributive bargaining had been of more benefit to the trade unions, related as it was to improvements in terms and conditions of employment and being less prone to management control and manipulation.[57]

Improving the terms and conditions of employment of their members, in particular with regard to pay and job security, has been the major concern of the unions. Whilst the TUC and certain unions at a national level have called for participation in change, as Willman has observed, 'bargaining over new technology has tended to take place in a decentralised fashion, with more emphasis on the traditional concerns of job security and earnings than on influencing innovation decisions'.[58] Of course, as we have seen, this particular trade union emphasis may not have been entirely a matter of choice, since managers have often so restricted the negotiable issues. This needs to be understood in terms of the long history of management–union relations and the institutions of UK industrial relations. As Child has noted, drawing upon a banking sector case study, 'Technology only becomes a negotiable issue once it affects terms and conditions, or health and safety. There is no procedure which admits the union to the technology decision process,' and:

> The unions' main grievance is that banks treat technology as a non-negotiable issue, except in relation to terms and conditions, and health and safety. Union demands are for participation before decisions are made so that the full implications can be discussed, rather than having to react to a *fait accompli*.[59]

Two main factors are identified as having prevented the unions from achieving this involvement: one is the reluctance of union members to take industrial action, the other is 'management's determination to retain exclusivity over decisions on new technology as a strategic matter and therefore to refuse to treat technology policy as a negotiable issue'.[60]

Some issues associated with technical change may, then, be seen as negotiable whilst others are not. In their intensive longitudinal study of the social processes associated with technical change at British Telecom during the late 1970s and early 1980s Clark *et al.* found no evidence of formal negotiations over the control issues which were raised (such as job tasks, skills, work organization).[61] At the same time, management did negotiate with the unions over staffing levels, job security and selection for training.[62] Clark *et al.*'s overall finding was that the unions had a limited yet significant influence upon technical change through bargaining and consultation. Clark *et al.* recognize, however, that commercial pressures and a new managerial industrial relations strategy following privatization may pose a threat to this trade union influence on new technology.[63]

The European Foundation studies, it will be remembered, found not only that collective bargaining was the predominant mode of trade union involvement in new technology adoption and introduction, but that it was commonly restricted to job-related matters.[64] There were good reasons for this: collective bargaining is a 'tried and tested' approach, is inherently flexible, and is well known and understood by the parties. However, its use as the prime method of regulation reflects the union's lack of influence on decision-making; strategic issues and matters of policy formulation are dealt with outside its framework.[65] This narrow focus can present some serious problems for trade unions:

> if technological change is part of a wider restructuring of the organisation. For the bargaining areas and the consultative forums, in being restricted to the plant or to job issues, were not able to deal with such global changes or gain involvement in the extensive planning that the management of the enterprise in necessity have to undertake.[66]

On the other hand, to go beyond collective bargaining to other types of formal involvement (such as worker directors) is, as Cressey puts it, 'to risk taking on responsibility without commensurate power and at the same time alienate sections of union support'.[67]

Wilkinson's case study research supports the drift of the findings above. Whilst observing that the design, choice, implementation and debugging stages of innovation all provide 'junctures at which actors can intervene to influence the direction of change', he found that 'The design and choice of technology were unquestionably management prerogatives, their technological choices rarely being considered matters for union or worker concern.'[68] This despite the fact that most of his case studies were of firms with batch production systems, undergoing constant incremental change and adaptation.

Given Wilkinson's interest in the shop-floor politics of technological change, it is not, perhaps, surprising that he focuses on the implementation and debugging stages, for it is here that 'people on the receiving end of technological advance – i.e. workers – can most seriously attempt to impose their own interests'.[69] The focus may also reflect the fact that he did not have access to 'top level' information, hence, in this study 'the motives of the most senior managers, and thus "corporate strategies", must remain largely unexplained'.[70]

During the 1980s, particularly the first half of that decade, UK trade unions made some use of New Technology Agreements (NTAs) as a means of attempting to regulate the adoption and introduction of new technology. Although they have since gone out of fashion, it is important to spend a little time on them, as they illustrate an alternative vehicle of trade union influence upon technological change, and there are lessons to be learned. An Institute of Manpower Studies survey published in 1986 identified 250 NTAs in the United Kingdom, of which the great majority covered white-collar workers. The NTAs were divided more or less equally between the manufacturing and service sectors.[71]

NTAs have been defined as 'formal agreements which attempt to involve unions in decision-making over the process of technological change, and attempt to deal with the effects such changes will have on work and conditions of employment'.[72] A distinction can be made between 'one-off' agreements, which seek to regulate the impact of a specific change, and 'procedural' agreements, which provide a set of rules for the parties involved in new technology adoption and/or introduction.[73] Rush and Williams, on the basis of their empirical survey of NTAs, identified five main approaches to employee involvement:

> *mutuality*, where no change occurred without mutual agreement; *negotiation*, where there was no change until negotiation procedures were exhausted; *consultation*, in which changes were discussed in advance with unions but were not linked to dispute procedures or 'status quo' clauses; *individual representation*, in which changes were discussed with the workers involved; or finally *no representation* at all.[74]

What of the impact of NTAs on practice? A Labour Research Department survey found major differences between 'model' NTAs, as laid down in policy documents and pamphlets produced by certain unions, and what had been negotiated in practice. Only a quarter of the agreements gave a guarantee of no redundancy, for example (despite this clause being a central plank of model NTAs), and only half contained a job security clause.[75] A survey by Williams and Moseley found that there was a requirement to involve unions at the planning stage in only one-twelfth of agreements; the rest of the agreements specified union involvement at the implementation stage only, or not at all.[76] Storey, in his insurance sector case studies, found NTAs in three companies, but observes that they 'fell a long way short of the aspirations contained in many draft "model" agreements. The provisions for "sharing the benefits" were noticeably absent or very thin. Hours had not been reduced nor salaries increased.'[77] In each of the three companies 'the great majority of the staff interviewed [85 per cent] did not know whether or not their company was signatory to a new technology agreement'.[78]

Overall, then, it must be concluded that NTAs had a limited impact. They were adopted in only a small number of organizations. Where they were adopted, they do not appear to have made much impact or real difference. Sometimes they were – at first sight paradoxically – too specific (on certain clauses) and yet open to interpretation on other issues such as associated organizational changes (perhaps in different clauses). Thus 'traditional' collective bargaining was seen to remain the key means of involving trade unions – and employees – in new technology adoption and introduction. It does not, *per se*, restrict the area of negotiations, can incorporate technology and other issues, and is inherently more flexible.[79]

As Gill put it in 1985:

The trade unions have had limited success in their policy of seeking to influence the direction of the new technology by bringing it within the ambit of collective bargaining through new technology agreements. They have been severely hampered by the fact that microelectronics has emerged during a period of recession, and their bargaining power has consequently been reduced. Most technical change is taking place without any kind of agreement, and where trade unions have succeeded in securing new technology agreements such agreements have fallen far short of their model aspirations.[80]

It must be concluded, then, that overall trade union involvement and influence over new technology *adoption* in the United Kingdom has been slight. There is little evidence of collective bargaining having been extended into the adoption phase; to put the matter differently, unions have not been invited by management into the design space, nor have they tried or been able to force their way in. Thus if and when they have been involved during the later introduction phase, their scope for influencing management decisions has been seriously circumscribed. A number of reasons can be put forward for this limited involvement. They can be divided into three main areas:

1 The social, political and economic conditions of the 1980s and 1990s have put the unions on the defensive. Managements throughout this period have had the upper hand and have not needed to involve unions and employees in new technology adoption in order to get it introduced and working. Hence the great majority of managers have not regarded new technology as a negotiable issue. They have often been able to employ a 'tell' – never mind a 'sell' – strategy, for example. However, some managers have been rather more subtle in their approach than economic and business conditions would allow. (In other words they might well have been able to 'get away with' a 'tell' strategy but have chosen to adopt a more accommodating, 'softly, softly' style.) It has also proved possible in some cases for managers to 'divorce' the adoption of new technology from any subsequent labour savings (blaming reductions, for example, on poor economic and/or trading conditions).
2 At the local (organization) level managers have often had the benefit of more knowledge and expertise (not least from outside the organization) about the range and nature of the possibilities and, of course, advance knowledge of what is to happen. One result is that the unions are invariably on the defensive.
3 The trade unions have often lacked the above expertise, as well as the resources and external help (at least to the same extent). There has also sometimes been a lack of a strategic response (which, of course, is hardly surprising, given what has been said above) and of a cohesive, co-ordinated approach, particularly where a number of unions are involved and some stand to gain more out of the changes than others. What is more, the policies they *do* have for new technology have themselves been criticized. For example, Dodgson and Martin have observed that their policies are largely a product of the 1970s rather than of the late 1980s.[81] Above all else, throughout the 1980s unions have usually lacked the capacity to threaten action or use sanctions in order to force managers to take their views into account.[82]

If, then, there is not much evidence in the United Kingdom of employee involvement in new technology adoption through trade unions, what of involvement through consultation?

Involvement through consultation

It is important to be clear about which particular meaning is attributed to the term 'consultation', for there are a variety of possibilities, ranging from institutionalized procedures for dealing with the employer/manager–employee/trade union relationship (this form is often termed 'joint consultation') to the simple passing of information by managers and supervisors to employees, but also including discussions between managers and employees, briefing groups, newsletters and questionnaire surveys of employees. Consultation is distinguished from collective bargaining or negotiation by its focus upon issues of common interest to both the parties as distinct from issues where there is a basic conflict of interest. (In this sense, consultation can have some affinity with integrative bargaining.)

An indication of the variety of forms of consultation that are available can be gleaned from a NEDO report based upon surveys of employee involvement in the introduction of new technology in the UK electronics industry:

> No single model of consultation emerged from the surveys. Practices vary according to the size, nature and needs of each business, the type of technology employed, as well as the prior history of industrial relations. Formal consultative arrangements were found to exist, in the form of 'joint consultative committees', 'works committees', and 'joint staff–union councils', which bring trade union representatives and management together on a regular basis, be it quarterly, bi-monthly, or monthly. In addition, 'briefing groups', often at the departmental level of 'participation meetings', usually on a company basis, are held once or twice each year in many firms. On a less formal basis, companies referred to liaison with shop stewards, discussion groups, and meetings with those individuals directly affected by change. Several firms mentioned a 'reasonably open' style of management as part of building an atmosphere where consultation is the rule rather than the exception.[83]

The NEDO surveys found that almost 90 per cent of respondents reported some form of consultation at some stage of new technology adoption/introduction. Unions were consulted at the planning stage in only one-third of cases, but in half if choice of equipment is included.[84]

Consultation does indeed appear to be the most common means of involving employees in new technology adoption and introduction. Indeed, Guest, in a study of worker participation in the United Kingdom based upon six case studies, found it to be the only form of participation used by managers when new technology was introduced.[86] What is more, this involvement occurred largely at the implementation stage. Cressey reports a similar result from the European study. This leap in employee involvement therefore occurs, as we have seen, when most of the major decisions have already been taken (largely by managers) and when the need for employees' commitment to (or at least acquiescence in) change is at a premium.

In certain instances it may be that managers use consultation in a much more strategic way as an attempt to circumvent the direct involvement of trade unions (i.e. through bargaining) and to preempt any opposition to the introduction of new technology. Child, in a banking sector study, found that head office management was 'determined to retain control of new technology development', in the process rejecting joint regulation with the unions, and 'relying instead on internal communication channels to signal any staff discontent'.[87]

In sectors or organizations which have a more deeply embedded adversarial relationship between management and work force, and a higher density of union representation, this employee relations strategy may not so easily succeed. Also, of course, bargaining and consultative approaches or strategies should not always be seen as alternatives, for they can clearly be complementary. This may particularly be the case where managers wish to achieve organizational as well as technological change, and want to secure their employees' commitment to that change.[88] Another vehicle for doing so draws directly upon the job redesign tradition and will be considered in the next section.

Involvement through job redesign

The implications of technological change for the design of jobs and the nature of work have a long history, dating back in modern times at least forty years to US studies of the social effects of assembly line technology and a UK study of the work group impact of changes in coal-mining technology.[89] By definition, studies of the implications of (and now, significantly, possibilities for) new technology and job design are more recent – dating from the late 1970s. Previous to this work, however, researchers such as Mumford had been looking at (old, i.e. non-new technology) computers and job design, informed by a socio-technical perspective.[90] Most of this work focused upon office and clerical jobs because, in the main, it was this type of work which was affected by the early computers.[91] It is at this job level that the majority of both researchers and managers see the greatest opportunity for employees to play a part in the change process; that is to say, for them not to be just the passive recipients of the decisions of others. What is more, and perhaps equally significantly, it can be argued that any changes associated with new technology must include the job level for them to make a real difference.[92]

There is a good deal of affinity between a job redesign perspective and a focus upon changes in working practices, as the latter often subsumes job redesign. However, interest in changes in working practices usually also involves looking at wider organizational issues, such as the employment relationship and management–employee/trade union affairs. These important issues are typically accorded no significant attention in job redesign studies.

The key question for our present concerns revolves around the extent to which employees have been involved in job redesign and changes in working practices associated with the adoption of new technology. I want to draw, first of all, upon the work of Beirne and Ramsay.[93] They have summarized a number of approaches in the literature to the issue of computerization and job redesign. (Although they are talking about office work, I see no good reason why their model cannot be applied to employees doing other types of work.) See Table 7, pp. 114–115.

The model consists of two main perspectives on job redesign: 'systems rationalization' and 'computer redesign'. The former emphasizes 'the scientific method and the dominance of managerial prerogatives' (hierarchy, division of labour, separation of conception from execution), whilst 'attempting to plug gaps in conventional technically dominated design approaches with strategies aimed specifically at acquiring information or generating consent . . . among employees in work areas targeted for technological innovation'. On the other hand, the 'computer redesign' approaches 'are fundamentally opposed to technology driven systems', they 'promote the participative design of computing systems as a legitimate end in itself, allowing users an opportunity for self-expression and trust. Rather than advocating the best "expert" design, adherents insist that participation is a means to ensure that proposed systems are acceptable and beneficial to all concerned' – management *and* workers.[94]

Each perspective is in turn divided into three sub-categories representing, sequentially, the building in of enhanced employee (or 'user', as is often the preferred term in this context) involvement either through systematic account being taken of their perceived 'needs', or through actual participation in the job redesign process associated with computerization. Briefly, the resulting six possibilities are as follows:

1 *Technocentric design* represents the extreme position of no employee involvement and is informed by a 'pure' Tayloristic ideology where design is the sole responsibility of computer specialists.
2 *Passive user involvement* makes some limited concessions for employees in order to facilitate implementation but, as with 3 below, the essential principles of Taylorism are retained.
3 *Ergonomic systems design* uses advances in computer hardware and software in order to try to prevent user resistance or recalcitrance; however, employee involvement if of an essentially passive nature.
4 *Socio-technical design* attempts to make 'systems design a joint venture in which users and professionals co-operate throughout the development process'. The focus is upon the job level and on achieving a 'fit' between the particular features of the computer technology and the needs and desires of users.
5 *Organizational design* is based upon the premise that job redesign cannot be divorced from organizational redesign. The focus is on the need for flexibility in response to uncertainty in the organization's external contexts, in particular for appropriate (i.e. flexible) job and structural responses. (We saw earlier that a key feature of new technology is its inherent flexibility.)
6 *Organizational politics* sees technology as a tool which can be used by groups within the organization to enhance their power *vis-à-vis* other groups. The search for power and prestige is a continuous process and is derivative of the conflicting interests of these different groups.[95]

It is only, then, the computer redesign options which can be said to involve some form of direct participation on the part of those affected by the introduction of computer technology. Beirne and Ramsay observe that a common contributory factor in the failure of

Table 7 Theoretical perspectives on participative job redesign in the office

	Systems rationalization			Computer redesign			
	Technocentric design	Passive user involvement	Ergonomic systems design	Socio-technical design	Organizational design	Organizational politics
Organizing concept	Centralized (specialist) design	Selective user involvement	Selective user involvement – human factors engineering	Participative systems design	Participative systems design	Participative systems design
Design strategy	Generic systems design – complete specification of technical features prior to implementation	Specific systems design – in organizational context of systems use	'User features' incorporated in design	Systems customization	Systems customization	Systems customization
Strategic objectives	Technical operating efficiency	User acceptance knowledge – acquisition	User acceptance	Organizational effectiveness Job satisfaction Motivation Self-determination	Organizational flexibility	Conflict resolution
Systems building procedures	Systems analysis Division of labour Cost-benefit analysis	Classification of conditional variables for user involvement:	User measurement: – questionnaires – interviews	ETHICS* method: – Job satisfaction analysis	Progressive decentralization, with increasing levels of	Compensation/ reward/incentive schemes

	– Necessary participants – Stage of development – Status of users	Product features design	– Variance analysis – Steering committees Participation by 'consultation', 'representation', 'consensus'	'turbulence' in organizational environments
Ideology	Scientific management	Scientific management	Human relations	Human relations	Several contending ideologies. In abstracted form: human relations

Source: M. Beirne and H. Ramsay (1986) 'Computer redesign and "labour process" theory: towards a critical appraisal', paper presented at the fourth annual conference, Organization and Control of the Labour Process, University of Aston, April
* The approach to computer introduction advocated by Enid Mumford, ETHICS being an acronym for Effective Technical and Human Implementation of Computer Systems. See, for example, E. Mumford (1983) *Designing Human Systems for New Technology: the ETHICS Method*, Manchester: Manchester Business School; E. Mumford and D. Henshall (1979) *A Participative Approach to Computer Systems Design*, London: Associated Business Press

systems rationalization approaches to reach the performance levels specified is the lack of recognition of the need to involve employees in the process of adoption and introduction. This, of course, is particularly disappointing because new technology is supportive of a range of choices in relation to job, work and social organization.

The role of choice in new technology adoption reminds us again of the importance of taking into account the objectives and strategies of the parties involved. Managers, for example, do not choose a participative ('computer redesign' in Beirne and Ramsay's terminology) approach for its own sake. They choose this type of approach, presumably, because they believe that it will be the most effective way of progressing adoption, taking into account the relevant internal and external contexts. In an earlier study of an engineering company I found that a key business objective was enhanced flexibility of response to customer orders. This involved certain social and organizational changes, such as harmonization of employment conditions, organizational restructuring, a new grading and payment structure, enhanced task flexibility and, not least, the adoption of new technology.[96]

It should not be implied from the above that all companies have all-encompassing strategies for achieving change through job and work redesign. As we saw earlier, managers may not have a labour strategy *per se* (never mind the possibility that it may be difficult to identify any sort of strategy – see chapter 2). They may have a 'locked in', unreflective approach to job redesign possibilities (which may mean that, de facto, Taylorism is the predominant form).[97] The point may be illustrated by referring to the research of Wainwright and Francis.[98] They draw upon socio-technical and organizational design perspectives in their study of IT adoption and work reorganization in a college of further education, a public-sector company in 'heavy manufacturing', a financial services company and an international insurance broker. They observe that although new technology allows a broad range of strategic choice *vis-à-vis* such matters as job redesign, little thought or time was in practice devoted to this area. Indeed, they found an *increase* in the centralization of decision-making with regard to technology and the associated changes (in order, managers argued, to facilitate standardization): 'the design approach adopted for advanced office systems is not given nearly enough consideration in many organizations, and is often a matter of conforming with existing practices ... rather than of making a deliberate choice'.[99] Wainwright and

Francis argue that data processing departments have too much influence over job and systems design, generating a technical emphasis. A possible solution is for 'user influence' to be tapped at the very earliest systems design phase, that is, at the R&D, technical specification and product design stages – just those which are often the province of the equipment manufacturer. This still begs the question, of course, of what form of employee involvement is being advocated and how it is to be organized. Very little information is provided by Wainwright and Francis about the involvement of trade unions in new technology adoption in their case study organizations, and indeed they state that 'it was not possible to interview trade union representatives'. There is a clue as to one reason at least why this happened in the section dealing with the college of further education, where 'no union representatives were interviewed since their involvement with the introduction of word processing had been slight'.[100]

The nature and orientation of instances of job redesign can be satisfactorily understood, then, only on the basis of an organizational and contextual location of events. Beirne and Ramsay describe the approach of the participative design proponents as 'liberal idealism, and as such insensitive to hidden agendas, contradictions, power relations and the enhancement of management control to which their perhaps genuinely radical intentions may open a path'.[101] Thus Beirne and Ramsay are critical of both the systems rationalization tradition and much of computer redesign. With regard to the latter, particular criticism is reserved for the work of Mumford and her 'participative' approach to computer systems job redesign. The essence of the argument is that many of her findings exemplify a limited form of employee involvement in which managers are still at the steering wheel and the workers are 'happily' riding along in the back seat. The argument is based in part upon findings from a survey of computer systems utilization in some Scottish companies where the authors found that:

1 Virtually all the initiative for participative design came from managers.
2 User groups largely involved middle and senior management; only 38 per cent of schemes included lower management and clerical staff, and only 3 per cent secretaries.
3 Two-thirds of design teams were composed of 'representatives' appointed by management.

4 Steering committees (which commonly had veto powers) were staffed almost entirely by top and middle management.
5 Non-managerial white-collar users were predominantly involved, if at all, in the implementation and operational adjustment phases (45 per cent of cases); they were asked to help identify problems initially in 28 per cent of cases, but that the involvement was superficial seems to be indicated by the fact that they were reported to take part in the decision to innovate in only 3 per cent of cases, and in the goal-setting process following it in just 6 per cent.[102]

These findings, along with those of the European Foundation study and case study-based research such as that of Wainwright and Francis, point to a general lack of meaningful employee and/or trade union involvement in new technology adoption. Indeed, one is prompted to wonder whether one is searching for a 'holy grail'! Yet there *are* instances of employee/trade union involvement, and, as is often the case with job redesign more generally, we can find them in Scandinavia, where there is a long history of innovation in job redesign and work reorganization. The UTOPIA project (UTOPIA is a Swedish-language acronym for training, technology and products from the quality of work perspective), for instance, involved collaboration between trade unionists, academic researchers and computer scientists, with the objectives of identifying and developing the conditions under which trade unions could participate formally in the design and development of technology, and in identifying alternatives to Fordism and de-skilling as consequences of new technology.[103] All the parties were involved in the development of the technology itself and its supporting systems, giving them the opportunity to use the design space to create meaningful work and an effective technical solution. The team developed a prototype text and image-processing technology for the typographic industry which retained typesetting craft skills in the use of the technology. However, it must be emphasized that the UTOPIA project was developed outside the usual commercial context, and has not led to widespread adoption elsewhere.

The social democratic infrastructure of the Scandinavian countries has been supportive of these more radical forms of job redesign, of course, whereas the incidence in the United Kingdom of even the rather conservative models of the socio-technical designer has been limited.[104] However, as well as reflecting different managerial ideologies and strategies, this may have something to do with the fact that UK unions have often been wary of managers' intentions in redesigning jobs, suspecting on occasion that the outcome will not be increased control by themselves over their work but, rather, an intensification of that work. At the same time, and somewhat paradoxically at first sight, it appears that many middle managers have been worried about losing control over employees, and hence have been wary of the job redesign proposals of senior managers.[105]

One final observation may be made in concluding this section; the fact that employees have been involved either not at all, or only marginally, in the redesign of jobs occasioned by new technology *adoption* does not mean that they will therefore have no impact upon the actual design of those jobs, that is, working practices, tasks, decisions about methods, appropriate tools and techniques, etc. There is a good chance that they will need to make day-to-day decisions about matters such as these, especially during the implementation stage of the new technology; in a very real sense, indeed, they are the only people who can make such decisions.[106] And, given that organizations experience a continuous process of change (varying over time only in respect of the amount and depth of change), there is likely to be a continuing need for exactly that sort of adjustment. So, whilst employees may not have been involved in the original design of the changed or new jobs, of necessity they are involved in 'design in use'. Incremental changes, taking place over an extended period of time, can lead to quite extensive changes in the nature of jobs and working practices.

CONCLUSION

We have seen that there is an extensive range of opportunities for employee involvement in new technology adoption and introduction, but that often they are not taken up (not least in the United Kingdom); similar points were made with regard to the participation of certain staff specialists, such as personnel managers, in the processes of adoption. Why is this the case? We found that in practice a number of constraints lead to this situation. They include issues to do with managerial objectives, strategies and decision-making, established power structures, linkages with other jobs/departments/sections/ divisions across the organization, the employment contract and any agreements which may have been concluded between management and trade unions (relating, for example, to working practices).

Whilst, however, most, if not all, of the key decisions may have been taken by non-users by the time the new technology is introduced into the organization, the active involvement of employees is necessary in order that the *potential* benefits can be realized. Thus senior and middle managers have an interest in gaining the users' acceptance of the new job designs and working practices. This argues for a responsible autonomy strategy. What happens in practice, though, as we have seen, is another matter.

Part II

Case studies in new technology adoption

Chapter 5
Bramley Building Society

This, the first case study chapter, will examine the adoption of a branch on-line terminal system for processing transactions with customers. The terminals are electronically linked to the Bramley Building Society's mainframe computer, located in the society's head office. Central files are automatically updated following a branch office transaction, eliminating the need for a second manual amendment of the file at Head Office. More detail is provided about the technology in a later section of the chapter. The case study shows how the society went about adopting this new technology whilst some major changes were taking place in its external contexts, including an intensification of competition and legislative changes. Focusing on the people and organizational issues associated with the changes, it considers the critical junctures in that process – in particular, in relation to the decisions taken, and the people who did the deciding. It draws attention to the objectives which were given priority, and describes the adoption strategy. It will be seen that, although computer specialists and administrative considerations led the adoption process, personnel considerations (and personnel specialists) came to play a more influential role as the decisions and changes unfolded.

THE ORGANIZATION AND ITS CONTEXT

The Bramley Building Society has its head office in the West Midlands, and a network of branch offices and agencies spread over a wide area, ranging from Yorkshire to Oxfordshire and from Gwent to Northamptonshire. The society was founded in 1884, and grew steadily through internal growth and mergers. It was ranked around twentieth among UK societies in terms of business volume during the earlier time period we consider, and sixteenth by 1993, when there were approximately 800 staff in total in the head office and the branch offices. Tables 8 and 9 show, respectively, the number of branch offices and total employees between 1975 and 1985/6. The increases on both measures between 1982 and 1983 (during which period the new technology was being introduced) were largely the result of a merger with a small building society, also based in the same town.

Whilst the on-line system was being adopted between 1978 and 1983 staff were represented through a staff association (which had obtained a certificate of independence in 1979). During this period between 60 per cent and 75 per cent of eligible staff had been

Table 8 Bramley Building Society: branch office numbers, 1975–86

Year	No. of branches
1975	38
1976	40
1977	42
1978	45
1979	47
1980	48
1981	49
1982	49
1983	61
1984	59
1985	58
1986	60

Table 9 Bramley Building Society: staff numbers, 1975–85

Year	Full-time	Part-time	Total full-time equivalent
1975	261	31	276·5
1976	288	26	301·0
1977	306	24	318·0
1978	311	24	323·0
1979	317	30	332·0
1980	328	56	356·0
1981	347	54	374·0
1982	349	53	375·5
1983	429	107	482·5
1984	425	92	471·0
1985	421	109	475·5

members. 'Eligible staff' included everyone up to and including regional and branch managers, which left out only executive management and personnel staff. This could have placed regional and branch managers in a difficult position, so they voluntarily withdrew from membership. Part-time staff had been allowed to join the association only since 1978. The association had a main committee of ten people, elected annually by the membership. An executive committee was introduced in 1981, consisting of the chairperson, deputy chairperson, treasurer and secretary. The negotiating team consisted of the chairman, deputy chairman, one other member of the main committee, and an external consultant employed on a contract basis. The importance of the role which such an external consultant can play should not be underestimated. Historically there has long been a low level of trade union representation in the building society sector, and in so far as there has been any form of employee representation, it was provided by the staff associations.[1] However, their true level of independence from the employer has been questioned, and they have not affiliated to the TUC. The consultant can assist the association on the basis of his/her relative independence and through the provision of negotiating skills and wider industrial relations experience. Not least, in a conflict situation, the consultant 'can take the flak and punch hard if need be, with no fears for his subsequent career'.[2]

Throughout its existence until the early part of 1983 the Bramley Building Society Staff Association acted largely in a reactive way, concentrating on progressing queries raised by members, the annual wages and hours negotiations, and the monthly consultation and negotiation meetings with management. It rarely took initiatives. It had become, in effect, moribund, with members showing little, if any, interest in its affairs. Management was very much in the ascendancy and faced no real opposition or even notable disagreement from staff or the association. The last formal or informal communication with a trade union had been in connection with a recognition claim submitted by NUBE in 1972/3, which had been rejected by the staff. The Personnel Manager estimated that there were around twelve BIFU (which had in the meantime been formed out of a merger of unions involving NUBE) members in the society in 1983, out of a total work force averaging around 530. The chairman of the staff association, along with a few other people, decided, in his words, 'to make a last-ditch effort' to see whether staff representation could be rejuvenated by transferring the engagement to BIFU. A ballot was organized in the building society by the Electoral Society, and the majority of those voting were in favour of the transfer; therefore, late in 1983, it duly took place. It was followed in February 1984 by an unsuccessful application by the union for recognition for negotiating purposes.

Let us now consider some of the key features of the changing contexts of building society operations during the period of adoption of the branch network on-line system. The quintessential change in context was that from a relatively predictable and stable environment to one in which there was a good deal of turbulence, linked with much intensified competition, and a burgeoning of new services and initiatives. Over the previous period business volume had grown on an incremental basis, having increased by an annual average amount of between 8 per cent and 15 per cent between 1969 and 1982.[3] The number of branch offices also continued to increase, along with assets and staff employed (see Table 10).

Whilst there had been increases on the dimensions referred to above, Table 10 shows that the number of societies had been

Table 10 Building societies, 1975–91

Year	No. of societies	No. of branches	No. of staff		Total assets (£ million)
			Full-time	Part-time	
1975	382	3,375	32,485	2,464	24,204
1976	364	3,696	34,673	2,704	28,202
1977	339	4,130	37,876	3,213	34,288
1978	316	4,595	40,870	4,062	39,538
1979	287	5,147	43,963	5,207	45,789
1980	273	5,684	46,418	6,309	53,793
1981	253	6,162	47,716	7,661	61,815
1982	227	6,480	49,102	9,047	73,033
1983	206	6,643	50,761	10,431	85,869
1984	190	6,816	51,660	11,454	102,689
1985	167	6,926	53,172	12,519	120,763
1986	152	6,954	55,830	13,436	140,603
1987	138	6,962	59,315	14,979	160,097
1988	131	6,912	63,874	16,243	188,844
1989	126	6,236	59,960	14,644	187,012
1990	117	6,051	61,254	15,128	216,848
1991	110	5,921	63,997	15,183	243,980

Source: Annual reports of the Chief Registrar of Friendly Societies
Note. The Abbey National converted from a building society to an authorized bank during 1989, and is therefore included in the figures only up to and including 1988

decreasing throughout the period, down to 152 by 1986, compared with 364 in 1976. This, of course, was due to merger and amalgamation activity. The expansion in building society business was connected with: an increase in home ownership at a time when the societies had a virtual monopoly of housing finance; the fact that people needed to save with a society in order to obtain a mortgage; the attractiveness of tax relief on mortgage interest; and legislative changes, such as the Housing Act, 1980, with its 'right to buy' provisions.[4]

Although total branch numbers increased, however, the *rate* of increase had slowed down. Rajan estimated that it had reduced from 11 per cent in 1978 to 3 per cent in 1982.[5] There were two main reasons for this. One was intensified merger activity, resulting in the closing down of branch offices where a newly merged society had two offices near each other. The other was renewed interest during the period in agencies as sub-branches, as against full-blown branch offices. Given that a society already had a branch in a main shopping centre, its 'next wave of expansion could only penetrate the secondary shopping sites in the suburban areas where neither the population numbers nor the projected business volume could commercially warrant a full branch'.[6]

A key change in the context of building society operations was the development of an increasingly competitive market for mortgages, savings and other financial services, both within the building society sector and across the wider financial sector. As Boleat put it at the time:

> A new and radically different competitive environment is evolving for building societies. It is an environment in which the banks, national savings and trustee savings banks, which are gradually moving into the private sector, are competing aggressively for savings and where the banks are also seeking to take a substantial share of the mortgage market.[7]

Competition on mortgage and savings rates intensified upon the formal abandonment of the building societies' cartel in 1983 (when the Abbey National withdrew), under which rates were fixed centrally by the Building Societies Association. Strictly speaking, societies did not have to charge those rates (indeed, some did not, preferring instead to increase their mortgage and savings rates slightly above the BSA recommended ones), but there was certainly much closer adherence to the recommended rates than has since been the case – many societies now preferring to fix their own rates. Whilst all this had been happening the societies still had to be closely attuned to the inflow of money from savers, in order to support their mortgage and other activities. They needed, therefore, to be watchful of base rate shifts, and to be ready to act quickly if necessary.

During the 1980s UK and foreign banks and insurance companies moved into the mortgage market in a much stronger way, and with a higher profile. At the same time, banks became keener to attract savings from customers via interest-bearing accounts. These moves increased competition for the building societies. However, the changing contextual picture in the financial services sector was not all about intensified conflict between societies, insurance companies and banks, for there were instances of two or more types of organization forming strategic alliances – sharing cheque card facilities and electronic point-of-sale systems, for instance. Within the building society sector itself, instances of co-operation included the sharing of ATM networks.

With regard to merger activity, it appeared as if almost no society could be excluded from the possibility of involvement. Following protracted discussions, the Alliance and the Leicester societies finally merged, as did the Midshires and the Liverpool. Subsequently the latter merged with the Birmingham & Bridgwater to form the Birmingham Midshires Building Society. These are examples of successful mergers; there were also abortive attempts. Examples included the Leeds Permanent and Leeds & Holbeck, the Woolwich and the Nationwide, and the Yorkshire and the Bradford & Bingley. On occasion the unsuccessful attempts were (publicly, at least) blamed on the computer – the different systems were 'incompatible', for example. One is entitled to wonder, however, why discussions went as far as they did before the 'wedding' was called off. Questions might be raised, for example, about top management attitudes and strategy. Were there other reasons than the incompatibility of the technology? Not only might some branch offices close if the societies overlapped in location, but something would have to be done about the possibility of two head offices, two boards of directors and two sets of senior managers.

A further aspect of the changing context of building society operations was the diversification of their activities. This had been made possible by the Building Societies Act, which came into force on 1 January 1987. The new services which could now be offered included cheque-book accounts, insurance, personal loans not secured on a house, and 'one-stop' house buying – estate agency work, the mortgage itself, surveying, conveyancing and insurance. The Act also created the Building Societies Commission (replacing the Registry of Friendly Societies) and the Building Societies Ombudsman, who mediates in disputes between the societies and their customers. The societies were allowed to become publicly quoted companies, subject to certain conditions. The latter stipulation meant that many of the new possibilities were not in practice open to all societies, for not all of them could meet the qualifying conditions of the Act. For example, to take advantage of the wider lending powers a society needed to have commercial assets in excess of £100 million. (This applied to such services as unsecured lending, property and land ownership, and holdings in subsidiaries such as estate agencies and insurance brokers.) Effectively this provision restricted such opportunities to the top fifty or so societies. Given also that at least 90 per cent of a society's commercial assets had to be first mortgages, conversion to PLC status appeared realistic only for the largest societies.

These contextual changes gave rise to an urgent need for societies, especially the large and medium-size ones, to develop their marketing and selling activities. They could no longer rely on people taking the initiative and coming to them, and, if they were hard-pressed with mortgage applications, rationing them through waiting lists and other means. Put simply, people would go elsewhere. At the same time, the societies had to be vigilant in ensuring that they attracted enough investment on a regular basis to service existing mortgages, thus generating acute sensitivity to interest rate movements in general, as well as to the rates being charged by competitors. Advertising in the press and on television became commonplace. New technology was used to provide, *inter alia*, longer 'opening hours' for some services, twenty-four-hours-a-day banking (cash dispensing, provision of statements, etc.), transaction recording, passbook updating, and information storage and amendment.

The external and internal contextual changes had repercussions on the structuring and culture of building societies. For instance, an urgent need arose for marketing competence within the organization, at both head and branch office level. In the main, it appears, existing employees were retrained for these roles (although there was an increase in outside recruitment of specialist staff where the skills could not be developed quickly enough). This implied a much enhanced requirement for training and development in order that staff could respond effectively to the changes outlined above, and to the introduction of new technology. Contextual pressures also encouraged senior managers to tighten up on costs and cost control through a variety of means, including Head Office attempts to exert tighter control over regions and branches.

On the basis of the above outline of the internal and external contexts of the Bramley Building Society, let us now turn to look at the technological changes which we shall focus upon in the rest of the chapter.

THE TECHNOLOGICAL CHANGES

Until 1968 the technology used by the Bramley society consisted in the main of accounting machines and typewriters. That year the organization purchased its first mainframe computer, which continued in operation until 1977. By 1975 this computer was becoming overloaded, so a new mainframe was installed in 1977. These first two computers were used to file details of investors' and mortgage accounts; they also greatly speeded up the calculation of interest payments, and did away with the need for the retention of passbooks for interest-calculation purposes.

The next stage in the use of technology by the society was the installation, during March and April 1979, of a computerized enquiry system at Head Office, based on six visual display units (VDUs) connected to the mainframe. The system was used for enquiries about investors' accounts at Head Office, but also enabled a service to be provided to branches in relation to customer enquiries. It replaced the previous, slower, manual system, where enquiries were answered at Head Office by reference to computer print-outs.

In May 1979 computer terminals were installed in the society's largest branch office, and they were linked up to the Head Office mainframe. This was the beginning of Bramley's branch office 'on-line' system. By April 1984 all the society's branch offices had gone on-line, and further additions to and developments of the society's new technology have continued since. They include joining the national Link system of ATMs which can issue cash, take deposits, check accounts and balances, and issue receipts.

Following the installation of terminals at the largest branch and at head office, there were no further on-line installations until September 1982, when the planned, sequential introduction began of the on-line system to all the branch offices. The installations were carried out by a team which spent three to four weeks in each branch office, moving on to the next one in turn. This sequential process followed a given telephone link throughout the branches connected to the link. Given that the starting point was a branch in the Head Office town, this meant that branches nearer the town on that telephone link would be connected first.

Key features of the on-line system included 'single-entry' key stroking, that is, data needs to be entered in a passbook only once, at the branch office. This action simultaneously updates the central files at Head Office, doing away with the need to take in customers' passbooks in order to calculate interest accrued, and helps to ensure that the society has an accurate and up-to-date record of transactions. All the managers with whom I discussed this matter said that the main principle of the computerization was that it should free cashiers from a lot of administrative work, and so give them more time to talk to customers. The time freed could be used to sell other services. In addition, balancing up at the end of the day would be a much quicker and more straightforward operation. The number of days when branch office staff had to stay behind after the close of business to perform this function was expected to be much reduced. On the debit side, on the other hand, if the mainframe computer failed, major problems resulted, including long queues and customer complaints. For security reasons such as these, the microcomputers in the branch offices were to have a limited amount of storage capacity, which, it was hoped, would tide the branch over until the system goes live again.

NEW TECHNOLOGY OBJECTIVES

The Assistant General Manager (Administration) stated that the main benefits of the computerized branch office on-line system were projected to be:

1 Increased productivity.
2 Improved service to customers.
3 Speedier processing of customer enquiries at branch office level, on the basis of the direct link to Head Office and the database.

It emerged later, during an interview with the Systems Development Manager, that another expected benefit was the opportunity of gaining more business at branch office level. (There is a link here with objective 1, provided additional staff are not taken on as volume increases.)

By the early 1980s the society was finding it difficult to expand the volume of its business. Existing branches were reaching the limit of their capacity but adjoining land for expansion was seldom available. Opening another branch near by could be expensive, and the new branch might compete with the old one for business. Thus a new branch might have to be in a less prominent position, off the high street. Many local authorities were not granting planning permission for new premises. These considerations prompted examination of the potential for expanding business within the existing branch network. Computerization appeared to be the answer.

What about the objectives for the first two on-line systems discussed above (the enquiry system within Head Office and the first branch office system)? According to the Systems Development Manager the enquiry system had two main objectives: to improve efficiency and to begin to get staff accustomed to operating such a system. Under the old procedure enquiries from branches (which arrived by post or telephone) were dealt with by locating the relevant computer print-out. This could be time-consuming. It had been projected during 1978/9 that within a few years the system would be unable to cope with the increasing volume of business. With regard to the first branch office system, it was believed that the computerization would improve Head Office's service to all branches, as Head Office staff would be relieved of some of their enquiries.

The service improvement objective was seen as having primacy over strictly financial considerations. Indeed, Computer Department staff believed that the investment in the on-line system at the branch office could not be justified in the latter terms, as the cost of the equipment, installation, telephone rental and calls was seen as generating a net deficit. However, as the Computer Department manager put it, 'The on-line system would improve Head Office service to the branches.' He appeared to be aware that there could be external pressure on the society to computerize all its branches in the near future. The installation was recognized as an early move to 'test the water' and make a start on learning some lessons from adoption – finding out more, for example, about the actual costs, benefits and problems. It would appear that the building society sector 'grape vine' was operating here, for the manager had heard during 1978/9 that the Halifax Building Society (the largest) was making a start on the computerization of its branch office network.

Whilst, then, no strategic decision had been taken at the time to computerize all the society's branch office network, given that the

Systems Development Manager believed that it was more or less inevitable that this would happen, it appeared to him to be prudent to take this limited step so that the Computer Department would be ready to introduce a widespread system should the decision be taken.
With regard to the objective of improving the service to customers, it is instructive to refer to comments made in interview by the Personnel Manager. Discussing the sort of changes in building society operations he expected in the light of intensified competition and the legislative developments, he voiced the belief that the societies would need to place much more emphasis upon the marketing and selling of their services, and on controlling costs, than had hitherto been the case. This implied the need for staff, especially at branch offices, to change their orientation towards customers from a passive to a much more proactive, selling style. Computerization could be expected to help achieve this change, by allowing staff at branch offices to provide services direct to customers, rather than, as previously, having to refer leads to Head Office. That often involved delay, the customer having to wait for a reply through the post. The Personnel Manager emphasized that he saw computerization as a tool, and not as 'the tail wagging the dog', that is, the changes were the result of management decisions and a strategy of moving in the service direction. None the less, it was recognized that the new technology would have its own immediate implications; for example, for the nature of the jobs of branch staff, and their productivity. They would need to learn keyboarding skills, certain operations would have to be performed on the computer before they could 'log off' at the end of the day, and so on.

It should be noted that the branch on-line enquiry system was used only for investment business. Mortgage enquiries were still centralized at Head Office and customers had to contact Head Office themselves, or branch office staff would do it for them by memo or telephone call. Senior management felt that, as this is usually more specialized work, it was better dealt with by specialist staff. However – and this nicely illustrates again the role of managerial choice – other societies such as the Halifax had decentralized most such work to the branches.

THE PROCESS OF ADOPTION OF NEW TECHNOLOGY

As we saw above, the first branch on-line system was installed in 1979 at the Bramley's busiest office, in its headquarters town. There were no further installations until September 1982, but by April 1984 all the society's branch offices had gone on-line.

What triggered adoption throughout the society? There appear to have been three main factors:

1 Senior and executive managers were impressed by the head office and branch installations.
2 A meeting between the General Manager and a representative of the technology supplier company early in 1980, at which the latter explained the further benefits of adopting the technology throughout the society.
3 The Managing Director, through his participation in Building Societies Association meetings, learnt that some of the larger societies were intending to introduce on-line systems into their branch office network. (A key reason was the difficulty other societies had been experiencing in finding suitable new offices, and in expanding existing ones, as with the Bramley.)

Executive management sought board approval for the adoption of the on-line system throughout the society. Following approval, a small working party was set up to progress the project. It consisted of the General Manager (Administration), the Assistant General manager (Branch Offices) and the General Manager. In spring 1980 they were given a demonstration of the new technology in operation in one of the supplier's offices. This presentation was geared to the financial sector, and to building society operations in particular, and was well received by the Bramley managers. A new working party was formed to look in more detail at potential suppliers and costs. Membership was the Assistant General Manager (Administration) (as chairman), the Systems Development Manager, the O&M Manager and the Computer Operations Manager.

Meanwhile, in November 1980, the Managing Director and the Assistant General Manager (Administration) visited a number of working installations of a range of suppliers' equipment in the United States. Demonstrations by technology suppliers were also arranged at the Bramley's head office. Early in 1981, following the board decision to introduce an on-line system throughout the society, a contract was signed with the selected supplier, and the implementation date was set for 6 September 1982, when the first branch office would begin the necessary conversion process.

Shortly after the signing of the technology supplier contract an implementation group was formed. It consisted of the O&M Manager, the Network Controller, the Computer Operations Manager, the Training Manager and the Premises Manager. During 1981 the group produced a leaflet on the new system for distribution to all the society's employees. Computer Department staff gave presentations on the system to managers and supervisors at Head Office and in the branch offices. These staff in turn passed the information on to their staff.

In summer 1981, before the implementation programme was due to begin, the Staff Association, influenced by its external consultant, presented a new technology agreement to management for comments. The response was that it would be more useful to set up a technical sub-committee to look at new technology developments on a continuous basis. The Staff Association agreed to this, and the first meeting took place in August 1981. Management presented a paper on word-processing, which included details of costs, staff involvement, review provisions, etc. There was little questioning of management by the Staff Association representatives. The strategy of management, according to the Personnel Manager, was to give computer implementation a trial run in a non-critical situation. (The word-processors were to be introduced in Personnel and O&M first, where few if any objections were foreseen). It was expected that as a result of this implementation management would be able to point to the benefits of the new technology.

After this initial meeting of the technical sub-committee no further response was forthcoming from the Staff Association for some time (not in fact until March 1982). Meanwhile, management was pressing ahead with preparations for the inauguration of the on-line system throughout the society on 6 September 1982.

It is notable that the origination and progression of the adoption process had gone some way before the society's personnel and training specialists were formally involved. This occurred when the Training Manager was invited to join the implementation group. It will be recalled that this is at stage 4 of the new technology adoption process, just before introduction. However, from this stage onwards, as the conversion of branch offices to the on-line system progressed, personnel and training specialists were more closely involved. There are four main reasons for this:

1 The Personnel Manager spent some time with the Computer and O&M departments, arguing that the people aspects and implications of the technological changes must be taken into account,

especially beforehand. In the words of the Personnel Manager, he had to 'battle with them to see the people angle'.
2 There had been increasing recognition on the part of a number of non-personnel/training specialists (not least, as a result of the Personnel Manager's efforts) of the importance of this matter. For example, the Assistant General Manager (Administration) began to circulate his annual computer/systems plan to the Personnel Manager for comment and discussion, allowing Personnel to make an early input into the planning process. Secondly, in 1982 the O&M, Computer and Personnel managers began to hold regular meetings to discuss current developments in the society and its contexts, and to decide what action should be taken. In other words, we find the beginnings of an informal matrix structure, where managers retain their functional specialisms but also come together on a cross-functional basis to discuss and tackle problems.
3 As we saw, by 1983 the Staff Association was becoming more active, and by early 1984 had converted itself into a branch of BIFU. It could now, therefore, be less easily ignored or 'fobbed off' by management and might require specialist attention.
4 Some of the developments in new technology that were now taking place (such as cash dispensers) were so pervasive in terms of their potential impact on staff that the people implications could be ignored only at management's peril, and this meant early (pre-introduction) attention.

MANAGING THE SOCIAL AND ORGANIZATIONAL ASPECTS OF ADOPTION

Let us begin this section by examining the role the Staff Association played in the adoption of new technology in the society. With regard to the original introduction of the on-line system, at the first branch office and at Head Office, the association had no involvement whatsoever, and did not raise any questions or issues. The first point at which it did raise the matter of new technology was, as we have seen, when it presented management with a draft new technology agreement in summer 1981. However, following the setting up of the technical sub-committee, it did not pursue the new technology issue again until March 1982. By then it was becoming clear that the on-line system was to be adopted on a widespread basis throughout the society. That month the association requested a meeting with management about the on-line system. At the meeting the Personnel Manager and the O&M Manager talked about the health and safety aspects of the new technology. They drew on reports of research in other organizations, for example investigations concerning VDU screens, posture and ergonomic implications. The association appears to have gone along with this angle, and did not raise any other substantive issues. Between September 1982, when the full branch on-line installation programme began, and March 1983 the only formal reference by the Staff Association to new technology was in the annual pay negotiations, where its argument for increased pay levels was based in part on the new tasks associated with the new technology.

By early 1983, however, awareness of the implications of the new technology introduction had begun to emerge on the part of at least some Staff Association members. Two matters appear to have been particularly salient at the time. First, the Computer Department staff were gaining leverage as the introduction of the on-line system proceeded. Some, at least, of the department's staff were aware of this fact, and two of them were members of the main committee of the association. So far it had been technically possible for management to switch the programs to an outside bureau; now this was no longer possible, owing to the amount of work involved and the sophistication of the programs. Manifestations of the changing attitudes of Computer Department staff included requests for additional allowances, and extra payment for working later in the day.

The other major issue emerging at this time was with regard to the position of branch managers. (They were eligible to join the Staff Association, and often did, sometimes taking the chair.) Their role in the society was changing as a result of the external contextual changes discussed at the beginning of the chapter. The nature of this change can be captured through the apparently paradoxical statement that they were gaining more discretion whilst at the same time coming under increasing Head Office control. It was, in other words, circumscribed discretion. The branch managers were being 'encouraged' to develop new business on their own initiative, simply informing Head Office of what they had done. Computerization facilitated this process, for it was now possible for all new business to be administered at branch office level, whereas previously the volume of work involved would have made it impossible. An illustration would be taking on a new contract to handle the payroll of a local organization, with the wages and salaries paid directly into the branch office. This sort of information could now be speedily placed on file via a terminal, whilst front office work continued as usual. On the other hand, branch managers were required to submit much more detailed reports to their regional manager (monthly) on all aspects of branch office business. The regional manager in turn reported to Head Office. A Head Office manager commented, 'It is no longer sufficient to put in a rather "glib" report to the Regional Manager.'

Given these developments, along with the fact that the number of openings for branch managers in the external labour market had reduced (as a result of building society mergers, rationalization, and a decelerating rate of branch office openings), and that some branch managers had been made redundant at other building societies, it is not perhaps surprising that, by early 1983, it was the branch managers who were making the running in the Staff Association. According to the head office and branch managers I interviewed, it was the cashiers who were acting as a constraint on the initiatives the branch managers wished to take through the Staff Association; the former remained a more conservative and divided group.

To conclude this section, let us examine senior management's strategy for dealing with the labour issues raised by new technology adoption. The first on-line system was introduced at the busiest branch in the society's network. Management were confident that the staff there would readily see the benefits to them of the new technology, given in particular that it was expected to relieve their work load. The latter had increased prior to the introduction of the on-line system, as management had deliberately not replaced staff who left. Part of their strategy, then, had been deliberately to engineer the high work loads.[8]

This branch represented, as the Personnel Manager put it, a 'toe in the water' for the society as regards new technology. Management were interested to see the response of the staff affected. The strategy also included getting employees acquainted with the new technology in a non-threatening (to job numbers) situation. The idea was that staff in the rest of the society would get to know about this (anticipated) favourable introduction via various forms of communication, including leaflets and the grape vine. Management's line was that it was nothing really new. The branch office staff were shown photographs of the new equipment, and told how much easier it would make their work. A training programme was provided at the branch, and staff were given turns on the new equipment, being told that they were the 'chosen few'.

Between late 1979 and 1980, after this first branch office and the Head Office installations, certain Head Office managers began to prepare staff for the widespread adoption of the on-line system. No definite decision had been taken at the time, but they calculated that the chances were high. The Personnel Manager and other managers began to plant the idea of the widespread adoption of new technology with the Staff Association, and with regional and branch managers. Managers were asked, for example, how new technology might help them with their jobs and how their jobs and those of their staff might change as a result of new technology introduction. They were subsequently told that they were expected to float possibilities about the on-line system with other employees.

Some staff did in fact make suggestions about how new technology might help their jobs, for example in reducing the length of queues. The Computer Department responded to the effect that they were hoping to develop a technology which would help to achieve this. A leaflet on the new system was produced and distributed throughout the society, showing photographs of the new hardware and describing its capabilities and benefits. Certain 'selected staff', as the Personnel Manager put it, began 'singing the praises' of the technology. At Head Office the Computer Department gave presentations on the new equipment, procedures and possibilities. Over a period of time these were given to all managers and supervisors at Head Office and in the branch network, and they were asked to tell their staff what had been discussed.

The Personnel Manager later discovered that some of the managers were not communicating as required with their staff. It appears that they themselves did not really understand all the details and implications. Indeed, there was a lack of communication within the society during the second half of 1981 and in early 1982 about the new technology. It had been assumed that the regional and branch managers would be communicating effectively with their staff. The fact that, as we have seen, the Staff Association was moribund at the time no doubt played a part.[9] In response to this situation, another communications exercise was initiated; another leaflet about the on-line system was produced and distributed; and branch managers and senior cashiers were brought to Head Office for presentations.

Shortly before the beginning of the installation of the on-line programme throughout the society, in September 1982, the new post of Training Co-ordinator was created. The appointee, who had worked for the society for eighteen months as a management trainee, had previous experience of new technology with a motor manufacturer. He was given the responsibility of developing the training provision for the cashiers who would be using the branch on-line system, and for helping to oversee the pre- and post-implementation training. In addition, five training assistants were appointed from within the society. The training section soon began to expand and develop its work, including identifying staff training needs on a broader basis, developing and running a range of courses (both at Head Office and in the branches), originating and changing job descriptions. This is a suitable point, therefore, at which to leave our consideration of the Bramley's adoption of the branch on-line system, and to move on to look at some key developments since then.

KEY DEVELOPMENTS SINCE 1986/7

The focus will, of course, be upon social, organizational and managerial issues associated with subsequent adoptions of new technology. The framework is broadly the same as the one used throughout the book. Following a review of changes and developments in the Bramley's external and internal contexts, the key technological changes and their associated objectives and strategies will be outlined. This discussion forms the backdrop for a consideration of the associated social and organizational issues. (The same framework is used in the next three case studies.)

External context

In the first section of this chapter we saw how it was becoming increasingly difficult by around 1987 to differentiate the larger building societies from the main clearing banks in terms of the services which were offered to customers. Since that time the financial services sector in general has become ever more subject to competition and the influence of the market place. The process of rationalization among building societies has continued (see Table 10) through mergers, amalgamations and take-overs (the largest twenty societies holding 92·5 per cent of the total assets of all building societies in 1991, the largest five 59·2 per cent and the largest ten 81·0 per cent).[10] Whilst some local societies still remain, the sector is dominated by the nationally based ones in particular, along with those societies (such as the Bramley) with a strong regional presence. One society converted to bank status (the Abbey National, in 1989), and, let alone whether the 'locals' have any long-term future, it is a matter of debate whether the regionals will survive intact in the long run. Of course, as noted earlier, it is only when societies achieve a certain size that they are allowed by law to offer a fuller range of services. The take-over of the Midland Bank by the Hong Kong & Shanghai made it abundantly clear that just about no financial services sector organization is immune from acquisition, either domestically or internationally. This has intensified the national and local societies' efforts to expand their asset bases, control their costs, increase their profits and drive margins down. It has also led to the much more explicit and concerted development of a strategic orientation by the larger financial service-sector organizations.[11] These major external contextual changes have had an impact upon the style and nature of management practices and employee relations. As Kerfoot and Knights put it:

> the industry has tended to respond by modifying if not discarding its previously risk-avertive and conservative traditions. In their place financial services have adopted . . . a policy of corporate growth through horizontal integration and the expansion of consumer markets. In their pursuit of success . . . [they have] adopted plans for strategic growth . . . Fearing to be left behind in the rush to diversify into associated financial services or to take advantage of markets that had a potential well beyond current levels of development, banks, building societies and insurance companies sought to abandon previously conservative and paternalistic modes of management. Attempts were made to displace these by strategic approaches to management which were thought to advance corporate control of internal and external business practices and enhance a company's competitive position in the market place.[12]

Cressey has recently reported upon the nature of the human resource changes which are implied by, and indeed have begun to take place in, the major European banks consequent upon the intensified competition and technological innovation. The changes are captured in Figure 5. Of course, these changes do not happen 'overnight', or all at the same time and to the same degree, and it can be anticipated that there will be variation across different organizations. This means that:

> The new, fast-changing environment currently coexists somewhat

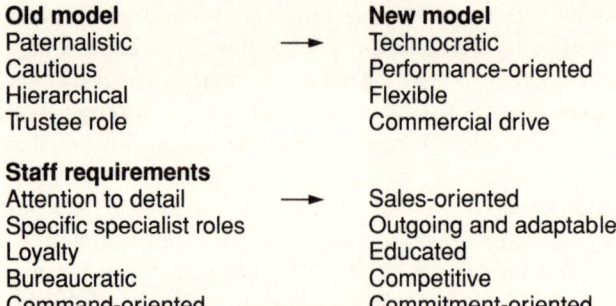

Figure 5 The emerging bank culture?
Source: 'Innovative experiences in European banking', *European Participation Monitor* 4 (1992): 3, reproduced with permission of the European Foundation for the Improvement of Living and Working Conditions

uneasily with the traditional, conservative banking environment in which many of the current generation of bankers began their careers. Indeed, many of the old cultural certainties about staff and employers' expectations are patently breaking down under the current strains in the financial sector. Such factors as the growing differentiation between banks' product profiles, the growing importance attached to measuring and rewarding staff according to their performance, the widening gulf between career and non-career staff, the segmentation of recruitment and training, and growing occupational specialization are all evidence of this.[13]

We shall see many instances in the discussion below of the changes which have taken place in the Bramley Building Society over recent years. Cressey and Scott go on to discuss the increasing need in the 1990s for extensive job reductions at the major UK clearing banks, in addition to the sort of changes referred to above. They argue that the growth in employment experienced during the 1980s has come to an end and will be replaced by a long-term reduction. They identify five main contributory factors:

1 General business conditions.
2 The labour-saving potential of the latest new technology.
3 The potential of that technology to bypass the branch structure.
4 Branch restructuring.
5 The pressure to reduce branch costs.

The analysis below of the Bramley will show how these sorts of environmental changes, including the actions of competitors in the financial services sector, have had an impact upon the society in areas such as technology and personnel resourcing and development. But if one change stands out during the 1990s from the earlier period of research seven years ago, it must be at the level of strategy, in all its various senses, including corporate, technological/IT and human resource.

Internal context

There have been significant changes here, along a number of dimensions. Indeed, change management is itself very much on the current agenda. The General Manager (Operations) – the ex-Personnel Manager from the original period of research – observed that the society had 'shifted away in a major way from anything like the paternalistic type of approach – but it's not clear what we've moved or are moving to'. The organization is more strongly performance-driven, with much more emphasis on measuring activities and teamwork. Because of competitive pressures, there are many more instances of cross-functional and outward looking/ market-oriented working. This manager expects a major erosion of functionalism over the second half of the 1990s and a re-focusing around service-chain and process management. Cross-functional teams have responsibility for solving business problems; the outputs of these teams go back to the functional areas for implementation. Team members split their time between the project and their departmental responsibilities, and have to delegate their work to cover for their absence. The agenda, unlike earlier, now has to be a corporate one, albeit a functional agenda will probably flow from it. If it does not, it is 'disallowed' because there will not be sufficient time to implement it.

The style of management has been loosened up, so that there are not many taboo subjects now. Senior managers are looking at the ways in which they might link long and medium-term corporate objectives into operating objectives throughout the organization. In the future, managers will be measured as much on their contribution to corporate objectives as on functional criteria. There is an attempt to carry forward certain desirable characteristics of the 'old' culture, such as trust and high(ish) morale. (As the General Manager (Operations) put it, 'The business is not too big to recognize the individual.')

There are a number of indications of the adoption by the Bramley of an HRM mode of 'managing the people resource', although it is interesting that human resource management is not a term which is in common currency in the organization. For instance, it was stated that the HR strategy is developed at the same time as the corporate strategy. In other words, the former is not simply derivative from the latter. The example was cited of demographic trends being taken into account when formulating the corporate strategy. It appears that the personnel function has not yet made the transition to an HRM mode. Apparently it has been unwilling or unable to refocus on facilitating and helping line managers to implement corporate and HR policies and practices through effective forms of involvement with their own staff. Instead it has defended what it sees as the specialist territory of personnel management, preferring to 'define, do and deliver', that is, act in a service/specialist rather than a consultancy role. Given this fact, it was no surprise to learn that Personnel had been peripheral to the changes – people-related or otherwise – which had been taking place.

What of collective representation in the society? We saw earlier that the Staff Association had become a BIFU branch in 1984. (Sole negotiating rights were achieved later that year.) This is still the case today, although the proportion of employees in membership is now less than 10 per cent and the branch has found it difficult on occasion to form a committee. (This may appear to be a drastic reduction in representation, but it should be noted that the highest level ever achieved was 20 per cent at the time of original recognition; it had hovered around 15 per cent for some time.) Close contact is maintained, however, with national and full-time BIFU officials. For example, discussions were held with them about the strategic direction the senior management team wanted to take, and the implications for employees. According to the General Manager (Operations):

> The thinking was that what we needed to do was so radical that, if they didn't understand where we were trying to get to, they wouldn't be able to see the logic of some of the things we were trying to do and therefore would want to resist them. They might not entirely like them, but they could 'hand on heart' say, 'That's the best that could have happened, given what the business needs to do.'

Again, indications of a HRM orientation, but also of the advantages to management of retaining some of the old values. This is also brought out nicely in a later comment: 'We have a fairly good record of job preservation and growing the business, so they had something to trust; but, having been through the process with us now a few times, they realize that it's not propaganda.'

Negotiations with the Bramley branch of BIFU, are now restricted essentially to the annual salaries round with respect to what the basic rate will be for the coming year. Even the scope provided here is shrinking, however, for the trend is to a greater proportion of total salary being made up of the performance-related element. Although the scheme was negotiated with the branch, its operation is controlled by management. The thrust is away from collective bargaining, in any event:

> It doesn't make sense any more to try and make an agreement that's going to affect the whole of the staff, apart perhaps from certain core issues around the employment contract such as annual leave or pension arrangements. What's happening now is, we are setting up fairly specialist operating units, such as Sales or Marketing, or processing units in administration, which have got a particular purpose. The sort of people we need to employ there is very different to what we need in the core business. For example, whether we need to stress teamwork or individuality varies a lot. So the employment relations that best fit the type of operation we are trying to run are breaking up now.
>
> (General Manager, Operations)

The prediction is that the society will increasingly reach local 'agreements' with parts of the business. An example cited was that a 'good fit' incentive scheme in financial services would not suit an administrative area, as it would not be the best way of measuring its work and rewarding it. In other words, there is a perceived need to cultivate more flexibility and choice. The restructuring and re-orientation around having more specialists than generalists is particularly evident in the branch network, to which we now turn.

It is perhaps indicative of the changes which have been taking place over the last few years that the terminology itself has changed from 'branches and the branch network' to 'retail units and the retail network'. In the new situation the managerial grades at branch level consist of three posts:

1 Customer Services Managers, responsible for developing the retail

unit as a sales outlet, i.e. maximizing the profitability of the outlet, optimizing customer service and retention (cf. the old branch manager).
2 Business Development Managers, concentrating on the intermediary, non-individual investor markets. These people are more akin to accounts managers, looking after corporate businesses.
3 Direct Sales Consultants, responsible for financial planning.

The current focus is upon developing the autonomy of the outlet, through such means as devolved responsibility for local marketing and staffing decisions. (On the latter, Customer Services Managers can decrease or increase staff at their discretion, but an increase would mean making out a business case and they would have to achieve the projected results, otherwise the extra staff would be lost.)

In addition to these posts there are a number of other new posts in the new structure, including Senior Sales Managers, Mortgage Centre Managers, District Sales Managers and Financial Services Managers. Space does not allow us to discuss the details of the restructuring; suffice it to observe that the expansion of staff numbers in the retail network has been in the specialist, managerial grades and that, overall, the skills base has been changed significantly. Because of the implications of these changes, all managers spent three days at an assessment centre being measured up against the competences which had been identified as needed in the future. Those who emerged as not having the requisite 'raw abilities' (and hence not being 'trainable' into the new roles) were offered early retirement, redeployment or, as a last resort, redundancy. According to the General Manager (Operations) it was found that quite a few of the managers did not have trainability potential, but it should be remembered that 'This was against a background of aggressive expansion planning, and what we were really saying was, "We can't mess about with this any more, we've got to have people who can deliver those results to us and know that we've got someone we can work with.'

The upshot was that around half the staff who were needed to fill the new posts were recruited from outside, from a variety of financial services companies, the common denominator being people who had some form of professional sales experience. There was no difficulty in attracting such staff because of the shake-out in the sector over previous years, particularly from the national building societies and banks, which had been shedding middle managers.

Technological changes

Three main developments have taken place since the original introduction of new technology into the organization:

1 The on-line system has been revamped into an extended Cobra system involving a higher degree of multi-functionality where, for example, transaction processing is linked to mortgage processing, to branch administration and to word processing. Paperwork is now produced only on an 'as required' basis. As a result of the changes, it is now possible to deal with an account enquiry by moving in and out of mortgage, insurance, etc., details, and then going back into the transaction. This facilitates branch office flexibility, as staff who are not currently dealing with customers can process mortgages or whatever at the counter. The aim is to take administration more or less completely away from such staff so that they will need to concern themselves only with directly interacting with customers.

2 The IS strategy for the business was redefined. This included the issues of what needed to be done with the society's mainframe provision, and what specialist applications were going to be required for the developing business. After an exhaustive and detailed consideration of the options it was decided to adopt a 'long, do-it-yourself' strategy, that is, an evolutionary approach over five years towards an open-system environment. This was seen as offering the necessary flexibility and also achieving a phased capital spending programme, so that cost–income ratios in IS will be driven down over a period of time. A transition strategy for IS staff has been adopted which moves them from a skill base around Cobol and a Bull mainframe to one around open systems. There are some important sensitivities during this transition period, and therefore a HR strategy is being implemented which involves providing some existing IS staff with Oracle training, bringing new staff in from outside the organization who already have this expertise, training some staff for maintenance work only, and switching current maintenance work to out-sourcing. In other words, quickly decreasing dependence on an internal resource whilst simultaneously building new expertise over a five-year period.

3 There has been a growth in the use of PC-based systems throughout the business and a strategy of moving towards end-user computing, with the users increasingly defining what they require

and managing the adoption process, supported by IS staff. Some PCs are networked, others not.

With regard to strategies and objectives, the starting point was the business strategy, which in essence says that the Bramley aims to become the leading provider of mortgage finance in the Greater Midlands area by the late 1990s. This means that it will also need to be a key player in the financial planning market. When the present IS Controller joined the organization in the early 1990s he asked for details of this strategy and then set about developing the IS strategy. It includes such elements as cost control and cost–income ratio control – very much business and not IS considerations. The Cobra project antedates much of this strategic IS/business thinking, and hence incorporates some elements which might not have been built in had the benefit of that thinking been available. Certainly the society would not now introduce a project which had a four-year time span, as Cobra had. The society's project management is organized over much shorter time periods of a year or less (the belief is that in an open-systems environment this is much easier to achieve), with each main element in turn broken down into six-week activity periods with 'deliverables' at the end of each.

Social and organizational issues

The emphasis has been upon trying to ensure that users have been involved at all stages of the development and implementation of the systems. For example, multi-level teams from the retail network were used to put Cobra in. The training was provided by operations staff (who had received team support training), not IS or personnel specialists, and the project was sponsored by the General Manager (Operations), and not the IS department. This does not mean that IS staff have had no responsibility for the success of the system, for a steering committee was established, consisting largely of non-IS people, where operations issues predominated, such as 'Is it to the quality required?', 'Is it producing the output required?'. Pilot schemes were conducted live in the branches, working with customers and building up staff acceptance, originally in low-volume branches, but then in high-volume ones. The General Manager (Operations) was of the opinion that:

> There is much more understanding now of IS issues in the business because of the end-user computing, with users being allowed to

define systems much more than in the past, and to own them, so that they're bringing something in. It's not IS doing it for them, it's their package. In some areas that's been less successful than in others, probably because the amount of systems expertise in the area wasn't that high, so they didn't recognise all the issues ... You then find a lot of defensiveness by the users. They 'own' it, they defined it, etc. This has revealed certain development needs amongst both staff and managers. Technology is so ingrained in the business now, it's so much part of what we do, that acceptability is high anyway. Everybody's dabbling with bits of technology ... It's never really been a problem, because it's always helped the job, got rid of routine work, etc.

This comment on the employee acceptability of new technology has strong echoes of the essence of the WIRS findings discussed in Chapter 4, and typifies the position found in the three case studies which follow. But this is to 'jump the gun'. Let us, therefore, move on to examine new technology adoption in the second building society.

Chapter 6
Park Hill Building Society

We shall see in this chapter that, whilst the branch on-line technology adopted by the Park Hill society was of a very similar nature to that adopted by the Bramley society, there were some differences in the social and organizational processes of adoption. A commentary upon the differences and similarities in the new technology adoption processes in the two organizations will be provided in the final chapter. There it will also be possible to draw upon two further case studies, taken from the engineering sector, which form the subject matter of Chapters 7 and 8.

As the external contexts facing the Park Hill Building Society are in essence the same as for the Bramley society, the discussion of this matter in the previous chapter can be taken as equally applicable here, and therefore only the internal context will be considered below.

THE ORGANIZATION

The Park Hill Building Society is based in the Midlands, and was ranked twenty-fifth in size among UK building societies (in terms of business volume) at the time when the first moves were made towards adopting new technology in 1985. It had just begun to fall from its peak number of eighty-nine branch offices, achieved in 1984 (see Table 11). The Park Hill has grown steadily in terms of business volume, branch offices and numbers employed. Table 12 details changes in staff numbers over the period 1975–87. Within these global figures, it can be seen from Table 13 that there had been some fluctuation between Head Office numbers on the one hand and branch offices on the other. Until 1986/7 staff numbers at Head Office had stabilized or grown very steadily, whilst branch office numbers

Table 11 Park Hill Building Society: branch office numbers, 1980–7

Year	No. of branches
1980	72
1981	80
1982	84
1983	88
1984	89
1985	87
1986	80
1987	81

Table 12 Park Hill Building Society: staff numbers, 1975–87

Year	Full-time	Part-time	Total full-time equivalent
1975	194	21	204·5
1976	216	21	226·5
1977	254	22	265·0
1978	272	27	285·5
1979	327	27	340·5
1980	352	39	371·5
1981	358	58	387·0
1982	386	67	419·5
1983	394	72	430·0
1984	390	86	433·0
1985	385	84	427·0
1986	387	83	428·5
1987	429	86	472·0

tended to increase in line with the opening (or, during 1985/6, closure) of branches. The larger increase in Head Office staff numbers during 1986/7 was attributable to three main factors:

1 A significant expansion of business, particularly in mortgage lending.
2 The recruitment of a number of computer specialists.
3 The lifting of an embargo on recruitment to many Head Office posts. (It had been in force for two years.)

The Head Office organization chart during this period is reproduced in Figure 6. It is worth noting that the mortgage and investment departments were combined in one department called Members' Accounts rather than being separate departments as had

Table 13 Park Hill Building Society: staff employed at Head Office and in branch offices, 1975–87

	Head Office			Branch offices		
Year	Full-time	Part-time	Total FTE	Full-time	Part-time	Total FTE
1975	71	7	74·5	123	14	130·0
1976	77	6	80·0	139	15	146·5
1977	85	6	88·0	169	16	177·0
1978	86	3	87·5	186	24	198·0
1979	105	2	106·0	222	25	234·5
1980	119	2	120·0	233	37	251·5
1981	132	3	133·5	226	55	253·5
1982	139	2	140·0	247	65	279·5
1983	131	1	131·5	263	71	298·5
1984	119	1	119·5	271	85	313·5
1985	127	5	129·5	258	79	297·5
1986	134	5	136·5	253	78	291·0
1987	175	5	177·5	254	81	294·5

Note: FTE = full-time equivalent

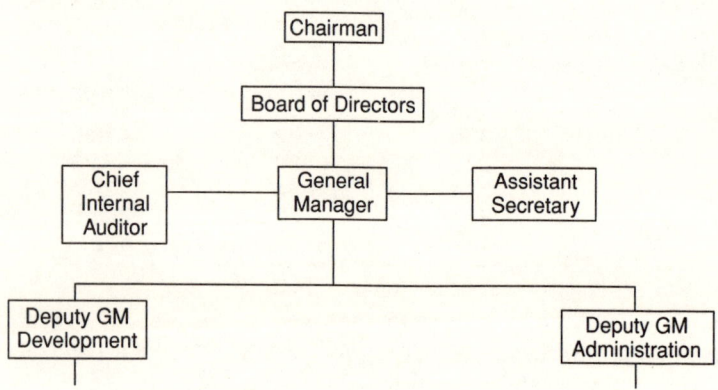

Figure 6 Park Hill Building Society: part organization chart

hitherto been the norm in building societies, not least in the Park Hill. This change, which was made early in 1985, was a result of two separate developments, one involving technology:

1 Management Services Department had been examining the work of the Mortgages Department and the Investment Department, and had concluded that they were basically very similar in terms of operating procedures and calculations.

2 During 1984 a software house had begun to develop new specialist programs for the society which were to be used on the existing mainframe. The basic unit of this software was a customer, as against investments or mortgages on the older software.

Certain staff (including the person who was to become the Members' Accounts Manager) had realized that the new software and information system would fit much more readily into an organization structure which was based on the basic 'unit' of a customer (or 'member'). We have another example here, then, of the reorientation which was taking place at this time in the building society/financial services sector around the customer, and of how this was impacting upon organizational structure. Against the backdrop of the structure of the Park Hill society, let us now consider some processual features of the society's mode of operation. These have been selected in order to help understand the society's new technology adoption process, and to distinguish changes connected with this adoption from those arising from other developments. They are:

1 Labour utilization and composition.
2 The Staff Association.
3 The changing role of branch network managers.
4 Project teams.

Labour utilization and composition

It is notable that Organization and Methods (O&M) was not established as a separate function until as late as 1978, when the society moved to the present, purpose-built head office. A group was formed to co-ordinate the transfer from the old head office and the person who headed it so impressed top management with his organizational ability that he was appointed to the newly created post of Organization and Methods Officer. It was not until 1982, however, following an investigation and report by external consultants, that O&M became firmly established in the society. The consultants had been called in by the Deputy General Manager (Administration) in the belief that 'there was scope for increased staff efficiency within Head Office'. They suggested various efficiency improvements, recommended that the society should introduce project teams (this recommendation influenced the society's choice of the project team concept for the adoption of new technology – discussed separately below), helped top management prioritize the future developments which were being considered at the time (mainly connected with computerization), and trained additional staff as O&M officers. By 1985/6 the O&M Department was investigating the branch office network. It is clear that by this time the external contextual changes discussed in Chapter 5 were putting pressure on the society to find more cost-effective working practices.

The consultants' exercise generated anxiety. The Staff Association chairman recalled that complaints were made by staff about the exercise, and that people were worried about the use that might be made of the information gathered. This was despite the fact that, some staff believed that the information gathered was of limited usefulness. According to the Staff Association chairman, 'The credibility of the exercise was low.' Rumours were circulating that the consultants had recommended staff savings of the order of 30 per cent at Head Office. It would appear that they had some substance, for, as from 1982, a policy of not replacing leavers was introduced (with certain specified exceptions) and staff were redeployed within the organization. The Staff Association chairman believed that the introduction and extension of computerization across the society was a major factor in generating the pressure for staff reductions. The effect of the policy on Head Office staff numbers can be seen in Table 13, which reveals a reduction of twenty staff between 1982 and 1984.

It was noted earlier that branch office staff numbers reduced somewhat after 1984. According to the Personnel Manager, the intention of senior management at the time was that staffing levels in the branches would stabilize, any increase in business volume being absorbed by the new on-line technology. There was no intention, certainly, of reducing branch office staff numbers through the computerization of the branch network: the expectation was that staff would be able to spend more time with customers. In any event, an absolute minimum of two people was always to be maintained in each branch for security reasons. In the lower-volume branches, whilst one person might be able to cope with the assistance of the new technology, management would not want them to be on their own.

A final observation on labour composition in the Park Hill Building Society is that whilst females constituted around two-thirds of the total labour force at the time, only 20 per cent of them were represented in management grades (defined as head of department or above at Head Office, and area and branch managers). We will not develop here an analysis of why this should have been the case, in part because we could not do justice to the matter in the space available, but also because the gender issue has been studied in some detail by others. Suffice it to say that the Park Hill seems to have been typical in this respect both of building societies and of financial services in general. The concentration of females in lower-level positions (particularly as cashiers) has enhanced the opportunities for males to mount the promotion ladder.[1] Ashburner, for example, found that the introduction of a new career grading system in one of the major societies relieved pressure on the promotion system for males but left a lot of female staff stuck at lower levels.[2] As she commented at the time, 'The power of patriarchal ideology remains largely unchallenged within the building society industry.'[3]

The Staff Association

The Staff Association was formed in 1978 following an ACAS survey of the society requested by the National Union of Banking Employees. The majority of those voting wanted Staff Association rather than NUBE representation. The association was issued with a certificate of independence in 1981, following an inspection by the Registrar of Trade Unions and Friendly Societies. Those eligible to join the association included everyone below departmental head level at Head Office and everyone below area manager level in the branches. The chairman, vice-chairman, secretary and treasurer were elected by and from within the Staff Association committee, which consisted of twelve people elected annually by the membership. A joint consultative and negotiating committee met four times a year and the chairman met the Personnel Manager regularly on an 'informal' basis. As with the Bramley society, the association appointed an external consultant.

The Staff Association negotiated with senior management on salaries, security, terms and conditions of employment, and general benefits. Around the mid- to late 1980s, 65–7 per cent of those eligible joined the association, the density of membership being higher in the branches than at Head Office. In contrast to the Bramley, no transfer of engagement to BIFU has taken place. The Personnel Manager was of the opinion, however, that if the Staff Association membership fees were significantly increased from their low level the result would have been a lower level of membership, and a consequent move by some of those remaining to switch to BIFU. The Personnel Manager's preference, looking ahead, would have been a better organized and more 'enlightened' association committee. He would like to have been able to provide training for the purpose. He foresaw obstacles, however, not least the danger of formally signalling to staff a loss of independence from management on the part of the association. We will look at the association's role in the adoption of new technology in a later section of this chapter.

The changing role of branch network managers

Until the end of the 1970s the Park Hill Building Society had two levels of management in the regions above branch manager level: Area Managers and Regional Managers. At that time there were four Area Managers, thirty Regional Managers and around seventy branch managers, with the reporting line shown in Figure 7. By this time it had become clear to management that the structure was unwieldy in terms of administrative costs and reporting relationships. Each Regional Manager, for example, was responsible on average for 2·33 branch managers. What is more, some of the Regional Managers lacked marketing and selling skills and knowledge. As the Personnel Manager put it, 'They went to visit the people they knew and felt comfortable with.' This in spite of the fact that the development of business at regional level was one of their two main responsibilities. (The other was branch monitoring.) The latter responsibility included a 'watching brief' over the branch managers, and in this respect they acted in effect as their line managers for certain matters, such as staff appraisal and development. The Area Managers had seven or eight Regional Managers reporting to them, and worked as a team with the Head Office Branch Agencies Manager. In the view of a number of Head Office managers, the branch managers at the time were essentially 'glorified cashiers', with administrative responsibilities in relation to their office but no selling or business development responsibility.

By the mid-1980s, given the intensification of competition and the widening range of services which could be offered (see pp. 126–9), it had become clear that the branch managers would have to put a lot more time, effort and thought into marketing and selling. The decision was taken to rationalize the branch network managerial structure. The Regional Manager post was abolished and replaced with twelve posts of Senior Branch Manager. The aim was to improve communications, facilitate in-depth training and enable the senior branch managers to take a more dispassionate view of their

Figure 7 Park Hill Building Society: branch network management hierarchy

new, expanded areas. The latter held regular group meetings and were informed by top management that they were expected to develop a 'semi-corporate strategy' for the branch office network, in addition to the specific marketing responsibility.

Whilst the above changes were taking place the Area Managers' role had continued; indeed, they had contributed to the changes. It was abolished, though, once the changes were complete. Two of their number became Administration Managers and the other two Development Managers (one specializing in operations and one in marketing) at Head Office. The Branch Agencies Manager post became Deputy General Manager (Development).

Project teams

The first project team in the society was formed in 1982 as a result of the new technology adoption process for the branch offices. As this is discussed below, we shall concentrate here on subsequent project teams. What was meant by a project team in this organization? The term referred to staff from different levels and functional areas who were brought together for a period of time to deal with a particular element of the society's business. The length of time the team remained in existence, like the number of members, varied according to the magnitude and complexity of the issue(s) under consideration. Eight project teams were in existence by 1987:

1 Users and Computer Technology.
2 New Legislation.

3 Data Protection.
4 Interest Rates.
5 Manpower Planning.
6 Contingency planning.
7 Housing.
8 Business Services.

The teams were chaired by a senior member of staff, who had primary responsibility for following up the decisions of the team. It was soon recognized that good project managers are not always 'born', and so training was provided. Another area of difficulty related to the tension which can arise between the 'pull' of the work of the team as against the 'pull' of departmental work. How is the time to be divided between the two, and who, if anyone, is going to look after the departmental duties whilst the employee is on project business? It was found to be easier for advisory and specialist, as against line staff, to get involved in project team work, partly because of the more discontinuous nature of their work, and partly because they often had society-wide responsibilities anyway. None the less, it was seen as equally crucial for line staff to contribute through membership of project teams.

The above developments created pressure for an additional level of management below the three which had existed for some time at the society's head office (according to the Deputy General Manager, Administration), that is, General Manager, Deputy General Manager and Head of Department. The reasoning was that, as there were relatively few managers in total at the three levels, and a number of them were members of project teams, the society 'now needs four levels of management, so that the departments can still be run when the head is away'. In the view of the DGM Administration, departmental staff should be trained and developed for this role of Deputy Head of Department, since there was a lack of people with the skills and experience to do the job when the manager was elsewhere. As departmental staff had experience only of administrative work, it was anticipated that it would take around ten years to create the fourth tier of management.

THE TECHNOLOGICAL CHANGES

At the time of my original research at the Park Hill Building Society, in the mid- to late 1980s, the following forms of new technology either had been introduced or were being adopted:

1 A mainframe computer.
2 A branch office terminal system.
3 'One per desk' microcomputers.
4 A distributed resource system.
5 An environmental control system.
6 A computerized telephone exchange.

The focus here will be upon the first three only.

The mainframe computer

The society purchased its first mainframe computer towards the end of 1978. Until then, and indeed for some years later, it had used an external bureau for many of its administrative and accounting requirements. By 1978 the bureau arrangement had become prohibitively expensive, and was not seen as providing the flexibility which managers required. An in-house mainframe was seen as giving the society not only more flexibility but also more control over computer applications.

A Computer Manager was recruited from outside the organization in 1978, followed by Computer Department staff. It took a considerable period of time to transfer data on to the mainframe; this was the reason for the parallel utilization of the bureau, which in fact was to last until 1982, when the transfer was complete. The nominal ledger and investment information were first put on the computer, followed in the summer of 1982 by mortgages. The society experienced a number of hardware and software problems during the first few years of mainframe operation. The capacity of the hardware was regularly updated, but the organization was chasing a moving target, for suppliers were continually changing and updating their products. It had been intended (in 1978) to use externally produced software, but in 1984 management decided the society should produce its own. (Again, flexibility and control objectives figured prominently.) As a result, software staff were recruited that year. In the words of the DGM Administration:

> The rate of development of the new technology was very rapid. Societies were dragged along by this, rather than the market. We wanted to handle all the accounts ourselves, and to link investment and mortgage accounts to managerial accounting. There was also an awareness that we would want to introduce an on-line system in the branches.

It can be seen from this that the integration of information was a further objective of introducing the in-house mainframe. However, software problems prevented the aim from being realized to any notable extent. According to the DGM Administration, these were:

1 Lack of control over the development of the system because of the external software.
2 The software did not exactly meet the needs of the society.
3 Liaison with the software house was handled exclusively by the society's computer specialists, with no involvement from the users-designate. Not surprisingly, the users' needs were not always adequately taken into account.

The branch office terminal system

The Park Hill society was rather later than the Bramley in introducing an on-line branch office computer system. As a result it was able to adopt a system which was not available when the Bramley was committing itself. It will be recalled that the latter's system consisted of microcomputers in branch offices linked via telephone lines to the organization's mainframe computer at the head office. In the Park Hill's system (henceforth termed the 'Devine' system) the microcomputer terminals in the branch offices were first of all linked to a minicomputer, which in turn linked into the Head Office mainframe. Some of the minicomputers were located at Head Office, but the majority were in the branch offices themselves. There were also a few branch offices on-line which did not have their own mini, in which case their terminals were connected to a nearby branch office's minicomputer. This system allows a minicomputer to be updated immediately a transaction takes place, and the mainframe when the opportunity arises. Unlike the Bramley society, only around two-thirds (rather than all, as with the Bramley) of the Park Hill society's branches got the on-line terminals. Management believed that branches with lower transaction levels could not justify the cost in relation to the benefits.

The key information processing benefit of both societies' systems is in essence the same: they do away with the need for the double inputting of data. Data are entered only once, rather than both at the branch counter and at Head Office. In addition the information is up to date and much more readily accessible.

How did the on-line adoption process begin? It can be traced, in

1982, to the awareness of some managers, in particular the Computer Manager, that on-line terminals had been introduced into a number of societies, and the recognition that this technology was likely to become the core branch office administrative technology of the future. It was foreseen that all but the smallest societies would adopt the technology and that it would play an important role in the increasingly intense competition for new business and customer retention. This intelligence about computer developments in building societies could be formally gathered from the quarterly meetings of an association of computer managers in the sector. The membership of the association consisted of those societies which had a particular supplier's hardware. Often the supplier attended the meetings to discuss problems and future developments (and, no doubt, to chase new business!). A 'grape vine' of computer specialists in the sector also existed.

The Park Hill's interest in the Devine system appears to have been sparked by a visit from a representative of the supplier company in 1982, when its advantages were described to the Computer Manager. As the latter put it, 'The branch on-line system seemed to be the way it was going, and the visit "whetted the appetite".' The Computer Manager followed up by contacting four other suppliers for details of what they had to offer. Apparently one had nothing suitable, one wanted to sell a software *and* hardware package (whereas the Park Hill wanted to produce its own software), one was very expensive (and in any event its system was not available at the time) and the other 'was not looking enough towards the future'. The Devine system, whilst not the cheapest, was seen as having the advantages of 'looking to the future' and of using the same programming language the society was already used to. What is more, and probably crucially, it received a favourable report when the Computer Manager contacted another regional building society where it had already been installed.

'One per desk' microcomputers (*OPD*)

'One per desk' was a brand-name microcomputer product of ICL; it was designed to be used literally on the desks of office and managerial staff. It was flexible in terms of applications, which include, for example, word-processing and spreadsheets, linking into a mainframe computer in order to access the data stored there, and with telecommunications connections to other OPDs anywhere in the world. In the Park Hill society OPDs were being used for the first three applications above, as well as others such as insurance quotations, enquiries, and daily updating of the mainframe computer with the final balance from the branches.

OPDs were first introduced into the society in 1986, when a few machines were installed at head office on a trial-and-error basis. Their benefits and potential having been demonstrated, they were then introduced into the branch office network. They do not have the ability of the on-line system to update minicomputers and the central mainframe on a real time basis. However, they are much cheaper and do not involve the major installation costs associated with the terminal system (which result from the need to build each terminal into the different styles of counters to be found in the branch offices, as well as the cost of the machines themselves).

The priority set for OPD introduction was to install the machines in all the branches that were not getting the terminal system. Subsequently, it was envisaged, they might also be introduced into the branches in the terminal network, as well as into the society's agencies.

NEW TECHNOLOGY OBJECTIVES

The General Manager, who, in his previous post of DGM Finance, had influenced the new technology adoption process, summarized the objectives as follows (no order of priority):

1 To provide a speedy and cost-effective service to members.
2 To provide a more efficient information system within the society.
3 To provide integrated data for individuals.
4 To provide an enhanced budgetary control and management information system.
5 To obtain a technology which was inherently flexible, in the sense that it could be added to subsequently.

It will be noticed that some of these objectives have an affinity with other, wider, objectives which were being pursued within the society at the time, such as the amalgamation of the Investment and Mortgages departments and the development of project team working. It is thus difficult to disentangle which, if any, objective took priority – the corporate, the organizational or the technological. Indeed, perhaps it is more accurate to see some of these so-called objectives as means to achieving the other, primary objectives. We shall return to these matters in the concluding chapter. It is worth noting here, however, that what can be clearly perceived is the influence of external contextual changes upon organizational decision-making and events. It begins to look as if some, at least, of those managers who were involved in the new technology adoption process drew no distinction between innovations in technology deployment and other forms of organizational response to contextual developments. In this sense, then, new technology *per se* may not have been regarded as particularly novel, still less radical, even during the mid-to late 1980s. Whilst new technology was seen as having the potential to enhance service provision, it would appear that had it not been available other ways of achieving this key objective would have been sought and found. It may be noted that the DGM Administration commented that, by the early 1980s, the Park Hill society was 'looking for improved speed and service, before the new technology was introduced'.

With regard to the specific objectives of the branch on-line system, the DGM Finance identified as central:

1 Direct inputting of information at the counter, resulting in a speeding up of information flows, the gathering of more timely position statements, the removal of double inputting and of reliance upon the postal system.
2 Improving the service to customers by speeding it up, reducing queues and making the service more personal.

The Computer Manager saw the major benefit as an improvement in the quality of the customer service which could be provided at the branch. This centred on the enhanced image which could be presented to customers, a reduction in queue length, and better presentation by staff. He also anticipated that the new technology would provide better data security, as well as keeping the organization abreast of the latest technological developments. On a strict cost calculation, in his view, the on-line system would not have been adopted. Interestingly, the Personnel Manager also commented that 'The time and effort saved probably couldn't be recouped *vis-à-vis* the cost of the counter-top system. It was more to do with keeping up with competitors, image and service.' All this points not only to the key significance of improved service provision but also to the fact that qualitative considerations can play a central role in the new technology adoption process.

No indication was given during my interviews with managers and employees, including that with the Staff Association chairman, of any intention to dispense with branch office staff as a result of new technology introduction. (See, though, the section on labour supply and utilization above.) However, there *were* seen to be Head Office staffing implications, largely owing to the elimination of double inputting.

THE PROCESS OF ADOPTION OF NEW TECHNOLOGY

The focus in this section will be upon the branch office on-line system. We noted earlier that it was not until 1982 that the society first seriously considered adopting this form of new technology. The Computer Manager played a key part in the initiation process, but, of course, financial support and board approval were necessary if the investment was to go ahead. The Deputy General Manager and Secretary played a central role at this early stage. Once the expenditure had been approved by the board and the Devine system had been selected, it took just three years (1983–6) to install across the designated part of the branch network. The branches with the highest volume of transactions were converted first.

The Computer Manager and DGM Finance recognized that it was important for other members of the society to become involved in the adoption process. With this in mind, they formed a Network Committee composed of the Computer Manager, the Assistant Secretary and Investment Manager (ASIM), the internal auditor, the Management Services Manager, a seconded branch manager and branch office representatives – a total of around twenty people. With regard to branch office staff, their pivotal role in operating the new system meant that it was important for them to understand and accept what was happening. The 'network representatives' on the committee were asked to obtain branch office staff comments on the new system, and feed them back to the Network Committee. At an early meeting it was decided that the seconded branch manager and the ASIM should draw up the system specification, outlining the facilities that the new system had to provide. It was to act as a guide for the Computer Manager and his staff in amending and writing the software.

In the event the Network Committee lasted only a short period of time, during which there were just four meetings. According to the Personnel Manager, 'The committee was too unwieldy. Different people were wanting different things, and there was a lack of a coherent view.' What is more, many branch office representatives did not get involved in a two-way communication process as had been envisaged. Apparently many of them showed little interest in the new technology.

The Network Committee was replaced by a project team, with the same composition, except that there were no branch representatives. According to the Personnel Manager, the team proved to be a more cohesive body. The ASIM and seconded branch manager presented the system specification for comment. Detailed specifications for all the main aspects of the on-line system were drafted, and plans made for the transfer from the manual to the computerized system. The Personnel Manager conceded that it had been a 'systems-oriented approach', but argued that 'the branch manager knew what the problems would be for the cashiers, and could get them taken into account'.

Whilst the network group may have become more cohesive with the reduction in size and change of composition, the danger of course was that it would become dominated by a 'computer systems rationalization' and managerial control orientation (see Chapter 4). However, a wider range of people and expertise were involved in the adoption process through the setting up of sub-committees of the main project team. Three sub-committees were formed: Siting, Training and Communications.

The training committee, set up in March 1983, focused upon the training needs of staff associated with the on-line system, and was composed of the seconded branch manager, the Chief Internal Auditor, the Personnel and Training Manager and the Assistant Training Officer. Other staff, such as the Computer Manager, attended certain meetings by invitation. The branch manager and Chief Internal Auditor were responsible for reporting back to the project team. The committee focused upon three matters:

1 Updates on the latest developments.
2 Progress reports from the personnel and training specialists.
3 The logistics of introducing the new system, for example the length of training time needed on a given computer in a branch office following conversion to the on-line system.

The participation of the personnel specialists in the training sub-committee was their first direct formal involvement in the adoption of the on-line system. However, the Personnel Manager had already been involved indirectly through a request from the seconded branch manager for his thoughts on how the branch office staff would react to the new technology. This meant, of course, that the Personnel Department had been formally involved only after the system specification had been written, that is, at stage 4 of the process of new technology adoption (the one immediately preceding introduction).

The communications sub-committee was given the responsibility for producing a newsletter about the on-line system for circulation among branch office staff, with the main objective of 'selling' the system; it was edited by the seconded branch manager. Seven issues appeared in total, the last in February 1984.

The project team and its sub-committees were wound up in January 1984, when the forum for discussion of developments in new technology in the society moved to the Computer Users Committee. This committee dated from the time when the society had introduced its first mainframe.

In the above discussion of the adoption of the branch on-line system it will be noticed that there has been no reference to the Staff Association. Why this was so will become clear in the next section.

MANAGING THE SOCIAL AND ORGANIZATIONAL ASPECTS OF ADOPTION

It can be seen from the preceding discussion that control over the adoption of new technology by the Park Hill Building Society was seen as a managerial prerogative by managers, technical staff and, perhaps, most employees alike. It is therefore not too surprising that the Staff Association should have had limited involvement in and impact upon the process. As the Personnel Manager put it, 'Members of the Staff Association just didn't see new technology as part of the Staff Association's business, or area of interest.' The Staff Association chairman's view was in sympathy with this. He commented that staff believed it was crucial for the society to keep up with competitors, and if that meant taking on new technology, then 'Fine, that's what must be done.' What is more, a majority of them were keen for the society to adopt new technology. This is in part because of what competitors were doing or about to do, but also because they accepted that the cashier's job would be made easier in some respects. For example, end-of-day balancing became more straightforward, and staff did not have to stay behind at the end of the day so often, or for so long, as in the past. In addition, staff saw themselves becoming more marketable as a result of their computer skills and knowledge. In so far as the Staff Association paid any attention to the adoption of the branch on-line system, it focused on the health and safety aspects of VDU operation; that is, new technology was used as a 'stick' with which to 'beat' management about improving security in the branches – a long-standing issue. It was also brought into the annual pay negotiations, but this did not appear to cut much ice with management. However, when a branch switched on-line, staff were automatically paid a little more as a result of accumulating a few more points on 'manual dexterity' in the job evaluation scheme, that is, for keyboarding skills. However, very few staff moved up the grading structure as a result. (Manual dexterity had a low weighting in the job evaluation scheme.) The Staff Association did not latch on to the much enhanced selling requirement (associated with the internal contextual changes connected to new technology introduction – see above) as an argument for re-evaluation of the factors and/or increased pay.

Let us conclude this section by returning to the matter of project teams. It will be recalled that the first was formed as a result of the adoption of the branch on-line system, and that teams subsequently spread throughout the society. Project teams also sparked off the moves to add a fourth tier of management below head of department level. Whilst I have been careful not to argue or imply that technological changes *caused* the adoption of project teams (indeed, as was argued earlier, they would probably have arisen anyway, if not *quite* as soon, because of the external contextual changes), I am none the less of the opinion that there is a close affinity between the use of computer technology on a widespread scale throughout the society and recognition of the need for project teams. This affinity has been described by Child:

> The unification of control through modern information technology encourages a corresponding integration and simplification in organisation structures. As the interdependencies between functional activities are made more visible through integrated control systems and shared data services, so the logic of team-working and networks emerges as the 'natural' basis of organisation rather than patterns of work and communication defined predominantly by departmental boundaries.[4]

Team working and organizational restructuring were in fact to figure among the most commonly advocated and sought-after forms of organizational restructuring and reorientation during the late 1980s and early 1990s. They are further exemplified in the engineering company case study which is the subject of the following chapter.

KEY DEVELOPMENTS SINCE 1986/7

Recent changes in the external contexts of financial and, in particular, building society organizations were discussed in Chapter 5, so we will move immediately to a few brief comments about changes in the Park Hill society's internal contexts.

Internal context

The society's current mission was summarized by the IT Development Manager as 'To consolidate the organization's position in its Midland heartlands, whilst also developing a national presence'. As with the Bramley, a much enhanced customer orientation was evident in a number of the comments made, and this had certainly been driving many of the changes in the IT infrastructure. The marketing function was more in evidence and appeared to have an enhanced role compared with 1986/7. There was recognition that customers were 'shopping around' the financial sector before deciding where to invest or place their mortgage business. This was a key source of pressure on the cost base.

The Park Hill was now the twenty-second largest building society in terms of assets – slightly up from 1985, when, it will be recalled, it was in twenty-fifth place. This movement is partly due to business expansion, but an important contributory factor must also be the reduction in the number of societies, and in particular the mergers and amalgamations which have taken place in the intervening period among other medium-size, regionally based societies. The Park Hill itself has not been involved in any merger or acquisition activity in recent years, but the possibility is by no means ruled out for the future. Continued growth is seen as resulting from at least two, and possibly all three, of the following:

1 Organic growth, as in the past.
2 The purchase of mortgage books from other financial organizations.

3 The take-over of smaller building societies. ('Join us before one of the nationals gets you and then closes you down.')

With regard to staffing, between 1991 and 1993 a new Chief Executive and a new General Manager (there are two General Manager posts) have joined, both coming from other building societies. The organization structures at Head Office and in the branch office network have been slimmed down. A management tier was removed in the former at the same time as the various functional areas were rationalized, the main objective being to create a stronger and more focused customer orientation. In the branch network the Area Manager and Regional Manager roles have been combined into just two (geographical) area roles, where each manager has both marketing and operational responsibilities. Branch managers are set sales targets on an annual basis and appraised against them. Partly as a result of failure to meet these objectives, some managers have been redeployed or have left the society. To quote the IT Development Manager, 'Paternalism is not as strong now.' Unlike the Bramley society, collective representation for employees is still available via a staff association, not a union. Of the 567 staff in post at the end of 1993, approximately 527 were eligible to join the association, and of these 449 were in membership, giving a density of 85 per cent. The association was consulted about a recent voluntary and involuntary redundancy programme, which involved both Head Office and branch network staff.

Technological changes

Little change in the society's IT infrastructure took place between 1986 and 1991, but since then a number of important developments have unfolded. At Head Office new customer accounting systems have been introduced, based on a package enhanced with management reports developed in-house. The package is customer-oriented, reflecting the recognized need to enhance service provision through a customer-centred approach. Additional systems to improve administrative information in such areas as deed control and house repossession have been implemented. A key element of current IT strategy is to move towards an open systems environment in order to achieve enhanced user friendliness and functionality, as well as reducing costs. A new mortgage application system was the first critical system to run in this environment. There are over 200 PCs in use across the society, many of them connected to the computer network. A new branch cashiering system is being investigated, with the aim of using new technology to achieve better service for customers by providing a faster response. It also incorporates greater flexibility for the implementation of further marketing support systems.

Social and organizational issues

The two major types of new technology referred to above were adopted through a project group structure. The groups' brief was to work from the business objectives informing the adoption of the particular example of new technology. Steering groups were set up to oversee the work of the project teams, with their membership consisting of the relevant senior managers (i.e. those from the departments and functional areas affected). A full-time project manager was appointed to lead the teams, which consisted of IT specialists and users on a full-time basis and other staff on a part-time basis (for example, training specialists where training was seen as an important aspect). Four such project group structures have been in operation since 1991, covering the following areas: software upgrading, the new network system, the merger of databases, and marketing opportunities. There have also been other, rather more loosely structured, groups where one person (either on a full- or on a part-time basis) may, for example, lead a group whose composition changes from time to time, but whose members are always part-time at best.

Regarding staff attitudes towards the technological changes, the IT Development Manager believed that they had been favourable because the technology was easy to use, it helped to keep the organization up to date, and employees realized that costs had to be controlled. This manager emphasized that, as the technology changes, so skill requirements change. Increasingly, in the emerging open systems environment, there will be a greater need for functional labour flexibility, project management skills and effective management of IT. The Park Hill society, as he put it, 'doesn't need or wish to be at the "bleeding edge" – we don't need to be pioneers – but it must keep up with the competition'. IT costs in total came to around 25 per cent of management expenses – a considerable amount of money, yet IT was not run as a 'business', as in the view of this manager, at least, it should be. In other words, IT needs to become a service function, charged out to departments on the basis of use. If it is calculated that the work will be cost-effective then it will go ahead. If not, it is necessary to think again. These observations provide illuminating instances of moves towards creating 'businesses within businesses' and of an impetus to the measurement of organizational activities.

Chapter 7
Don Ltd

In this chapter and the next we examine the adoption of different varieties of new technology in two engineering companies. Following the same structure as with the building societies, we begin with the internal and external contexts of Don Ltd, the first of the companies to be considered.

THE ORGANIZATION AND ITS CONTEXT

Don Ltd is the South Midland plant of an American-owned manufacturer of capital equipment. The company has three manufacturing plants in the United Kingdom, located at some distance from each other and producing different versions of essentially the same product. Differentiation is based upon size, one plant producing a small version of the product, another a medium-sized one, and the third – the subject of this case study – a large version for incorporation in a variety of items of capital equipment. Don Ltd was set up to produce a new product for the company, one which it was known would be subject to regular alterations. The other two plants were manufacturing well established products, involving relatively few production changes. The plant producing the small version of the product is also the UK manufacturing head office. It is the UK location for Manufacturing Services and for the mainframe computer, which is linked to the other UK plants and to the company's corporate head office in the United States. Apart from Customer Services, the plants do not have a sales and marketing specialism. The UK Sales and Marketing head office is located in London.

The Don plant was built by another engineering company on a green-field site in the late 1960s, some distance from the main West Midland conurbation. At the time it was one of the most modern factories of its type in Western Europe.[1] It was bought by Don's parent company in late 1972. Production began in January 1973 with twenty people, most of whom had worked for the previous owners. The business objective was the manufacture, on a small-batch basis, of a new range of large items of capital equipment. Don Ltd inherited a functional plant layout of mills, lathes, etc., but in early 1975 it was changed to group technology, with all the machines needed to produce a defined product range located together in cells.

The company competes in a highly competitive global market against companies from Japan, North America and Western Europe. Periodic and fierce pricing wars occur on a regular basis, often instigated by heavy discounting on the part of the Japanese producers. This generates shock waves throughout the industry, resulting in drives to reduce costs and improve competitiveness through improved efficiency, productivity and quality. Given that Don Ltd has concentrated on producing an intermediate product, it has been very dependent on the success of the final producer. During 1986/7 it began to reduce this dependence through buying some of the companies concerned. Notwithstanding the competition, the company has been profitable during the 1980s and 1990s, often being the most successful of the UK plants.

Throughout the 1970s and early 1980s the trend of Don's output was upwards, but during the mid-1980s it plateaued at three or four items a day. A peak of eight per day had been achieved early in 1982, but a rapid fall-off occurred later that same year, continuing into 1983; an upturn to four or five items per day had been achieved by the time the original research took place between 1985 and 1987. Troughs and peaks in output levels were experienced on a recurrent basis. However, a significant difference between the troughs of the 1970s and those after 1982 is that the former were always relatively small, short-lived and upward from a basis of nil output in 1973, whereas during the latter period, when output had plateaued, troughs were sometimes much more significant in their impact. Increasingly the company responded to fluctuations in demand through alterations in the mode of labour utilization. For example, if demand increased, efficiency issues might be addressed, or an extra shift introduced; if demand declined, further moves in the direction of functional flexibility might be made (such as getting 'core' machine operators to perform 'non-core' tasks like cleaning the work area). The scope for adjustment in numerical flexibility was limited, for, by the mid-1980s, the company had few workers who fell into the flexible category – essentially canteen staff and two or three sandwich course students – but, in any event, management preferred not to draw a core-periphery distinction because of its divisive nature and possible negative connotations. (Factory and office cleaning and security were already out-sourced by this time.) The first priority for adjustment in response to market changes was in the subcontract machining work which the plant had begun taking on about 1985. One reason for this subcontracting had been to utilize spare capacity. In a situation of falling demand, attempts would be made to gain more of that type of work. The next line of defence was seen as the option of changing cleaning and then security to in-house sourcing. Notwithstanding the reluctance to make the core-periphery distinction explicit, by 1986 Don Ltd was using short-term contract labour. Sixty people were taken on on this basis, although the number subsequently fell to ten through the migration of some employees into the full-time work force. During negotiations with the unions over the introduction of short-term contracts, management agreed that the number of people on such contracts would not go above 20 per cent of the total manufacturing work force.

The main shop-floor job categories were operators, maintenance workers, and an assembly and test group. Functional flexibility for the operatives meant them being able to work with manual and NC or CNC machines, as well as being trained in at least three out of a total of seven possible skills (milling, drilling, boring, turning, etc.). The work is done in teams, each team having a balance of skills. Operators are trained in additional skills according to business requirements, moving along the job grade and gaining extra pay for each additional skill acquired, up to and including three skills.

An important element in the design of this grading structure was management's wish to accommodate semi-skilled and skilled jobs on the same scale, or rather to abolish the distinction altogether because of its potential to impede labour flexibility. Whilst there had always been a degree of functional flexibility in the plant, the new grading structure provided a further move in that direction. The old grading structures for staff and shop-floor workers are shown in Figures 8 and 9. They can be contrasted with the new common (staff and shop-floor) grading structure, shown in Figure 10.

As an illustration of the new structure, take the shop-floor operator grade. It was divided into Machine Operators X and Y. The latter undertook less skilled jobs such as materials handling, with three practical skills the maximum that could be acquired. The former

Don Ltd   175

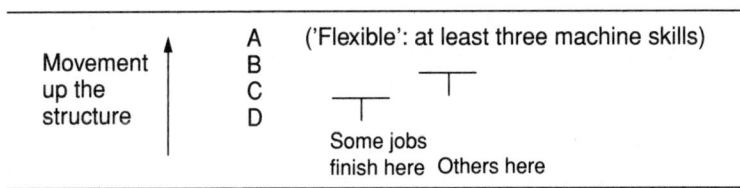

Figure 8 Don Ltd: old grading scheme for shop-floor workers
Note: Practical tests were involved throughout before any move from one grade to another. Each grade also entailed a 'theoretical' test

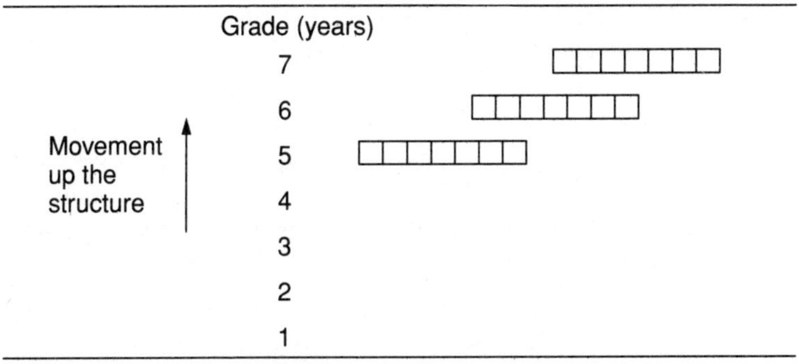

Figure 9 Don Ltd: old grading system for staff
Note: Purely service (time)-related, incremental, with grades overlapping

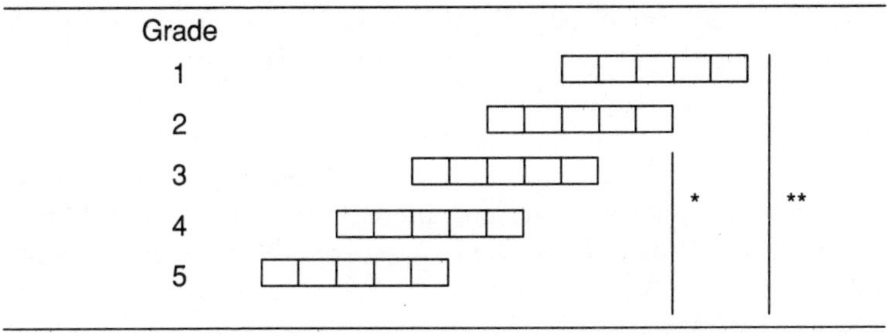

Figure 10 Don Ltd: new grading scheme for staff and workers
Note: * Old manual grades compressed into grades 1–3; ** old staff grades compressed into grades 1–5
Notes on the new grading structure: (a) 'Theoretical' as well as practical tests are distributed throughout the grading structure; (b) In principle the top of each grade can be reached within five years, i.e. movement is by one increment at a time; (c) There is the possibility of promotion across grades

category dealt with jobs for which three machine modules were available as well as two support or planning modules (one of which might involve training others in one of the machine modules acquired by the job holder).

A total of eleven grades were replaced by five new grades covering both staff and shop-floor jobs. These changes in the company's grading structure formed a part of management's strategy for harmonizing employment terms and conditions across the plant. By 1985 all the remaining differences between staff and shop-floor workers (in these terms), apart from appraisals, had been removed (appraisal at that time not being used for shop-floor workers). The Personnel Manager, reviewing the history of labour utilization at the company, commented that 'the enlargement of manual jobs had been taking place for some time, right back into the early 1970s. The greenfield site had very much facilitated this approach; that's to say, the plant had started afresh, without any encumbrances of custom and practice.' He cited examples of the early adoption of functional flexibility, such as mechanical engineers taking on electrical jobs (and vice versa), and continued:

> So they [the shop-floor workers] got used to this idea gradually. Eventually, however, they reached a 'plateau' where there was nowhere obvious for them to develop other than taking on some non-manual tasks, and this, in fact, is exactly what is happening now.

Instances were also to be found of the reverse happening – that is, staff taking on manual tasks. For example, materials requisition staff asked if they could spend some time helping shop-floor workers in the conduct of their jobs so that they would appreciate the problems better. A notable exception, however, to the take-over by shop-floor workers of non-manual tasks related to the production and editing of programs for CNC and NC machines. Programming and editing remained firmly with the process engineers. We shall return to this issue later in the chapter.

At the time of the original period of research at the plant (1985–7) there were around 520 employees, 300 of whom were shop-floor workers, 200 staff and twenty managers. Apart from managers, everyone's terms and conditions of employment were negotiated at plant level by one of the two recognized unions: the AEU, representing shop-floor workers (with 100 per cent of eligible membership), or TASS, representing staff (with 80 per cent). Managers' terms and conditions were determined centrally, at the UK manufacturing head office. Whilst there was a high level of union representation, then, it did not appear to have led to a major collective divide between workers and management. Contributory factors would seem to have been the relative newness of the plant (with its green-field origins), which meant there had been no build-up of 'custom and practice' over a lengthy period of time, and the 'low-key' managerial style, which was deliberately fostered and nurtured. On the other hand, it should not be assumed that management had everything its own way. Take the new grading and payment structure. According to the Employee Relations Manager it was essentially 'about buying employee commitment, and pushing decision-making down to the work groups themselves; it was also about making labour more flexible and productive.'[2] The unions' response was that any such changes must be linked with increased pay, otherwise they would not accept them. Senior management somewhat reluctantly accepted this.

Let us now turn to another aspect of the internal context of the organization, structure. A major restructuring had taken place in the early 1980s, when three separate manufacturing 'mini-businesses' were created, each under its own Business Manager. The organizing principle was group technology, with all the day-to-day staffing needed for each business being located within the unit itself. (There remained a small Factory Manufacturing Services function, with responsibility for cross-factory matters.) Figures 11 and 12 illustrate the organization structure before and after the changes. The rationale for the change was as follows:

1 A wish to minimize the drawbacks of a functional structure, in particular the danger of not treating issues or opportunities in a cross-functional, integrative way. A number of specialists (such as Finance and Training) moved from central staff departments to the businesses, often leaving only a few staff at the centre.
2 It was felt that manufacturing was becoming too big from an employee involvement and identification point of view. The business groups were an attempt to recreate a feeling of smallness. (There were approximately 100 in each business, as against 300 in manufacturing as a whole.)
3 To encourage people to take on more autonomy at lower levels of the organization. The businesses became separate cost and responsibility centres.

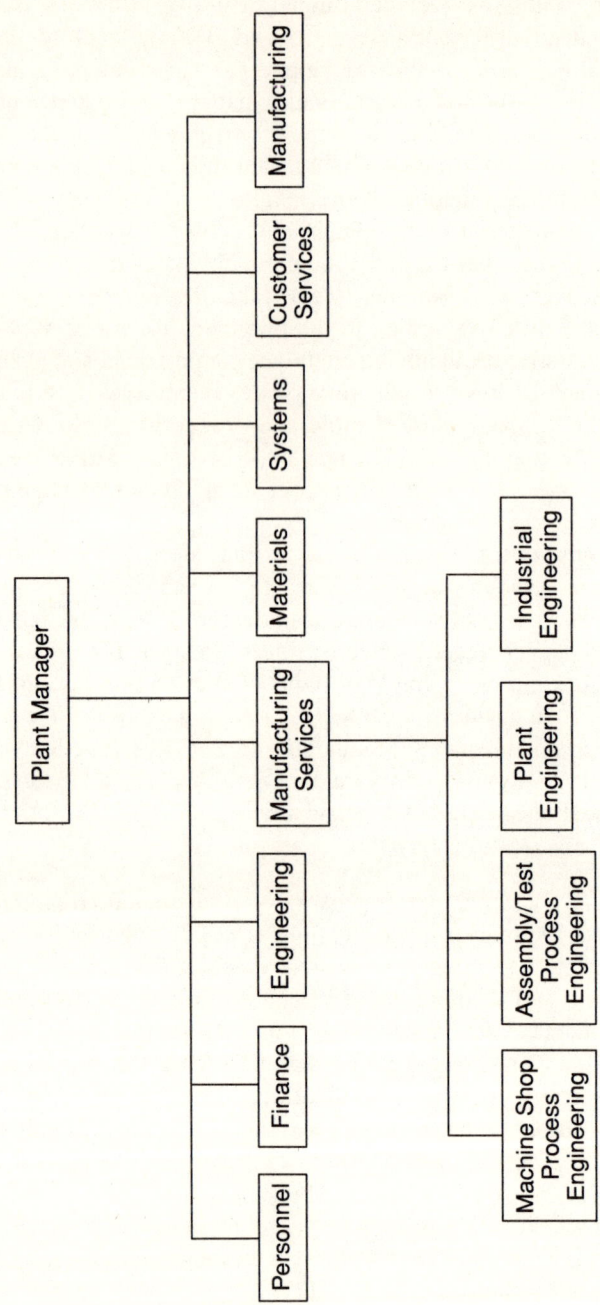

Figure 11 Don Ltd: part organization chart, 1973–81

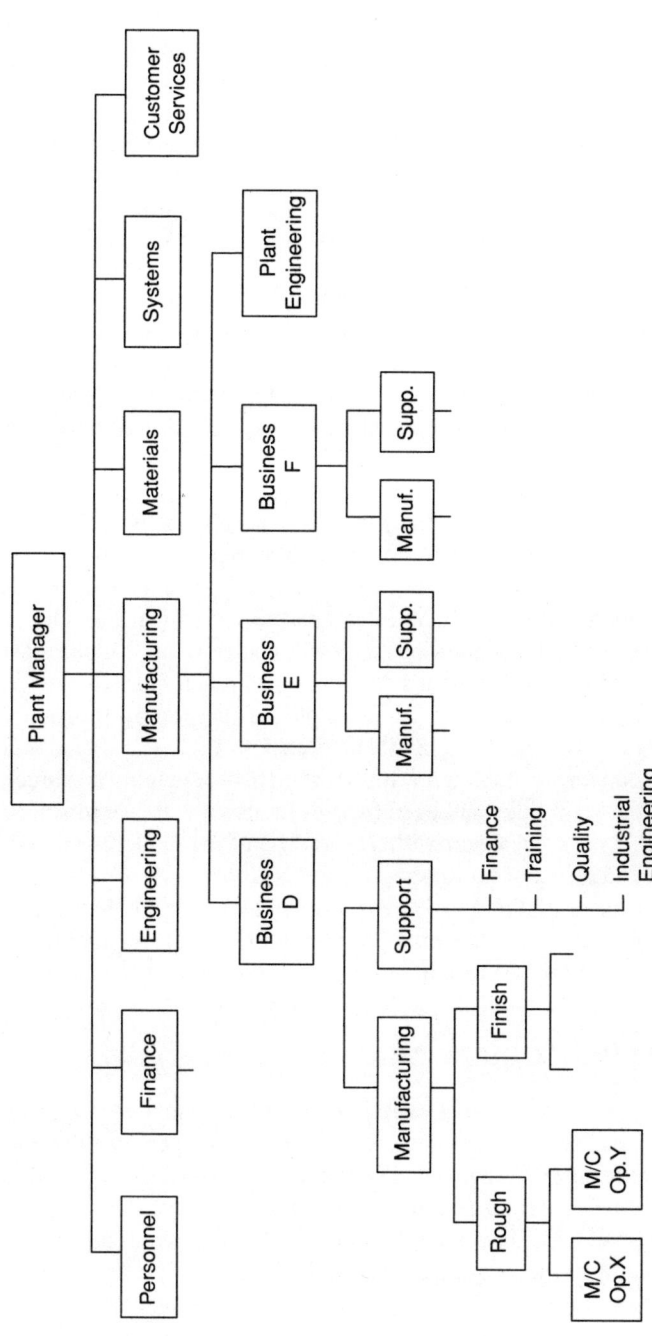

Figure 12 Don Ltd: part organization chart, January 1982 to date

4 To increase the emphasis on production quality.
5 A wish to overcome, or at least reduce, the conflict between Manufacturing and Manufacturing Support Services by attempting to weld them together in the businesses. The Personnel Manager commented that under the old structure the latter liaised informally with Manufacturing 'but had important longer-term interests – for example, machinery maintenance – these interests sometimes conflicted with Manufacturing's interest in getting production out'.

The reflections of the Employee Relations Manager on the organizational restructuring some five years after it had taken place offer food for thought. He argued that organizational changes are likely to have only marginal effect unless change takes place at the job level, otherwise it would mean 'just shuffling organizational structures around'. In his view, for example, the Manufacturing/Manufacturing Services change had made little difference; in practice it had not served to devolve responsibility to work groups. This reflected a 'partial failure to realize that there is a collective bargaining barrier to the creation of changes'. He went on to argue that 'The unions and workers will not be bothered if it's just an "organizational chart" change, but if it affects their jobs they will want paying.'[3] In his view the new grading and payment system had had much more impact on work and jobs (in the sense, for example, of facilitating functional flexibility) than the organizational restructuring. The Personnel Manager concurred, but felt it was important to bear in mind that much stronger business links had been forged. In his view the significance of achieving physical proximity should not be underestimated, especially in terms of facilitating integration.

On the basis of the above overview of Don Ltd's external and internal contexts we can now turn to look at the technological changes upon which we shall be focusing in the rest of the chapter.

THE TECHNOLOGICAL CHANGES

By 1987 the company had a variety of new office and manufacturing technologies. The former included a computerized personnel record system, teleconferencing, electronic mail (linking all the worldwide plants of Don's parent organization), and microcomputers for a range of applications. The new manufacturing technology consisted of NC and CNC machine tools, programmable logic controllers, semi-automatic storage facilities, computerized test equipment, robotics, computer-aided design/drafting (CAD) and a flexible manufacturing system (FMS) cell. Many of the NC machines had been bought from the previous owner of the plant. The FMS cell (installed during the summer of 1987) consisted of three machining centres linked via pallet loading, and incorporated automatic tool changing. From Don's take-over of the plant in 1973 up to 1978 a total of ten NC machining centres and CNC machine tools had been installed (some custom-built for the company), and in 1978 a decision was taken to purchase only CNC machines from that year onwards.

CAD was introduced in January 1984, following a similar installation at the parent company's North of England plant a few months earlier. Don's three CAD work stations were linked to the UK mainframe at the latter plant and, by the late 1980s, into the other UK plants, as well as the main US plant. The work stations were located in an open-plan office (where manual draughting continued to take place) and were used mainly for generating drawings from designs created in the United States, where some 90 per cent of design work was carried out for the company worldwide.

In the sections which follow we shall restrict the discussion to the adoption of CNC and CAD.

NEW TECHNOLOGY OBJECTIVES

These can be summarized as follows: to reduce costs, improve quality and increase flexibility. The 'spark', or initiative, which set the adoption process for the switch from NC to CNC in train was a question put (in 1978) by the Machine Process Engineering Manager to the Manufacturing Services Manager, 'Should we go over to CNC?' It was known that the company's US plants had already done so. The investigations which followed revealed that a CNC machine would cost around £24,000 more than an NC machine, and the project team found itself unable to justify such expenditure by the company's usual financial and economic criteria. However, they took the view that CNC was the right technology from a strategic point of view, and recommended adoption. With regard to CAD, the Manufacturing Services Manager saw the essence of the objectives as residing in 'the logic of having more highly skilled people producing higher-quality work at a higher output level'. More detail on the decision-making processes for CNC and CAD are provided below, but it is worth noting here that the company is by no means alone in finding it difficult to justify new technology in financial terms. As I have observed elsewhere when reporting findings on new technology objectives from a number of companies (including Don Ltd):

> A number of managers were of the opinion that the investment in the new technology could not be justified in the short term in financial terms; they believe that it would be so justified in the longer term but, in the meantime, they believed that strictly financial criteria should not be allowed 'to rule the day', and that other benefits more than compensated for the lack of a short-term financial justification, such as the expected compatibility of the new technology with other new technologies expected to be adopted in the future.[4]

It is important to locate Don's new technology adoption process, particularly the (stage 3) investment decision, in the wider context of the company's UK manufacturing policies and strategies. Approval of the expenditure from the UK manufacturing head office could not be taken for granted. For example, when Don Ltd sought approval to purchase a CNC machining centre the response was 'No, get an FMS,' but the FMS still had to be justified financially. According to the Manufacturing Services Manager, this proved no easy task, especially as Don had a history of introducing new technology incrementally, and had thus accumulated a good deal of up-to-date technology. In the event, as this manager put it 'We just managed to get the figures "right" to be able to buy.' He observed that it was easier to get permission for the purchase of new machinery to replace worn-out technology, even if it meant doing so as an 'overnight, *en bloc*' leap (i.e. radical innovation), involving significant expenditure, than if a plant had a history of incremental innovation in technology (and hence was more up to date) but wanted to purchase just one additional new machine.

THE PROCESS OF ADOPTION OF NEW TECHNOLOGY

Let us first turn to the adoption of CNC machine tools. As we have seen, the company already had a number of years' experience with NC machine tools, from which CNC had derived, so the switch to CNC did not involve an 'overnight' change to a technology with which the company was completely unfamiliar. What occurred was a process of incremental change, that is, the piecemeal adoption of one or two CNC machines, perhaps to replace some manual lathes and/or NC machines. A particular advantage of this approach is that it facilitates organizational learning, that is, gradually becoming accustomed to the new technology whilst the proven technology is still in use. It also helps to forestall reluctance on the part of managers to invest in new technology because, for example, they believe the financial figures won't justify it, or because they think it safer to wait and see what competitors do. There may, indeed, be something to be said for learning from the mistakes of competitors; on the other hand, competitors may be planning their next move in the meantime, and may get so far ahead that the chances of catching up constantly recede.

Let us now look at the CNC adoption process in detail. As noted earlier, it effectively began in 1978, on the initiative of the Machine Process Engineering Manager. A project group was established, consisting of plant and process engineering specialists. After looking at eight different CNC systems they narrowed the choice down to two for more detailed investigation. A report was produced which outlined the capabilities of the various makes and models of machine. Two generic facilities of CNC machine tools appear to have made a particular impression: the ability to edit on the machine, and the relative ease with which maintenance staff would be able to carry out diagnostic work. The process engineers were in favour of CNC adoption throughout the plant. Compared with NC, CNC made their job easier, for it meant less 'to-ing and fro-ing' between their office and the machines, and fewer occasions when they would have to mend or replace spoiled tapes. The only disagreements within the group were over which make and model should be purchased.

There were problems in recruiting maintenance staff with the requisite electrical and electronic skills. (The company already had a number of staff with the former but not enough with the latter for the incoming CNC machines.) Management took existing staff, or recruited new staff, with electrical skills and then gave them electronics training. They wanted to place such staff on the existing maintenance grade, with no additional pay for the extra skill. The maintenance workers argued that a higher grade was warranted, and that it should be created by adding a new grade on to the existing structure. According to the Personnel Manager, they were using the bargaining opportunity provided by the creation of the new electrical/electronic maintenance engineer job category to extend the grading structure so that most, if not all, of them would get on to this grade in time. Apparently, they had for some time resented not having more opportunities to earn higher pay for increased flexibility. Negotiations took place between management and the AEU. Management proposed the creation of a new post, Control Systems Engineer (CSE), on a staff grade. The expectation was that the other maintenance workers would do the bulk of the work, only calling on the CSEs when they could not solve the problem themselves. (As the Personnel Manager put it, 'The CSE was seen as a sort of super troubleshooter.') The AEU accepted the proposal.

Apart from the occasional 'local difficulty' such as this, CNC had a trouble-free adoption. The incremental nature of the process clearly contributed, but there were a number of other factors:

1 The green-field origins of the site. As we saw earlier, management put the emphasis from the beginning upon flexible job designs; this was facilitated (or, perhaps, necessitated) by the company's gradual increase in size from a handful of staff. Indeed, at a later stage, when the organization had grown in size to such an extent that it had to be restructured, task flexibility was motivated partly by the wish to maintain a feeling of 'smallness'.
2 Because it was based upon skill acquisition and flexibility, Don's pay and grading system could accommodate new technology. Lack of flexibility in the grading structure could, of course, have inhibited the process, for example where the new skills were not included in the job evaluation scheme, or where they had only a small weighting. Thus, if there was a need to pay employees more for using the new technology, it might have necessitated an *ex gratia* payment (with the danger of knock-on effects) or reconfiguration of the payment and grading system. That could have been expensive in time and effort; on the other hand, not taking action could have led to festering industrial relations problems.
3 When the change-over to CNC was made the plant was experiencing a period of growth. Although there were output fluctuations, the trend was upward; it did not peak until 1982. Thus there was no need for a reduction in labour supply – indeed, staff were still being recruited. As the Employee Relations Manager put it, 'It was a successful introduction – there were no "collective" problems. The 1970s was a period of expansion, so there was no link between new technology and higher productivity/redundancy. CNC was introduced on a piecemeal basis, hence there were no overall effects.' He also observed that the payment system had helped 'because the company was paying for skills possessed,

rather than adopting a "job description" type of approach. This culture was developed in the 1970s, when output was expanding.'
4 The process engineers were closely involved in the adoption process. This encouraged acceptance. They also stood to benefit in time through the insertion of the additional grade.
5 As the Manufacturing Services Manager put it, 'We didn't get hung up on the skill question.' He was referring to the problems which can occur when new technology is introduced to an organization which does explicitly distinguish between jobs in terms of skill, such as as between skilled, semi-skilled and unskilled jobs. Multifarious demarcation, payment, control, equity and other issues are often closely interwoven with these distinctions, and new technology can upset them. (There are also obvious implications for the potential for labour flexibility.) Apparently one of the company's other, much longer established, plants in the United Kingdom did get into difficulties in this respect when new technology was introduced, not least because it *did* make the distinction.
6 'Management had a clear strategy of a low-key approach to the introduction of new technology, which placed the emphasis on it being "nothing really different"' (Personnel Manager). The observation needs no further comment, as managerial strategies for new technology, including this 'softly, softly' variety, were discussed in Chapter 2.

Let us conclude this section by contrasting the processes through which CNC was adopted with those associated with CAD. We noted in the case of the Bramley Building Society how organizational learning can occur with second and successive waves of new technology adoption in a given organization. The CAD adoption process at Don Ltd shows that such learning cannot be taken for granted – indeed, that (in a reverse of the foregoing) a relatively unproblematic first adoption can be followed by a troublesome later adoption.

The initiation of the CAD adoption process can be traced to October 1983, when the Manufacturing Services Manager at the North of England plant of the company (which, it will be recalled, is also the location of the head office of UK manufacturing) proposed to US corporate headquarters the purchase of one CAD installation for that plant, to enable its potential to be evaluated over a one-year period. The response from the United States was to the effect that three CAD installations should be bought, one for each of the UK plants. Don's

CAD unit was introduced into the plant in January 1984, three months after the request. The union representing the staff affected (TASS) had not been involved at all, nor had the relevant middle managers. This despite the fact that the same managers, in the CNC adoption, had been encouraged by higher management to involve the workers affected – now they were not being involved by that same higher management. Many of the technical staff were asking questions such as 'Why here?' 'Why no training?' 'What's in it for me?' and, not surprisingly, their managers were finding it difficult to give immediate and satisfactory response. Despite the criticisms levelled at Don management by staff with regard to the approach to CAD adoption, it was strongly suspected by the Personnel Manager that the employees 'were basically in favour of the adoption of this new technology for, amongst other things, it provided them with the opportunity to gain experience on the new equipment, and thereby to make themselves more marketable'. (There are echoes here of the findings reported in the WIRS surveys – see Chapter 4). What is more, fortuitously as it happens, management were able to build CAD operation into the new pay and grading system (about to be introduced, in April 1984) by moving designers into a tagged-on skill band. Management assured employees that no jobs were at risk as a result of CAD installation and, by April 1984, arrangements were in hand for CAD operators to have externally provided specialist training.

MANAGING THE SOCIAL AND ORGANIZATIONAL ASPECTS OF ADOPTION

The focus here will be upon the social, organizational and industrial relations implications of the production and use of CNC tapes. We will draw upon a number of the issues discussed in Part I, such as skill and de-skilling, managerial strategies and trade union and employee responses. Researchers have recognized for some time the significance of the social and organizational contexts of tape production as a touchstone for a range of outcomes from the machining process, not least those to do with questions of management–worker power and control.[5]

The early NC machine tools were of two main types: one that could be programmed at the machine and one that could not. Only the latter machines found widespread adoption. This could have been because some managers believed that NC necessitated the separation of programming from operating. Thus they acted accordingly in respect of the staffing of the programming function and the operation of the machine tool. 'Accordingly' here implying, of course, a Taylorist form of work organization, where planning and conception go to technical staff (typically process engineers or, even more specifically, 'NC programmers'), and operating (a new, de-skilled *job*) to a different group of workers – machinists, or operators. Hence it could be said that a redistribution of conceptual skills had taken place, from the job of operating the old manual lathes to the new job of programming computer tapes by process engineers. Note that, if the same workers were now operating the NC machines, they could also be said to have been de-skilled in a personal sense by comparison with the work they used to do. If semi- or unskilled workers, however, had been taken on as operators, they could not be said to have been de-skilled in the same personal sense, although clearly they would have been performing de-skilled work. Numerical control, then (especially after the early years of its introduction, when the non-machine programmable model had achieved supremacy), left (or, to be more specific, appeared to leave) most managers with little choice in respect of the organization of work. With CNC, however, because a microcomputer and control panel are attached to the machine tool (rather than, with NC, the machine simply having the ability to read information on a disc or tape – the tape having been produced separately from the machine tool), managers were much more clearly faced with a choice: whether the machinists should do the programming as well as the operating, or whether programming should stay with the process engineers. (It should be borne in mind that most companies introducing CNC already had NC machines, and hence a separate programming section). The latter option was far and away the more popular in practice.[6] Suffice it to say that there was often a wish not to upset the *status quo*, and to retain if not increase control over the machinists.[7]

What happened at Don Ltd? With NC, planning, programming and editing had indeed been separated out from machining, and given to the process engineers, whilst the machinists had received training in NC machining skills. The machinists had lost some elements of their job (in particular, conceptual skills and knowledge) to the process engineers but had gained new skills connected with operating NC machine tools. (This should not be taken to imply that they were no longer required to use their knowledge, experience and tacit skills in their work, for it was as necessary as ever that they should do so in order that production might proceed effectively.)

When CNC machines were adopted by Don Ltd, then, it was in a context where a separate machine tool programming department already existed, with established agreements and working practices affecting planning, programming, editing and operating. As might have been predicted, programming work went to the process engineers. The reasons managers gave for this decision were:

1 If programming and/or editing had been given to the operators, the process engineers would have objected strongly, given that they regarded it as their work.
2 Tape production takes some time, If it is done away from the machine, the machine can be kept running on another program in the meantime.
3 The machinists would have wanted more money for the extra work. On the other hand, it was already part of the process engineers' job, and, given that they were on a service-related payment system, they would be paid nothing extra.

Management's view was that there was little change in the nature of machining work on CNC as compared with NC. There were some more marked differences for process engineering, however. With CNC the program could be retained in the machine tool's memory and the process engineers did not need to load a tape every time a job was to be run. Tape prove-out was more straightforward, as it could be done entirely at the machine itself, whereas with NC the process engineer had to keep moving between the machine and the office, in order to punch out a new tape. CNC allowed editing of the program at the machine, although, again, it by no means self-evident who should perform this operation, as will be seen below.

At Don Ltd the formal position was that tape editing was done by process engineers (on both NC and CNC). When CNC was introduced, therefore, only they were given the keys allowing access to the control panel attached to the machine. However, it was not long before, as the Manufacturing Services Manager put it, 'one of the keys went missing', and it came to management's attention that machinists were editing CNC tapes.[8] This was a much more common occurrence on the night shift, when an 'illicit' key was used to gain access to the panel. The formal position on night shifts was that if there was a need to use the control panel the process engineer on standby would be called out; in the meantime, production on that machine would have stopped.

It follows that the 'illicit' editing could be said to have suited management, as it kept production going and avoided the need to pay call-out fees. It should be emphasized that it was not the case that the machinists were doing the editing for financial gain (they were not on a bonus system or piece rates), or in order to take a break by short-circuiting the program (they would be transferred to another machine if theirs broke down). The managerial problem, however, was that they were not using the edited tape to obtain a new master tape when the job had been completed, so updating the tape files (as the process engineers would have done). It meant that the next time the tape was used the same problem would recur. It also raised the question of who would be held responsible if damage occurred (for instance to the tools or the workpiece) as a result of a tape being edited illicitly. Management had connived at what was happening, and it might be difficult anyway to determine who had caused the damage. There could even have been an informal arrangement between the process engineers and the machinists on night shift not to call anyone out unless it was absolutely necessary.

Given problems like these, it is not perhaps surprising that some managers should have expressed a wish for the company to move to the formal position that operators performed editing work. As one of them put it, he 'wished the keys had been given to the operators in the first place'. Management, however, was captive of its previous decisions. One option considered was to accommodate routine operator CNC tape editing in the new payment and grading structure as an extra skill. The operators and their union, the AEU, expressed interest in this. Management's approach, according to the Personnel Manager, was to argue for having a 'balance of skills' within a given work group, where part of the training, and a potential subsequent responsibility, of the job holder would be file updating. The process engineers' response to this 'kite-flying' was that the operators would simply not be able to do the work (in contradiction to what was already happening informally). On balance the Personnel Manager was in favour of the work being given to the machinists, but observed that 'management would need to prepare for this by showing the process engineers how their jobs could take up the slack', i.e. that they would be able to do other things they were unable to do now for lack of time, these tasks being at the same level of responsibility as tape editing, or higher.

In essence, then, Don Ltd's strategy for the adoption and introduction of new technology was to create a climate where new technology would be accepted by all employees, if not, indeed, welcomed. It was a deliberately 'low-key' approach, with management working with the trade unions where necessary, and taking the line that the new technology was not very different from what had gone before. The Personnel Manager commented, 'If Personnel was to go in in a high-profile way, it would immediately be assumed that something drastic was about to happen – for instance, job shedding.' The emphasis was on trying to ensure that the managers involved were sensitive to what was happening; that the people affected were involved in helping to resolve any problems; that the payment and grading systems were appropriate, and that, if job loss was to be involved, ways of dealing with it had been formulated beforehand.[9] In other words, 'production and technology changes on the one hand, and people and labour requirements, aspects and implications on the other, had always been planned for and implemented together, rather than sequentially, as often appears to be the case'.[10] The company's personnel specialists do not appear to have seen themselves and their work as somehow distinctly separate from what happened on the shop floor; indeed, it was often quite difficult to distinguish between 'staff' and 'line' in the company. What is more, it appears that, as the Employee Relations Manager observed, 'this sort of distinction would not be particularly meaningful to employees'. Personnel specialists did on occasion take a rather higher profile – interestingly, often as a result of wider organizational changes, such as the introduction of the new pay and grading scheme, harmonization, or during the annual wage negotiations.

The overall impression is that the adoption and introduction of new technology were not seen as a major issue by managers or employees. Of course, things might have turned out differently had management not taken its strategic, low-key approach. At the same time, it should be remembered that it was not dealing with a quiescent work force: the great majority of employees were represented by a trade union, and a number brought with them experience of working in other factories, under different control regimes.

KEY DEVELOPMENTS SINCE 1986/7

External context

Two developments in particular have had a notable effect upon the context of Don's operations since the time of the initial research:

European and US emission standards, which have provided an impetus to R&D spending in the sector, and the demand from customers for an ever more fuel-efficient product. Don has introduced electronic fuel monitoring and fault-finding systems and, like its competitors, is constantly looking for ways of achieving greater power output from a given unit. New types of materials are being examined with a view to lowering weight and reducing corrosion.

As Don's product reaches the final customer through distributors, the company has also been looking closely at these organizations, assessing the quality of the service they are providing, helping them to improve it and to provide it in a more cost-effective way. Distributors are being monitored for quality and can now sell Don's product only if they have the necessary certification from the company, indicating, *inter alia*, that they have the requisite expertise in Don's products and servicing requirements.

With regard to market share on a global basis, Don Ltd is the leading supplier of its main product line (which accounts for 75–80 per cent of its business), followed by other US and some UK companies. A number of take-overs, management buy-outs and amalgamations have taken place in the sector in recent years. The tendency has been to preserve both the identity and the manufacturing plants of what were separate companies, however, and, as a result, it is not always clear to the end-customer whether it is comparing the products of distinct and unrelated organizations or those of companies which are ultimately all part of the same group. Don's parent company in the United States recently purchased one of Don's main customers, and as a result has come under pressure to supply its product at a cheaper price. At the same time, other customers have been expressing concern that they will be undercut on price – a difficult 'balancing act' for Don management! There is increasing evidence of manufacturers worldwide purchasing end users in order to guarantee a market for their product. This can also occur in the reverse direction, guaranteeing supply: for example, a customer of Don's parent company bought an interest in the company, part of the agreement being that it would take certain product ranges only from there. Other companies have come to similar arrangements through part ownership, whilst still producing and marketing their own products in different ranges. Manufacturers are finding it more and more expensive to pursue R&D, design, engineering and production across all the product ranges. The main market opportunity now is seen to be in Russia, where the comparable locally produced product is inferior owing to lack of investment over a long period of time.

Internal context

Little change had taken place in the intervening period in management style, employee relations strategy and representation, or organization structuring. When asked why he thought this was the case, especially given that, according to the research record, a good deal of change has taken place in other companies, the Personnel Manager replied:

> Because it works. The company is doing well, making a lot of money, and is working flat out – seven days a week, including a temporary weekend shift, to meet demand. This also means that there's lots of overtime. There has been a big increase in efficiency over the last three to four years, and it has resulted in the plant being given the promise of being allocated production of the new product. This has provided a sense of security for employees.

The plant is running at full capacity, with virtually continuous working in some areas, partly so that other areas (bottlenecks) can be in production six days a week. Output is running at an average of fifteen units a day with around 580 staff, compared with the four or five of the 1985–7 period with around 520 staff. In the late 1980s, however, the plant was under a lot of pressure, as it made a loss for four or five years. A key factor in explaining the upturn since then, besides the achievement of internal efficiencies, was the change in strategy by certain end customers, from using one particular source of power to using a different one (i.e. Don's main product), which is much cheaper, more cost-effective for its purpose and cheaper to install, as well as far more flexible. This reorientation reflects certain social and political changes which have taken place in society at large. (Unfortunately I cannot outline them here, for to do so might be to reveal the identity of the company.)

Technological changes

Overall, there has not been much change in the technology employed by the company since 1986/7. However, in terms of new technology in the product, the view is that the present basic model has reached the end of its development and a new model is at the design stage.

With respect to AMT, a number of the CNC machines have been upgraded or renewed. The majority of CNC stock is still used in a stand-alone mode, and the FMS, which was on the point of introduction during the earlier study, is running twenty-four hours a day, six or seven days a week. A high priority is attached to ensuring that it is fully employed, in order to maximize its utilization, given its high cost. Of course, the level of orders and hence of activity makes this relatively easy to achieve. CAD, which is being used exclusively for design and draughting work (there being no electronic link into CAM), has become so central to Don's operations that, as the Personnel Manager puts it, 'We couldn't do the business without it.' With regard to IT, as well as being linked electronically to Head Office in the United States and every other company in the group, Don has links into some key customers for invoicing and other administrative purposes. Tele-conferencing has been replaced by video-conferencing.

The company is in the process of moving out of light machining for anything other than key components, by sub-contracting such work. As the above manager put it, 'There are other companies which can do this work much more efficiently. What we are good at is development, assembly, testing and supplying the customer, and that's what we are going to concentrate on.' Standard ratios are used to measure performance, one of the key ones being people per product per day. It has gone down from ninety-plus in 1992 to fifty-plus in late 1993. This has been achieved through small but continual incremental improvements (to use the Japanese term, *kaizen*); the suggestions for improvement have come from individuals and cross-functional teams. The objectives for new technology adoption were expressed in summary terms by the Marketing Support Manager as to 'Make money, survive and grow the business profitably.'

Social and organizational issues

It appears that employees and the unions have generally welcomed any technological changes. (As before, two unions are recognized: the AEEU, which has a density of 98 per cent, and MSF, with a density of 90 per cent – up 10 per cent from the former TASS level of 1986.) This was put down to the following by the Personnel Manager: 'People are quite keen that we have the best tools to do the job with. If the company is pumping capital in here, there's a certain guarantee of some future and security.' There is a major thrust at

Don Ltd and throughout the group on training and quality. Audited quality standards and awards are in place; the impetus to quality has, in the main, come from within the company, and the cross-functional teams referred to above function partly as quality improvement teams. The Personnel Manager again:

> We've always trained, but never to the level that we do now. We're seeking quality like there's no tomorrow, and the company is committed to having the Baldrige award in the States like pronto – they'll have it, it doesn't matter what it costs or what it needs, they're going to have it.

Interestingly, there is no talk of human resource management in the company and little talk of multi-skilling. On the former, the view of the Personnel Manager was that even if his title was changed to 'Human Resource Manager' it would make little difference, for 'Whatever we call it, we're going to do similar things. Our role is to manage the people, in conjunction with the business managers, as a resource.' On the latter, this is simply not an issue, for:

> We have good flexibility now. We have as much flexibility as you'd ever want. If we flexed them any further they'd begin not to be experts in the base skills. We don't want to make a storekeeper into an electrician – but the mechanic, there's nothing to stop him doing electrical work, or the electrician doing mechanical work.

A nice illustration of what are perceived by a key actor to be the limits to multi-skilling and flexibility. This completes our examination of new technology adoption at Don Ltd. Let us move on to consider the management of new technology adoption in another engineering company, Meadows & Butler.

Chapter 8
Meadows & Butler

THE ORGANIZATION AND ITS CONTEXT

At the time of the original research Meadows & Butler was an operating company within the engineering division of a diversified UK holding company. (There were three other divisions.) The engineering division included four other companies, dispersed across England. Meadows & Butler had two plants, the main one (the focus of the case study in this chapter) located in the Midlands, the other, much smaller, in the North East. The company dates back to the early years of the twentieth century, and was bought by the holding company in 1972. (Unless otherwise indicated, reference hereafter to 'the company' or 'the organization' means the Midland plant of Meadows & Butler.)

In 1986 Meadows & Butler employed approximately 400 people, and had a turnover of £25 million. It supplies a specialist product to both public and private organizations, and was the UK market leader, with 40–50 per cent of the market, during the 1980s. The UK sector consisted of ten firms, two of them foreign-owned. The intensity of competition increased during the 1980s, especially from one of the foreign-owned companies, which had a factory in the UK. Volume levels stayed relatively static throughout the period, but began to increase somewhat from around 1986.

In 1978 the company made a loss of £500,000 on a market share of 5 per cent, but by 1986 this had been turned into a profit of over £2 million on a share of 50 per cent. The dramatic improvement was attributed to an improved product, an overall increase in selling prices, marginal only rises (sometimes a fall) in raw material costs, and wage increases only slightly above the rate of inflation (which in any event were more than offset by productivity gains). The turn-around was achieved with an old-established factory which had been experiencing a number of problems (e.g. in terms of layout and logistics – see later). Indeed, these became so inhibiting that in summer 1985 the company transferred to a purpose-built green-field site, on the outskirts of the town.

The move appeared to have been sparked off by a chance opportunity early in 1985. Meadows & Butler had been told by the holding company that they could not further develop the existing site. Around that time the company occupying the site next door went out of business, and the factory became available for purchase. A local developer was keen to make a quick profit by knocking both factories down and converting the sites to retail use. He approached Meadows & Butler and agreement was reached on a package which included the developer building them a new factory at a discount. The old sites became a supermarket.

There were two main reasons why management was keen to transfer to a new site: problems at the old one and a rationalization programme in the Engineering Division. Let us look at them in turn. Problems at the previous site centred on the fact that the factory was hemmed in on all sides by offices, shops and a main road. It was where the company had started up. As output expanded over the years, all available space had been taken up in a haphazard way, leaving no room for expansion. The result was that a good deal of time was spent moving materials backwards and forwards around the factory, with a consequent loss of efficiency and effectiveness.

With regard to rationalization, there are two main senses in which the word is used here. First, a new site provided an opportunity for the production layout to be planned and organized systematically, so that a more efficient flow of materials and parts could be achieved, with machinery located in logical sequence (likewise for the stores and offices). Secondly, the relocation would accommodate a rationalization of the work of the Engineering Division companies, through a transfer of work from another group company located in the south of England. For the latter company this meant selling off a large piece of land (and thus the contraction of the site) and refocusing upon a reduced product range. Employee numbers were reduced from 1,000 to 300, with some being offered the opportunity to move to the Midland site.

The upshot of the changes was that Meadows & Butler increased the number of its employees from 225 at the old site to 400 at the new one and doubled its production capacity. The reorganization resulted in a short-lived drop in profits, but the company now had one of the largest and most modern factories in the sector in Western Europe. Certain key changes in staffing and managerial posts took place immediately following the relocation. These included the creation of a chairman role (roughly equivalent to the Managing Director role at the old site), the appointment of a new Managing Director (the person appointed had previously been managing director at another Engineering group company), and the creation of two new board posts in the form of an Engineering Director and a Parts and Service Director (both post-holders having held similar jobs at the southern plant). Figure 13 presents the new senior management organization chart. The majority of the changes were in production and engineering. This was because, as the Finance Director put it, 'these are the areas where we have been experiencing the greatest problems, because there have been so many changes in the product, and, at the same time, a substantial increase in output, from eight and a half units a week to twelve and a half, due to an increased market share of an expanding market'.

There is no personnel specialist on the board; the Personnel Manager reports to the Finance Director. The former acts in a 'clerk of works' mode, in the sense that:

> All authority for action is vested in line managers. Personnel policies are formed or created after the actions which demonstrate the need. The policies are not pre-set, nor are they seen as an

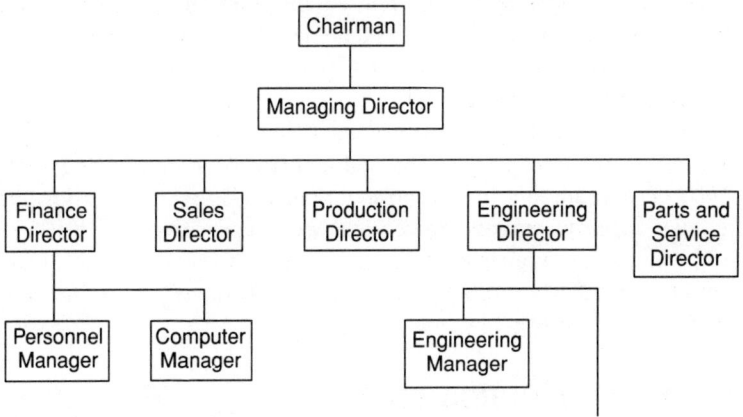

Figure 13 Meadows & Butler: part organization chart

integral part of business policy. . . . Personnel systems are created in an *ad hoc* way. The main systems require the recording of information after the decision is taken, collecting information together and providing whatever standard letters or statements are thought necessary, and will essentially be generated for financial information.[1]

As in Tyson and Fell's model, we find that 'The Personnel Department will administer basic routines, undertaking record keeping, first-interviewing some applicants for employment, preparing letters and documents on instructions.'[2] The welfare role is also well developed, and the Personnel Manager had no specialist qualifications. However, *contra* the model, he had previously been the Works Manager, taking up the personnel post in 1979 following over forty years' experience with the company.

Industrial relations were split off from the personnel specialism, and were the responsibility of the Works Manager. This person, along with the Managing Director and Finance Director, formed the management team for purposes of negotiation with the unions. The AEU had far and away the highest level of representation of the six unions representing manual workers, with around 55 per cent of shop-floor employees out of a total union density of 60 per cent. A Works Committee met management once a month for discussion and consultation purposes, with staff as well as the shop floor represented. Staff had no union representation, but their pay award tended to be close to the settlement with the manual unions. They had a merit payment system, based upon the distribution of a global sum, the amount of individual awards being decided by line managers. An output bonus, based upon factory performance, was paid to all employees at the same rate.

The growth of the company created tensions in the company's centralized mode of control, and led to attempts at more delegation, and a certain amount of decentralization. It also resulted in greater reliance upon systems and procedures, with implications for information technology requirements. It is of interest, however, that (apart from the new Parts and Service Director post) there was no increase in the number of organizational tiers.

THE TECHNOLOGICAL CHANGES

During the period of the initial research, four main types of new technology were introduced into the company:

1 Word processors.
2 NC and CNC machine tools.
3 A minicomputer-based accounting, inventory and production control system (henceforth referred to as IPCS).
4 CAD.

In what follows we shall consider only the latter two forms of new technology. (I have discussed NC and CNC adoption in this company elsewhere.)[3]

Prior to December 1980 the only new technology used by the company took the indirect form of using the services of a bureau in order to support the financial system. Earlier that year work began on identifying a computer system with the ability to incorporate materials requirements planning, accounts, payroll and production control requirements. When a minicomputer-based IPCS was introduced in December it was the first introduction of new technology into the company, and it resulted in the termination of the bureau contract. The adoption and introduction of the technology were handled entirely by Meadows & Butler staff, and represented the beginnings of the development of in-house competence in new technology.

By the time the company came to introduce CAD, in July 1987, the effects of the changes and restructuring within the Engineering Division were such that much of the adoption and introduction process was organized on a divisional basis, resulting in the simultaneous introduction of CAD installations into a number of the plants. Let us look at the organizational details of these developments.

NEW TECHNOLOGY OBJECTIVES

The objectives which influenced the company's adoption of the two new technologies to be discussed here will be considered in turn, taking the IPCS first.

IPCS

In order to understand the objectives set for the new IPCS computer system, it is necessary to set them in the wider context of problems facing the company in the months preceding the beginning of the adoption process. In essence these were production inefficiencies, changes in the nature of the business, and poor or non-existent management information. Let us illustrate each in turn.

On production inefficiencies, stock and work in progress records were inaccurate, with the result that parts were not ordered sufficiently in advance and were not there when needed. Parts were being manufactured that were not required, whilst those that were required were produced too late; as a consequence, workers and machines were sometimes idle, waiting for materials. According to the Finance Director, the main objectives in adopting the IPCS were 'to reduce stock levels, as well as to tell the company what to buy, and when, and what to make, and when'. The company was undergoing a strategic refocusing, from producing one-off 'specials' to order, and lowish quantities of a standard product, to higher volumes of a standard product incorporating options based upon common parts.

With regard to information problems, management did not know whether a given unit could be produced by a certain date, or what the result of producing that particular part would be in terms of the impact upon production elsewhere in the plant. Given that senior management was planning to operate on smaller profit margins per item, but with a greater turnover of items, this was seen as a problem which was only going to get worse. In addition, because it was not known whether there were sufficient quantities of the right stocks, salesmen were committing the company to orders when no one knew whether or not they could be met by the due date. (To move ahead a little, even with IPCS the salesmen were still not sure about this at the time of taking an order, but it became much easier to check the situation with production staff, and to reschedule and reorder if necessary.)

As a result of all these problems the key issue for management had become 'How can computerization help to resolve them?'. The view emerged that what was needed was a computer system which, *inter alia*, had a Materials Requirements Planning (MRP) facility in order that there would be the capability, as the Computer Manager put it, 'to define what we are going to build, and to break it down into a set of requirements, on the basis of which to be able to place orders for components far enough ahead to be able to get the best price or to properly schedule our own production'. The Computer Manager, along with the Technical Director, specified the requirements for the new system as follows.

1 Software
   (a) *Operating system.* Must be easily understood by non-computer specialists, so that the organization did not become over-dependent on the Computer Manager (in case he was absent or left the company).

(b) *Production software*. A 'tried and tested' system was preferred, but one which was not too old, and therefore 'still had some life left in it'. The system should be relatively easy to program and reprogram.

(c) *Accounts software*. Because accounting systems have externally set standards, the view was that the new system would be acceptable so long as it was at least as good as the old one.

(d) *Payroll*. The transfer of the payroll to the new computer was expected to lead to a reduction in costs as compared to the old manual system. This would help to pay for the computer itself.

2 Hardware

(a) *Size/expandability*. It was seen as important for the computer to have spare capacity in order to avoid the need to reinvest after a short period of time as demands upon the system increased. At the same time it had to be possible to add to the hardware as required for a 'reasonable' length of time.

(b) *Reliability*. The computer system must be reliable in operation for a number of years.

(c) *Service*. The computer should be readily serviceable and have a good back-up provision from the supplier. This must include rapid response times.

3 Supplier. Meadows & Butler wanted one company to supply both the software and the hardware, to avoid being passed from one supplier to the other in the event of problems. Management also felt it was important to have confidence in the information provided by the supplier.

4 Price. Whilst no upper limit seems to have been set on price, it is clear that the company was looking for a system which would meet most, if not all, of the above requirements at the lowest possible cost. It was recognized, however, that the level of cost involved had to be balanced against the meeting of requirements. The company chose the more expensive of the two systems on the final short list on the Engineering Manager's recommendation.

CAD

The first consideration of the suitability of CAD for the company took place in 1983–4. (This is discussed later, at pp. 204–5.) Nothing happened until 1986, when the Engineering Manager (who was to take the leading role in CAD adoption) drew up the following list of objectives for CAD (not in any order of priority):

Improved accuracy
Increased speed
Assembly drawings
Automatic calculations
Extra possibilities
Standardization
Co-ordination
Personnel
CAM

'Assembly drawings' refers to a CAD feature whereby, in order to obtain a full drawing of a finished article, it is not always necessary to draw all the separate parts (as would be the case with manual draughting), since individual part drawings are called up from memory and incorporated into the full drawing.

'Extra possibilities' refer to the ability to ask 'what if' questions and see the results displayed on screen, the facility to rotate the design or drawing in 3-D, colour coding, automatic production and maintenance of parts lists, ease of retrieval and amendment of previous drawings, and the facility to produce high quality brochures for customers as an output of CAD (rather than having to buy them in from specialist printers).

'Standardization' and 'co-ordination' need to be understood in the wider context of the developments that had been taking place in the Engineering Division. This was referred to earlier, suffice it to note here that it was recognized that CAD would contribute to the rationalization process. CAD was expected to help achieve standardization across the various companies in the division, which were increasingly working together. This objective was made explicit in the minutes of the Engineering Division's first formal CAD meeting (held in December 1986), when the following reasons for having a common approach to CAD were put forward:

1 Shared learning.
2 Purchasing power.
3 Drawing common parts/symbols at one company only, then distributing them to all the companies.
4 Interchange of personnel.
5 Better maintenance response.
6 Possible benefits of common hardware.
7 Interchange of parts, and therefore of drawings.

'Personnel' related to the concern that, if CAD was not adopted, it would become increasingly difficult to retain skilled people, particularly those at an early stage of their career: they would want to keep abreast of the latest technology, and would be prepared to leave the company in order to do so. On the other hand, the introduction of CAD was seen as helping to attract good recruits to the organization.

'CAM' refers to the technical possibility of the output of CAD being linked electronically to computer-aided manufacturing (for example, CNC machine tools) through providing CAM part programs. Although Meadows & Butler had only a few CNC machines at the time, this was seen as a facility which could become useful in the future, particularly on an inter-plant basis.

These, then, were the key objectives set for the IPCS and CAD by Meadows & Butler staff at a crucial juncture in the company's history. They were in essence technical, systems-level objectives, connected with the emerging corporate and manufacturing strategies for continued competitiveness, profitability and viability in the global market place of the later 1980s and beyond. Let us now look at the company's adoption process for these two forms of new technology.

THE PROCESS OF ADOPTION OF NEW TECHNOLOGY

The initiation of the process of adoption of the IPCS can be traced back to the appointment of the company's first Computer Manager in 1979 (the person appointed having been a design engineer with the company). He reported to the Technical Director. Three key senior staff (the Computer Manager, Technical Director and Managing Director) were now all from a production/engineering background, and it is not perhaps surprising that the computer system which was installed had a similar orientation. As the Engineering Manager put it, 'Because it was the Technical Director who was pushing for the computer, production got more emphasis than it might otherwise have done, and the system chosen is definitely production-oriented.'

An early decision was taken by the Computer Manager and the Technical Director to select a computer system which would incorporate MRP, accounts, payroll, production and stock control. During the early period of his appointment the Computer Manager identified a number of deficiencies in the organization's provision for dealing with these functions (see pp. 199–200). Over a period of three months he visited a number of equipment suppliers, eight being subsequently invited to submit quotations. On the basis of price and functionality the list was narrowed down to five, whereupon further discussions took place, reducing it to two potential suppliers. A capital expenditure proposal was then submitted to the board, using the financial figures provided by the shortlisted suppliers. The first choice of the Computer Manager and Technical Director was supported by the board. Whilst this work was progressing, the Computer Manager visited organizations which had purchased the two systems for demonstrations of the technology in use. (He also spoke to ten other companies which had bought the equipment, having been given a list of telephone numbers by the suppliers.) Both suppliers used the same software, so it was effectively hardware and support which were being evaluated, with the emphasis on the latter.

It is of note that what particularly impressed the Computer Manager and Technical Director on visits to one particular IPCS supplier's system in operation (and, indeed, clinched the order for that supplier) was that the system was being used by two companies in very different, yet equally effective, ways. One had a financial emphasis and the other an MRP/technical emphasis. The Computer Manager observed that 'Both knew what they wanted and where they were going. They were using IPCS differently but effectively.' This underlined the potential of the system, especially its flexibility. When, on the other hand, the Computer Manager visited an installation of the other supplier, he found a system which 'had been allowed to stagnate' (largely because the person responsible for its adoption had left the company). The damning aspect of this was not poor utilization *per se* but the fact that the supplier was so out of touch with the company as to arrange a visit in the first place. (Remember, supplier support was now the key focus.)

What about CAD adoption? Meadows & Butler's awareness of the potential of this technology's features was first raised in 1983/4 through two feasibility studies: one conducted by the Engineering Manager (using a government grant) and the other by a consultant at no cost to the company. Both reports came to the same conclusion: that, whilst there were a number of factors in favour of adopting CAD, the time was not right, given the imminent move. They recommended waiting until the company had settled in at the new site.

In 1986, following the relocation, the thoughts of the Engineering Manager returned to CAD adoption. In the meantime he had enrolled on a Ph.D. programme at a university business school, where he had been given a project brief to 'investigate, select and implement a CAD system'. The terms of reference were clearly chosen advisedly, for the intention was to use this work to help introduce such a system at Meadows & Butler.

The Engineering Manager approached a number of suppliers to see what they had to offer. The essence of the response, as he put it, was 'Everything's wonderful.' Because he did not have enough knowledge of CAD at the time he was not in a good position to assess such claims. He therefore enrolled on a CAD course at a local technical college and talked to a number of consultants. One of the latter was an independent consultant who had been examining the benefits offered by new technology to the manufacturing function across the Engineering Division; this person also recommended CAD adoption.

Having extended his CAD expertise and elicited wider in-company support, the Engineering Manager paid some additional visits to see demonstrations at suppliers. He then drew up a plan for the further progression of CAD adoption by the company. It included a CAD specification, cost justification, board approval, supplier selection, and implementation during summer 1987. The specification document made reference to the following: company profile, drawing office procedures, volumes of data, manuals ('It is envisaged that a proportion of the justification for CAD investment will be derived from an enhanced ability to produce manuals. The company wishes to improve its image with its customers by the production of far more comprehensive and accurate manuals'), CAD requirements (hardware, software, support), requirements for the quotation details (for example, 'The costs of training should be listed separately,' and 'A list of existing users of similar-sized systems is required so that references can be obtained'). The cost justification obtained board approval in November 1986. It contained six main features, listed in Table 14.

The Engineering Division employed the pay-back method for the cost–benefit analysis of proposed investments. The period over which the calculation should be made was a maximum of two years at the time. The Engineering Manager estimated that the pay-back for CAD would be 1·7 years for a system with one or two work stations with three-dimensional designing/drafting, or a growth path from two

Table 14 Meadows & Butler: CAD cost justification

Quantifiable
1. Improved drawing office efficiency (on the basis of drawing office labour becoming more productive)
2. Increased sales (on the basis of a projected improvement in service to customers)
3. Reduced scrap and rework (because of the greater accuracy of the new system)

Non-quantifiable
1. Recruitment/Personnel*
2. Image:
    (a) Technological
    (b) Via enhanced quality of quotation documents*
3. CAM*

* Discussed under 'New technology objectives', above

dimensions (2-D) to three dimensions (3-D). In the view of the Finance Director the 1·7 figure was spurious, as was any strict financial calculation, for such an investment 'was not capable of financial justification', and, in any event, strategically 'it was right to "dip a toe in the water"'. The Engineering Manager commented that 'the board know they have to make allowances for new technology like CAD, where they *must* adopt – otherwise we would get left behind by competitors'. Following the board approval, the next two stages were to send out the CAD specification to suppliers, and then to visit the shortlisted ones for demonstrations. Before going on to this, however, we need to discuss certain broader developments which were taking place in the Engineering Division late in 1986, for they affected the progress of CAD adoption at Meadows & Butler.

It has already been seen that in 1985–7 a process of rationalization of the Engineering Division took place, involving the transfer of work, parts, machinery and people between the constituent companies, the major rationalization being between the southern plant and Meadows & Butler. In connection with these developments, incompatibility problems had been experienced between the different makes of minicomputers at the two plants. Management resolved that the same sorts of problems must, if possible, be avoided with CAD adoption. The need was recognized from an early stage of CAD adoption to find out what, if anything, the other engineering companies were planning to do in this area, and to work with them if they were planning CAD adoption. Staff at the other companies took the same view, as did the group-level technical consultant.

In December 1986 a report was prepared by the group Information Systems Manager summarizing the systems thinking about CAD within the division. It indicated that all four companies were either already considering CAD or would be likely to benefit from it, and that some had more money to invest than others. The CAD specification produced by the Engineering Manager at Meadows & Butler was referred to in the paper, as was his action plan and estimated pay-back of 1·7 years. The paper also mentioned that 'An idea was suggested, but not pursued, of a central CAD function available to all [the engineering] companies. It is thought unlikely that such a system would be beneficial.' The possibility was never seriously pursued because the companies preferred to retain their own CAD competence and staff. Meadows & Butler's experience of using the mainframe computer at the southern plant had not endeared it to the idea of sharing. The Finance Director stated bluntly, 'Centralized computing does not work.' He explained the difficulty of pinpointing accountability if there was a problem: the computer department at the southerm plant reported to that plant's management, not to Meadows & Butler's, whilst the latter must 'be in control of their own computer people'.

An inaugural CAD meeting of the engineering managers and directors of the four companies, along with the group chairman, was held shortly after the report had been circulated. The key outcome was agreement that it would be beneficial to pursue CAD adoption on a group basis. It was felt that all the companies would benefit immediately from 2-D draughting. All wanted 3-D at some stage for design work, although some saw a need to go to 3-D immediately, whereas others would move later, once they had gained experience in 2-D. Interestingly, in view of Meadows & Butler's Engineering Manager's pay-back period of 1·7 years, the minutes stated that 'All think it will be impossible to cost-justify, especially as consensus is to depreciate over three years maximum.' The key benefits were seen as automatic production, maintenance and amendment of parts lists. The advantage of much improved manuals was also recognized, as was the fact that 'Commonality of systems between companies (*not* a centralized system) would aid interchangeability of drawings and experience'. It was decided to identify by the end of February 1987 a system which would satisfy all the companies' needs, and the managers agreed to redefine their requirements for CAD as a group, based on the specification of Meadows & Butler's Engineering Manager.

Following the December meeting, the Engineering Manager sent the CAD specification to ten suppliers, receiving nine replies. At a group meeting early in January four of these suppliers were put on a short list for the February visits, on the basis of their system not being prohibitive in cost terms and appearing to meet the requirements at least in broad terms. It was also decided to tighten the hardware specification and to specify the software requirements in order to obtain more readily comparable responses. The suppliers were visited in February by the CAD group and asked to produce a demonstration drawing of a basic component produced and/or used by the companies.

Another group meeting was held in March, when the quotations and demonstrations were analysed and compared. A table was drawn up, listing the costs stated in each of the quotations (seven in all) for the three major stages of introduction which had been identified. Phase 1 covered the initial system which was to be installed and phases 2 and 3 covered the addition of work stations, monitors, digitizers, etc., in time. The table had two columns for the average marks awarded out of ten by the group for each quotation (derived by comparing each system with the standard). One represented an assessment of the system's performance and ease of use, the other the group's impression of the level and quality of support which would be forthcoming from that supplier. This process produced a first and a second choice, and the Engineering Division chairman was given the responsibility of renegotiating a 'bottom line' price with these suppliers for hardware, software, initial training and maintenance and support. The quotations turned out to be within £190 of each other, so the first choice was put forward for approval, via capital expenditure proposals, to each board of the group companies.

The final plan was to introduce a 2-D system into each company as soon as they could afford to do so (this meant more or less immediately for Meadows & Butler and the southern plant) and to introduce 3-D, as appropriate, at a later stage when the company could afford it. The group-based adoption process ensured, of course, that all the companies would have a compatible (indeed, the same!) system, to facilitate intra-divisional work.

MANAGING THE SOCIAL AND ORGANIZATIONAL ASPECTS OF ADOPTION

With no union representation of staff and technical employees there was no question of management–union consultation or negotiation over CAD or IPCS adoption. Moreover, as we have seen, both new technology adoption processes were controlled and dominated by engineering specialists. The engineering function originated the proposals and was, almost exclusively, involved throughout the subsequent adoption stages. The only other notable actors were the Finance Director and, in the case of the IPCS adoption, the Computer Manager.

Financial considerations were also influential, and they *could* have made a difference in respect of CAD adoption had the Finance Director wanted to challenge the 1·7 year pay-back period calculated by the Engineering Manager. Although he believed the pay-back would in fact be over the two-year maximum specified by the company, he was happy to accept the proposal on strategic grounds. Notice that there was never any question of justifying the CAD investment through projected savings on design/drawing office labour costs through reducing the numbers employed. (Remember, however, that one objective alluded to in the cost–benefit justification was to make drawing office labour more productive.) Furthermore, there was a recognition that savings could be made on the cost of producing technical manuals, and that improvements could be made in the quality of the manuals through the CAD investment. The connection between achieving them and the possibility of increased sales was also recognized, and these benefits *were* attributed direct to CAD introduction. Primrose *et al.* found that because in many firms the manuals are ordered by the marketing department direct from subcontractors, without drawing office involvement, any projected savings are attributed to Marketing rather than forming part of the CAD cost–benefit analysis.[4] In ways like this, some of the benefits of CAD may be omitted from the cost justification, thus militating against the investment. This factor may be particularly significant where a company sticks rigidly to traditional capital investment appraisal techniques (such as pay-back), instead of allowing that new technology has distinctive features and should be financially assessed in a different and more appropriate way. Primrose *et al.* list twenty-nine possible benefits of CAD under the following main headings:

1 Drawing office savings.
2 Increased sales from reduced delivery times.
3 Increased sales from other causes (for example, quicker and better presented quotations).
4 Reduced stock levels.
5 Reduced production costs.
6 Cost control.
7 CAD–CAM link.[5]

Clearly, it would be unreasonable to expect every CAD installation to realize all these benefits, but it seems safe to assume that a number are achievable, making a narrow focus in the justification upon cost savings in the design/drawing office unduly restrictive and inhibiting.

Whilst a good deal of attention was paid by the company to the engineering and financial implications of IPCS and CAD, the people alternatives and implications received relatively little consideration. The one personnel specialist in the organization had virtually no involvement (simply advising on how assistance might be obtained for CAD training). At the same time, there do not appear to have been any notable employee relations problems with IPCS and CAD adoption. Contributory factors here included the relatively few people directly affected, the lack of unionization among the staff concerned and, above all else, the fact that the order book, and hence the number of employees, was increasing throughout the period. The rationalization of work in the Engineering Division had far more impact in that area.

KEY DEVELOPMENTS SINCE 1986/7

External context

Two contextual developments in particular have had the effect of reducing the size of the product market in which Meadows & Butler is competing over the last five or six years, resulting in a situation where all manufacturers are operating at lower volume levels: the introduction of compulsory competitive tendering (CCT) in local authorities (LAs) from 1989, and the Community Charge (or 'poll tax'). With regard to CCT, the result has been that private operators now have around 25 per cent of a market which had been provided directly and exclusively by LAs. They have achieved this through significant increases in efficiency which, in turn, have 'encouraged' many LAs and their direct employees to move in the same direction in order to retain the work within the LA domain. The Finance Director of the holding company (see later in this section) expressed the matter as follows:

> They [the private companies] have achieved this by making inroads into what was a grossly inefficient system in the first place, whereby LAs were dominated by union practices which determined work would run on a 'task and finish' basis. That is, once a certain number of streets had been driven down and the refuse collected, the employees were finished for the day, with the result that some were finishing by late morning and then doing a different job in the afternoon. Private companies said, 'We can do it much more efficiently. We will have larger and more efficient vehicles, reorganize the rounds, and have people working eight hours a day.'

In some areas, what is more, the refuse vehicles were 'double-shifted', that is, used for sixteen hours a day, with two crews. The example of Birmingham was cited to illustrate the impact all this had upon the existing internal organization, which was restructured in order to head off the possibility of losing the work to an external company. Previous to CCT, Birmingham had approximately 120 refuse disposal vehicles; facing the CCT threat, collection rounds were reorganized, larger vehicles were purchased, and the fleet was reduced to forty-six.

The Community Charge had a depressant effect upon the vehicle market because of the lower effective collection rates as compared with the situation before its introduction. Local authorities had a range of statutory services to provide, and when it came to the choice between maintaining the level of such services or buying new refuse vehicles, new vehicles came second.

In this depressed market Meadows & Butler has increased its market share from a low 40 to a high 40 per cent, with the resulting higher volume going only part way to compensate. There are two main competitors, each with 15–20 per cent of the market, and three or four other companies taking up the rest; the former two organizations, along with the majority of the latter, are foreign-owned. Since the original research there have been no mergers or amalgamations in the UK sector.

How has Meadows & Butler achieved this dominance of a contracted UK market? There are two main factors: new product development and enhanced internal efficiencies. The new product introduced in 1993 was designed to enable more efficient operation by workers, and thus to appeal to customers' search for ever more cost-effective modes of utilization. Working practices were redesigned, thirty redundancies were declared, spending programmes and overheads were reduced, restrictions were placed upon capital expenditure and greater use has been made of CAD for vehicle design and development (resulting in reduced lead times, which have more than offset the costs involved). Much of this is discussed in more detail below.

The company has taken more interest in export markets in recent years (some 25 per cent of output goes abroad) and foresees a greater percentage of production going overseas in the future, particularly to Western Europe. A key factor is a pending change in European legislation relating to vehicle safety. It is anticipated that the UK standard, which has been in operation for some ten years, will be adopted in a European standard. The fact that Meadows & Butler's product has been developed to meet that standard for some considerable time is expected to work to the company's advantage. On the strength of this, and an analysis of the age and number of vehicles in service in the United Kingdom (which indicates that a number of those which were purchased in the late 1980s will need replacement by 1995–6), there is an expectation of growth from around this time.

Internal context

In January 1989 there was a management buy-out of the Engineering Division of the original holding company. The new company went public in October 1992. The Finance Director of Meadows & Butler became the finance director of the new group in a 'lean and mean' head office consisting of himself and the group chairman, with secretarial support. Since 1989 some of the constituent companies have been sold off, whilst new ones have been acquired, resulting in a portfolio of five operating companies. (Unless specified otherwise, the discussion below relates purely to the Meadows & Butler plant of the holding company.) As at January 1994 Meadows & Butler had a total of around 570 employees, some 400 of them being located at the sole manufacturing plant in the Midlands (the rest being employed in the thirty or so parts and service depots scattered throughout the country).

On the employee relations front, major change has taken place since the late 1980s. In essence it has involved a reassertion of management control in the context of significant external contextual changes and threats, as discussed above. Reflecting upon the climate of employee relations in the company during the 1980s, the Finance Director observed:

> The greatest fault of management was that it was a highly successful company, with an excellent product and increasing market share, therefore it was always straining for additional output. Whenever, therefore, there were any confrontations with the unions, the attraction of achieving higher and higher profits was such that it was easier and cheaper to buy the unions off. In the later 1980s, when the structural changes in the market place occurred, the company began to experience quite severely declining profits, but had a union which had gained in strength, with particular individuals who were much more powerful than management, and the unions were dictating on pay, working practices, etc. It became an almost intolerable situation for the company, and had to be brought to a head, and this could only be done by a full-scale confrontation. That happened in late 1992, when the union convenor was summarily dismissed on the grounds of being a disruptive influence, and the message was spelt out to everyone on the shop floor, individually and collectively, why the company was taking this drastic action. At the same time, all the working practices were changed. A new document was put to everyone: 'This is the new order for [M&B] to go forward into the 1990s with. If you want to be part of the company, you will sign.'

A central element of management's strategy was that unit labour costs should be reduced, and this aim was achieved through a new bonus system which generated lower overall levels of payment than the previous one. There was no discussion, let alone negotiation, of the changes with union officials or employees: they had the option, of course, of threatened or actual strike action, and in the past they had exercised it, resulting in management backing down. On this occasion, however, Meadows & Butler's senior managers and the holding company chairman said that if the changes were not accepted the company would be closed down. As the Finance Director put it, 'This time the message got through that we meant it.'

With regard to union recognition, the same unions (dominated by the AEU, which is the largest and negotiates on behalf of the other five unions) are recognized as before for shop-floor employees (with around 50 per cent actually being members), whereas there is no representation of staff, again as before. Whilst, then, there has been little change in industrial relations structuring and representation, change does appear to have taken place in respect of the nature of management–union relations and attitudes. The Finance Director expressed it as follows:

> We're quite happy under normal circumstances to negotiate with a representative body, but we have to be able to feel that the people we are dealing with are people we can trust, and that they will relay the information accurately to the rest of the shop floor and not distort management's message.

With regard to changes in working practices, it is of interest that there was no strategy of moving towards a multi-skilled work force (or functional labour flexibility). Rather, management put in train the possibility of labour mobility if and when this suited business conditions, subject to the employees involved receiving the requisite training. This does imply, of course, that a certain level of multi-skilling will occur in practice. What senior managers were much more intent on achieving was acceptance by shop-floor workers that management had the right to manage as it saw fit, including moving workers around as necessary. (Under the old regime employees would simply refuse to do a different job or undertake retraining.)

> The company is not trying to ban unions, but to define where their rights and responsibilities are, and likewise for management; at the end of the day shopfloor operations are a management responsibility, and these have to be geared up to production efficiency.
>
> (Finance Director)

The restructuring of Meadows & Butler's ownership has had an important impact upon its ability to attract capital for investment purposes. In the old structure, before the buy-out, proposals had to go to the main group board (whose membership included many people without manufacturing or engineering industry experience) for approval, where they competed with proposals from the other non-engineering companies in the group, many of which were more profitable than the Engineering Division and as a result found it easier to get their proposals accepted. The change of ownership created a group of top, senior and middle managers dedicated to engineering and with a common philosophy: the way to gain and maintain a competitive edge is to lead on product development and demonstrate that you have a better product than competitors. Proposals for investment in new technology are more likely to be found acceptable in this climate. At the same time the constituent companies of the new group operate in a decentralized mode, with autonomy on such matters as developing and designing new products. The holding company exercises control through setting annual budgets (and leaves the companies alone as long as they are operating within those budgets), group reporting systems, three-year strategic plans, and through the two group managers attending all the monthly board meetings of the operating companies (participating in the latter as 'knowledgeable, non-executive directors').

Technological changes

Since the original research in 1986/7 no more new technology has been introduced into the company, although Meadows & Butler and one of the other group companies (the southern plant) are now at the point of beginning to update their CAD systems, and Meadows & Butler's IPCS system is scheduled for replacement. In addition, the number and utilization of PCs has increased throughout the company, for word-processing, spreadsheets, etc., with a mixture of networked and stand-alone installations. There has been some degree of software standardization. There are no plans for any other new technology adoption, and this includes the CAD/CAM link included in the original CAD investment proposal. The Finance Director commented:

> This was a spurious justification in the first place. The type of product we make and the engineering requirements flowing from it were never such that we were going to have a CAM link anyway – it was something that was listed and sounded good.

All the other projected benefits of CAD have been achieved, including reduced design-to-production lead times, the creation of an external image of the company as modern and up-to-date, the attraction and retention of staff with the requisite skills and knowledge, the enhancement of sales documentation, and increased design efficiency. Having said that, it is of note that the Finance Director still believes that CAD cannot be effectively justified in conventional financial terms: he argued that CAD investment is largely instinctive and is done for a number of unquantifiable reasons. There has certainly been no reduction in the number of design staff at Meadows & Butler. Indeed, quite the reverse over the last few years, because of the wider range and greater complexity of the products.

Social and organizational issues

Some interesting differences are emerging between Meadows & Butler and the southern plant in respect of the CAD installations that are being proposed. Given the 'stand-off' approach adopted at group level *vis-à-vis* the operating companies, they are creating certain tensions for the group managers who will have the final say on whether the proposals go ahead. The southern plant is pursuing a multi-functional, high initial cost, work station-based system, whereas Meadows & Butler prefer a PC-based system in which applications software is added on an incremental basis over a period of time, thus building up gradually to an extensive work-station system. It may be fine in itself for each plant to pursue systems which are presumably more appropriate to its needs, but group managers have to consider the different implications for financial requirements, including cash flows. The southern plant has a work station-based system with eight CAD seats, and wants to double the number so that all its design engineers are covered. The cost would be around £200,000. Meadows & Butler, on the other hand, has a CAD system nearing the end of its useful life, and wants a completely new system, also requiring sixteen seats, but its proposal, being PC-based, will cost only £120,000.

The managers and engineers of the two companies have not collaborated over their CAD proposals, and managers at group level have been left to compare and co-ordinate the progression of the new technology adoption. These managers are reluctant to impose solutions from the centre, for that would be to run the risk of the 'not invented here' syndrome. That is, if a solution is imposed which is not the one the company wants, it may not be committed to making it work, and if there are problems it may say, 'Well, we didn't want that system, anyway.' The group approach to trying to resolve the matter has been to begin with Meadows & Butler's proposal and, having examined it, to take it to the southern plant and say, 'This is Meadows & Butler's proposal – why can't you adopt it?'. In other words, get the southern plant's staff to justify not accepting it, rather than the other way round.

With regard to the IPCS system, although it is beginning to 'creak', the approach has been not to focus on the replacement of the computer system *per se* but to look at the possibilities on a wider basis by taking the opportunity to examine other information system requirements at the same time. (For example, only part of the product range is controlled by materials requirements planning.) The company is about to recruit someone who will have the broad brief of examining IS provision and future requirements in general, and then going on to make recommendations for IT requirements.

It appears that IT and CAD will play an even more important role in future, in the context of a corporate strategy which emphasizes the superior quality of the company's products, which are difficult to imitate. Competitors may eventually bring out a comparable product, but by then Meadows & Butler plan to have enhanced theirs. Thus the time taken to develop new products is projected to continue to shorten, resulting in new products which have shorter and shorter life cycles.

Chapter 9
Conclusion

The discussion in this final chapter is divided into two main sections: (1) an overview of the key findings which have emerged from the four case studies, and (2) some reflections on the implications of these findings, as well as of the findings of the other research presented in Chapters 2–4, for our understanding of the social, managerial and organizational processes connected with the adoption of new technology.

ISSUES RAISED BY THE CASE STUDIES

These will be considered under the headings of objectives, strategies, and employee involvement, representing the three main elements of the new technology adoption process.

Objectives

Financial and economic objectives predominated in all the organizations, along with technical objectives in the building societies and production objectives in the engineering companies. However, these objectives were by no means the only ones to be found, and they were not adopted and pursued in an unreflective, unbending way. For example, it will be recalled that in all four organizations managers said that on a strict financial calculation they might well not have adopted new technology. They did so because they were pursuing other objectives as well, such as improving customer service, or they could see strategic reasons why the new technology should be adopted. At Meadows & Butler the Finance Director had reservations about the CAD financial appraisal; he understood why it had been provided but recognized that many of the benefits of CAD could not be adequately quantified *ex ante*, and that such calculations were therefore likely to be spurious. He supported CAD adoption for strategic reasons.

A further point which arises from the above illustration is that an element of ritualism can be said to have been present in Meadows & Butler's capital investment appraisal procedures, in the sense that they were being followed in the letter but not in the spirit. I would not wish to argue that there is no need for such procedures and controls, for it appears to me that there is much to be said for the rigorous examination of proposals, certainly where significant expenditure is involved. The initiators then know it will happen and therefore that it will not be a case of 'anything goes' (where capital expenditure would be in danger of getting out of control). In any event, a number of even small to medium size proposals can soon add up to a very large commitment of funds.

A second illustration from the case studies involves Don Ltd. Broad company-wide objectives for new technology were set at corporate level and, for the UK plants, at the UK manufacturing head office. Hence, as the Plant Manager put it, 'there was not much room for manoeuvre at [Don Ltd], and therefore any financial justifications are in a sense spurious, other than trying to work it so that we get the particular machine we want, as against others'. Besides the ritualism issue, this example also prompts the question: 'If Don's senior managers were less politically attuned would they end up with a type or make of new technology that they did not really want?' Even where there is this political realism, success is not guaranteed, however, for, as we saw, when Don sought approval for a CNC machining centre from the UK manufacturing head office they were told to get an FMS cell instead. Even then they got the one Head Office wanted them to have rather than the other way round, not least because at the time, it appears, there was a corporate policy of standardizing on FMS equipment.

It can therefore be seen that organizational structuring, processes and procedures impact upon new technology objectives. This applies at the corporate, divisional and plant levels and in terms of the impact of decisions taken at one of the 'higher' levels upon behaviour at 'lower' levels. We saw how the different ownership and structuring of Meadows & Butler after January 1989 provided an engineering focus throughout the company, and created a climate which was more supportive of investment in manufacturing, that is, a climate in which the company was no longer competing for capital with non-engineering companies in front of a board which represented a diverse range of interests. Others have noted that the establishment of profit centres in the various divisions of a company may encourage over-concentration by the managers of those divisions on financial returns and the tendency to take a short-term view; or to put the matter differently, it may not encourage enterprise and imagination.[1] If it is accepted that many of the benefits of new technology are indeterminate, it is perhaps not surprising that 'approval is sometimes gained only through intricate manoeuvring within the internal political system of the firm, which may sometimes require elaborate subterfuge'.[2] A proportion of managers' salaries is often based on their success in achieving the budgets they have been allocated or the targets they have been set, and, in any event, they may be appraised in those terms. Thus systems of reward and recognition need to be changed in order to encourage better-quality and more imaginative investment proposals.

The fact that financial and economic objectives did not by any means dominate the new technology adoption process is exemplified by the range of other objectives which were also identified. In the building societies these centred on improving the management information system and data capture and security, and, increasingly throughout the later 1980s and into the 1990s, using new technology to improve customer focus and service. In the engineering companies the focus was upon production objectives such as improving quality, accuracy and scheduling, increasing flexibility and throughput, and (increasingly in the 1990s, as with the building societies) getting closer to the customer.

In the building societies a key objective was to keep abreast of new technology innovation in the financial sector through not putting off adoption and introduction. At Park Hill, for example, the belief was that the longer the decision to invest was postponed the more difficult it would become to take the 'leap'. Whilst it may be tempting to wait for the latest technical development, and thus steal a march on competitors, the danger is that the wait may go on too long, with the society slipping further and further behind competitors which have 'dipped a toe in the water'. Remember also that this applies not only to the technology *per se* but also to the organizational and social changes related to the introduction of new technology.

With regard to social and organizational objectives, a key finding of the case studies was that no organization had labour reduction as an explicit objective. Contextual factors need to be borne in mind, however. All the organizations, for example, were expanding in terms of business volume during the period under consideration. However, they also had the objective of increasing labour productivity, so labour reduction is implied, in the sense that fewer people are likely to be taken on than would otherwise have been the case. In this respect the job 'loss' can be said to have been concentrated in the local community in terms of a reduction in the number of vacancies. The reverse situation could also hold, that is, *ex ante* (rather than *ex post*) reductions. The Bramley Building Society affords an illustration. At the principal branch office, where the on-line system was first introduced, staffing levels had been deliberately held down before the new technology was brought in so that management would be able to point to a reduction in work intensity. We simply do not know the extent to which this happens more generally in the economy and, in any event, it is often very difficult to attribute labour reduction to a specific cause or causes. Managers are invariably able to point to a variety of factors; decreased business volume and lower margins are only two of the commoner ones.

Regarding new technology control and skill objectives, no reference was made during my interviews to managers wishing to change the extent or nature of the control exercised over employees or the level of skills possessed by the staff affected. Indeed, the only such mention was at Meadows & Butler, in connection with CAD helping the retention and recruitment of skilled staff. This should not be taken to imply that it was not recognized in the case study organizations that the introduction of new technology would (or might) have implications for skill and control. (Indeed, there were a number of references to how skill composition would change after its introduction.) Rather, they were not seen as new technology objectives but as the consequence of those objectives. The analysis of CNC introduction at Don Ltd illustrated many of these implications, pointing up in particular how management's past decisions constrain the room for manoeuvre in the present. It will be recalled that, formally speaking, the machinists had been de-skilled, yet in practice they were doing the work of process engineers, with management connivance. At the building societies it was recognized that branch office staff would need some new skills (such as keyboarding) whilst losing others. With regard to control, the financial, economic and technical objectives of improving budgetary control, improving the management information system, and integrating information, all had implications for the nature of the control exercised over managers as well as employees.

Strategy

Continuing the labour issues and implications theme, extensive evidence was found, both in the case studies and in secondary material, of the adoption by management of a 'softly, softly' strategy towards labour when introducing new technology. Three of our organizations took this approach – the building societies and Don Ltd.

Why was a 'softly, softly' strategy popular? At the building societies business volume was increasing and some competitors had already introduced, or were adopting, new technology. It had become clear that new technology would play an increasingly central role in enhancing service provision and improving management information systems. Senior management at the Bramley and Park Hill societies recognized that they needed the technology, and needed it quickly. This meant that they could not afford any major staff problems arising from its introduction. In other words, there was a premium on gaining employee commitment to the use of the new technology. Whilst this did not pose any major challenge to managers, given the internal contexts of these organizations (see Chapters 5 and 6), they nevertheless had to tread carefully so as not to upset the *modus vivendi* based on the paternalistic norms which were so much part and parcel of building society culture at the time. Indeed, by the mid- to late 1980s there were already some indications of fragmentation, for example direct external recruitment into managerial functions such as information systems, marketing and personnel/training, as against reliance on internal labour markets. External recruitment had indeed developed to such an extent that by the 1990s senior managers were being taken on from other societies (see Chapter 6): there was particular interest in obtaining staff with professional sales experience (see Chapter 5). All this had been made possible both by the changed competitive climate of the 1990s, in which 'no poaching' agreements were very much a thing of the past, and by the availability of senior and specialist staff as a result of the rationalization processes which the large national societies were undergoing. There was evidence of a much stronger strategic orientation (in all the senses of the term 'strategy') at the Bramley society, and the attenuation of conservative and paternalistic managerial styles, illustrated, for example, by an enhanced performance and measurement control system. At the Park Hill society the current mission (1993–4), which included a much-enhanced customer orientation, was helping to drive the changes taking place in the IT infrastructure.

At Don Ltd technological changes had occurred on an incremental basis since the opening of the plant in the early 1970s, hence it was easy for management to argue that CNC 'was nothing really new'. The organization was growing, albeit on a gradual basis, and management recognized the importance of gaining employee acceptance of the new technology; an explicit labour strategy for new technology had been developed. Corporate and UK manufacturing head offices were designing and, in some cases at least, influencing the various strategies (business, manufacturing, technology) being pursued. (However, there appeared to be more room for the exercise of discretion on the labour front.) Given this, it is perhaps more accurate to talk about Don Ltd developing *tactics* rather than strategies (other than with regard to labour). CNC introduction, for example, was funded from the plant's annual investment budgets, and was the responsibility of line (engineering) managers. UK Manufacturing head office *told* the company to install CAD, and which configuration it should obtain.

At the Bramley Building Society elements of a new technology labour strategy could be detected at various phases of adoption, such as in the choice of the busiest branch office for the first installation, the holding down of staff numbers beforehand, and the 'floating' of the new technology possibility. Yet personnel specialists were not formally involved until the later stages of adoption. However, informally, in an advisory capacity, the Personnel Manager had been exercising influence from an earlier stage – not least in respect of the matters referred to above – and personnel specialists did become more formally involved when introduction approached, and at an earlier stage in subsequent adoptions of new technology. Questionnaire surveys, it seems to me, run the risk of not picking up these rather more subtle forms of influence, and it may therefore be the case that the WIRS surveys have underestimated personnel specialist involvement in new technology adoption and introduction as a result.

The case studies, then, provided evidence for the existence of all the varieties of organizational strategies which were discussed in Chapter 2, that is, corporate, business, manufacturing and labour. Not all the companies had explicit strategies in all these areas. However, Don Ltd came close, although the proviso about tactics mentioned above needs to be borne in mind. Some companies had clear strategies in certain areas but lacked them in others – Meadows & Butler, for example, had a manufacturing strategy but were less strategic in their approach to the management of labour. The building societies had developed labour strategies for new technology adoption, and were increasingly taking a strategic view in the marketing of their products and the servicing of customers. In summary terms, then, in the majority of areas these organizations were taking a strategic orientation towards the adoption of new technology in the increasingly turbulent external environments of the later 1980s and early 1990s.

Employee involvement

In all the case study organizations adoption was dominated, especially during the early stages, by technical/administrative or engineering considerations. If a labour strategy could be identified, it was usually seen as flowing from corporate, business or manufacturing strategies. In so far as labour issues were even considered the orientation was a financial or economic one, that is, labour was a cost of production which could be reduced through head-count loss or increased productivity, as a result of introducing the new technology. For example, in the CAD justification submitted by the Engineering Manager at Meadows & Butler, drawing office productivity was projected to increase by 25 per cent. Even then, questions can be raised as to whether there was an element of 'window dressing' – giving the accountants and senior managers the 'hard' quantitative information they were imputed to want (as, indeed, may well have been the case!) in order to gain approval of the proposal. It was argued earlier, again drawing on the Meadows & Butler data in particular, that there could be a touch of ritualism here.

Qualitative issues and implications of new technology adoption, such as job redesign and changes in working practices, were often not considered (if at all) until the later stages, or were treated in a derivative – in a sense, technologically deterministic – way. This is perhaps hardly surprising, given that it was computer/engineering/administrative managers who were driving the adoption process. Personnel specialists either had no involvement (as at Meadows & Butler), were brought in only after the decision to invest had been taken by others (for example, at Don Ltd, where their key role was seen as being to 'get the infrastructure right') or came in at a later stage (as at the building societies).

The organization where this technical/engineering/administrative dominance was least in evidence was Don Ltd. Here corporate, business, manufacturing, technical and labour issues were developed and thought through in concert, at the extra-plant level and at the plant itself in some instances. Don was the only organization which could reasonably be said to have a sophisticated employee relations strategy. What is more, following an organizational restructuring, training specialists had been transferred to the business units, where they reported to the relevant Business Manager rather than to the Personnel Manager. This gave them the opportunity to become more readily involved in new technology adoption. (Whether they took the opportunity was another matter, of course.)

What about employee involvement in new technology adoption? It is clear that this was limited, and at best largely superficial, in all the case study organizations (as well as in the great majority of organizations studied by other researchers), apart from an attempt to involve the staff affected just before introduction – when, of course, most, if not all, of the key decisions had been taken. In part, this is a reflection of the fact that the case study organizations are UK-based, for, as we saw in Chapter 4, a higher level of involvement is to be found in certain other European countries, notably Denmark and Germany, where external contextual factors have had a positive influence. But it also had much to do with the technical and administrative or engineering orientation of the organizations, most of which employed a systems rationalization approach of the passive user-involvement variety. At the Bramley Building Society there was no involvement of user representatives or delegates in the team which progressed the new technology adoption process, not even in the implementation group. However, there was some indication of rather more – and earlier – involvement of users on subsequent occasions when new technology was adopted in the 1990s. The open systems environment to which the Bramley (and the Park Hill society) was moving facilitated and encouraged this – a nice example of the importance of seeing technology as an engineering system. At the Park Hill society branch office staff had a brief involvement at stage 4 before the seconded branch manager replaced them. In neither society did the staff association exercise much influence. At the Bramley the association made an attempt to get involved, but it was readily deflected by management. At Meadows & Butler the IPCS and CAD adoption processes were led by engineering (as well as, in the former case, computer) managers, with no user, union or indeed personnel specialist participation. The decision to introduce new technology, the configuration, make and model to be bought, along with the associated changes in information systems, working practices, job design, grading and payment systems, etc., was regarded in every case by the participating managers as the unilateral preserve of management.

ADOPTING NEW TECHNOLOGY: SOCIAL, MANAGERIAL AND ORGANIZATIONAL PROCESSES

The discussion and analysis of new technology adoption throughout this book has been conducted with the aid of a model which addresses three key aspects of the process: the contexts (external and internal) of adoption, the content of adoption, and the processes involved in moving through the four stages, from initiation to planning and systems design. With the aid of this model we have used primary and secondary material to examine what happens when specific forms of new technology are adopted by organizations, focusing (but by no means exclusively) upon three particular elements: strategy, objectives, and the involvement of the people who will be using the new technology. Strong links were found between all three aspects of the contextual model, for instance between changes in external contexts, changes in internal contexts, and the technical changes themselves. Further illustrations of these links – and, indeed, the difficulty sometimes experienced of discerning whether a change was to be seen as emanating from 'out there' or from 'in here' – will be provided below. This, the concluding section of the book, will draw upon this model and focus as a means of organizing a discussion of the key themes and findings which have emerged. In order not to repeat the points addressed in the first section of the chapter, however, many of the issues considered there will be taken as given and will form a backdrop for the ensuing discussion.

External contexts

Let us take the changing nature of the external contexts of organizations as our starting point. Besides the well known intensification (and, in some cases, globalization) of competition, there are four elements of context which have stood out as particularly influential:

1 Customers.
2 Suppliers.
3 The technology itself.
4 The corporate/divisional group within which the relevant firm is located.

Of course, not all aspects are equally relevant, or relevant to the same degree, to each organization. For example, (4) applies only to the engineering companies, and (2) applies much more strongly to the building societies. Let us take each in turn.

Customers

Interestingly, customer focus, as a key objective which new technology may help to facilitate, was not picked up as significant in my search of the secondary literature. It was hardly ever mentioned as a new technology objective, for example. Yet in the case studies it was referred to in all the organizations as at least an important objective. Indeed, in the building societies it was seen as central, even more so (if it is not a contradiction in terms) in 1993 compared with the mid- to late 1980s. The reasons were discussed in the case studies; they include the Building Societies Act, 1986, increasing competition from other financial institutions (the Bramley and Park Hill societies), changing customer preferences and the demand for more choice and flexibility (the former plus Don Ltd), the contracting out of local authority services, and European Community health and safety legislation (Meadows & Butler), customer demands for more resource-efficient capital equipment (Don Ltd). New technology was helping the building societies to achieve this customer focus through such things as reducing the time taken to deal with enquiries, the offering of more services and the twenty-four-hours-a-day availability of certain facilities. At Don Ltd it was the incorporation of new technology in the product offered to customers which was enhancing service provision (this new technology, in turn, having been produced with the aid of new manufacturing technology). All this, of course, generated the requirement for a much enhanced marketing and selling capability. Note also that, despite this customer focus, and despite the fact that it had intensified during the intervening period, there was no reference to Total Quality Management in any of these organizations. I do not, however, intend to discuss or speculate why this was the case, merely to note the fact.

Suppliers

It will be recalled that at the Bramley Building Society an influential factor triggering adoption of the on-line computer system throughout the branch network was a meeting between the General Manager and a representative from a technology supplier company. At the Park Hill society the Computer Manager had gained intelligence about what other societies were doing, or planning to do, through building society computer managers' meetings, which were often addressed by supplier representatives. A visit from such a representative to the society had also helped to spark interest in an on-line system.

Technology suppliers, whether of hardware or of software, appear to have had less influence in the engineering companies. Here various forms of new technology had been available for a longer period of time (NC/CNC, for example, since the 1940s and early '50s), hence members of these organizations had built up internal knowledge of and competence in AMT in a way that building society staff could not possibly have done with IT. Thus they were nothing like as reliant upon what supplier staff could tell them or do for them. Putting it another way, the engineering companies had experienced incremental technical change over a period of years, whereas the new technology coming into building societies in the early to mid-1980s was a radical departure from what had gone before. Drawing on Friedman and Cornford's four phases of computer systems development, we can generalize by saying that engineering companies have been moving through them since the 1940s, whereas the building societies' time period for the same stages has been condensed into around fifteen years from 1980, for both sectors have now reached the fourth stage of attempting to realize the strategic potential of new technology (see Chapter 1, p. 4).[3]

The role and influence of new technology suppliers upon new technology adoption by organizations is a neglected area of research, and I have commented upon some of the possibilities in Chapter 3 (see pp. 82–3). Suffice it to say here that, *ceteris paribus*, we can expect their influence upon the internal arrangements and policies of adopting organizations to be greater where hardware and software problems predominate and where staff lack the requisite skills and knowledge. In a more mature phase of IT use, where user issues predominate and organizations adopt an open systems architecture, perhaps there will be an attenuation of the influence of suppliers? The 'jury is still out' on this one.

The technology

Technology has been placed in the external context category, but in many respects it could equally well have been defined as an element of internal context, for, as discussed earlier, it is both 'out there', that is, available from the suppliers referred to above (so long as the organization can afford it), and 'in here', in the sense of the software being developed or amended/added to in-house. Indeed, there is an increasingly wide range of choice about which particular configurations of hardware and software to have, mixing and matching and developing the products of a range of suppliers.

By the time of my return visit to the Bramley Building Society, technology had become such a part of the way of life that, according to the General Manager (Operations), it was not an issue any more. Both this organization and the Park Hill society were in the process of moving towards an open systems environment. At Don Ltd the technological innovations since the earlier period had been in the product itself, whilst incremental updating to the existing technologies had been the order of the day for process technology and IT. Meadows & Butler had updated some of the existing technology. In sum, then, it would seem reasonable to assert that, for all these organizations, new technology had become, by 1993 at the latest, 'simply' an everyday element of working life. It was the way in which it was used and the purposes it was used for that were seen as the crucial issues.

Corporate/divisional group as the context of plant-level operations

As noted above, this is relevant only to the two engineering companies. Let us take each in turn. At Don Ltd we saw two instances where the particular type of new technology and the timing of its introduction were effectively dictated to the plant either by the corporate head office or by the UK Manufacturing head office. FMS was imposed by the latter, instead of the CNC machining centre which Don Ltd had requested, and Don's first CAD installation came via an application which UK Manufacturing head office had put to US corporate level for its own installation. None of this obviated the requirement, however, for Don Ltd to put in the necessary financial justification before approval was forthcoming. With the CAD installation a serendipity element was also present, in the sense that the new payment and grading system had just been completed, and it was readily able to absorb the skills and knowledge requirements of CAD. With regard to Meadows & Butler, we have already commented on how the new ownership structure as from 1989 lent more support to investment in the engineering companies, with a (new) board dedicated to engineering and having a common philosophy. We also saw how the old Engineering Group within the previous ownership structure of a diversified range of companies co-ordinated the adoption of CAD, and benefited from sharing knowledge and information. The most recent example of corporate-level influence upon the plant level has been with regard to the social and managerial processes involved in the replacement of the old CAD installations by newer systems, Meadows & Butler preferring a different solution from the southern plant. And, as we saw, the two projects have significantly different financial implications.This time there has been a lack of co-operation between the plants, and group level has effectively been left to co-ordinate the proposals, perhaps ending up, albeit reluctantly, cajoling the southern plant into a solution nearer to Meadows & Butler's, at least in terms of cost.

Issues therefore arise about the extent to which plants (and, indeed, divisions) should be allowed a 'free reign' in respect of their new technology proposals, and, conversely, about the extent to which control and/or intervention is advisable from above the plant level (for example, in order to have compatible systems across plants/ divisions/corporate levels, which are thereby able to talk to each other). This sort of analysis would benefit from knowledge gained from the centralization versus decentralization/divisionalization experience and debate, but it is too far away from our concerns to be taken up here.[4] Finally, it may be noted that although it was not possible in the research project reported upon in this book to interview managers at the corporate or divisional level, it is probably safe to assume that different views on the same new technology adoption and introduction would have been forthcoming if we had, to judge by the Warwick survey of multi-establishment organizations.[5]

Internal contexts

What, then, of internal contextual developments? From the variety of aspects of such contexts which have been considered, we shall

Conclusion   231

select for brief discussion here just three: (1) changes and developments in managerial style and employee representation, (2) labour flexibility, and (3) personnel management.

Managerial style and employee representation

In so far as the four case study organizations are concerned, there has been little, if any, change in the institutions of industrial relations and the level of employee representation over the six or seven-year period from 1986/7, yet the (senior) managerial approach towards employees has shown some notable changes in three of the organizations. At the Bramley Building Society there is a very low level of union membership, but then, this was always the case. At the Park Hill society the level of Staff Association membership has actually increased by around 20 per cent, but even in this organization there cannot be said to be any significant collective representation of staff – a situation no different from that found in 1986/7. In addition, we noted earlier that the conservative, risk-averse, paternalistic culture has been modified, if not altogether abandoned, in favour of – what? Perhaps it is too early to say, but we talked in Chapter 5 of the 'new' culture having a stronger performance and measurement orientation, more flexibility, more focus on outputs and the customer. The practices and attitudes inherited from the past do not always sit easily with the emerging performance/results ideology of the 1990s, Yet, at the same time, there was awareness (see Chapter 5, for example) that there is something desirable to be retained from that past. At Meadows & Butler there had been little change in the institutions of industrial relations and employee representation, yet a significant change in the nature of the management–employee relationship had occurred. To borrow some terminology from a debate of the mid-1980s, it can be expressed as a reassertion of management's 'right to manage', or, to put the matter slightly differently, as an intensification of management (direct) control.[6] Don Ltd was the only organization to show no notable change on any of these dimensions.

Labour flexibility

During the original period of research this issue was explicitly on the agenda of only one of the organizations: Don Ltd. That company had a long history of labour flexibility, particularly of the functional variety, which could be traced to the green-field origins of the plant, such that even at that time flexibility (or 'versatility', as they preferred to call it) was nothing new or remarkable. So, far from Don Ltd moving towards or trying to achieve 'full flexibility' in subsequent years, whatever that might mean, in the opinion of the Personnel Manager (interviewed in December 1993) the company had attained as much flexibility as it needed. If employees were flexed any more it was likely that certain organizational benefits, such as the deployment of specialist knowledge, would be lost. To borrow from Clark, the reality of practice was that 'limited flexibility equalled full flexibility'.[7]

Of the other case study organizations, functional labour flexibility was either being explicitly practised by 1993 (Bramley Building Society) or was on management's agenda. (Of course, it is well known that building societies – and other retail financial organizations, for that matter – had long had numerical labour flexibility in the form of part-time staff in the branch networks.) Meadows & Butler did not have a strategy of moving towards functional labour flexibility, but under the new managerial regime the company 'reserved the right' to adopt it on a piecemeal basis as and when it suited them, or, to put it another way, 'when business conditions required it'.

As a final comment on the changing internal contexts of the organizations we have been studying, let us turn to the practice of personnel management.

Personnel management

Taking the building societies first, we saw that during the original adoption of new technology in the early to mid-1980s personnel specialist involvement was limited and came late in the day, towards the end of this phase, albeit there was evidence that thereafter involvement increased (particularly at the Bramley society). It was interesting to discover that during the second major wave of new technology adoption in the 1990s the involvement of Personnel was equally, if not more, restricted. At the Park Hill society, adoption was overseen by senior managers from the departments affected and was progressed in teams led by a full-time project manager, the teams consisting of the users and other staff as appropriate on a part-time basis. It was only in the latter capacity that one *might* find personnel specialist involvement, for example if training was perceived by the full-time members of the team as an important issue. At the Bramley

Conclusion 233

society the second wave of new technology adoption was also led by the relevant users and line managers, sponsored by the Operations (and not the IS) Department, with training provided by operations staff and not by personnel specialists. This is just one illustration of how personnel specialists have been marginalized in the society in recent years (see Chapter 5 for other examples), Yet it would appear that there have been opportunities for them to take a more central role, for the organizational and technological changes have been recognized within the society as having significant people/staffing implications. Personnel *considerations* are higher on the organizational agenda, but they are being addressed by and through executive and line management rather than the personnel function. Notwithstanding that many of the elements of human resource management are in place in the society, the label was not used. This was despite the fact that the ex-Personnel Manager, now General Manager, Operations, was very much aware of the HRM debate – indeed, this manager came close to arguing that it was the personnel specialists who were getting in the way of the organization embracing HRM more fully!)

Of the engineering companies, Meadows & Butler had no history of personnel specialist involvement either in technical change or, indeed, in the management of the firm more generally, and this remained the case in the 1990s. Whilst it therefore meant that the people issues connected with new technology adoption and introduction were handled by executive and line managers, there was little evidence of the company operating in an HRM mode, explicitly or implicitly. At Don Ltd, on the other hand, there *was* a history of personnel specialist involvement in technical change – through a deliberately low-key strategy – and this organization (like the Bramley Building Society) was also avoiding use of the HRM label, despite the fact that it had a good number of the elements, as defined by HRM commentators, in place. The current Personnel Manager preferred to retain that title.[8]

Adoption content

This, of course, centres on the particular form taken by the new technology, but we have found that it is impossible to study or talk sensibly about the content of new technology adoption without also considering the social, economic and financial, managerial and organizational content, changes and issues which form the context of, and are connected with, that particular technical content. It *is* important, however, to know of the technology *per se*, for it can make a difference. (Remember the discussion of 'engineering systems' in Chapter 1, and recall the detail provided in the case study chapters on this matter.) We talked of a 'constellation' of objectives for new technology adoption and a variety of possible strategies for achieving those objectives. We also talked of how the particular objectives and strategies (if, indeed, it is justifiable to talk of strategies at all) which have been chosen are very much the result of who has participated in the objective-setting and strategy-formulation process. This immediately prompted us to ask, 'Who has *not* been involved in the process, and therefore not had an opportunity to contribute to the formulation of the objectives and strategies? Why not, and with what consequences?' Much support was found for Buchanan and Boddy's findings from their own studies that technical change triggers processes of organizational decision-making in which strategic choices emerge.[9] The element of choice, in a variety of senses – technical, organizational, in relation to labour control and skill possibilities, *vis-à-vis* the process of adoption itself, etc. – was found to be of central significance in terms of which particular choices were made out of the range presenting themselves to the actors involved. Indeed, were they aware that a choice existed? To talk about these matters is to move on to issues to do with adoption *processes*, so let us conclude with a few observations on this matter.

Adoption processes, and to conclude

Whilst there are undoubtedly choices to be made with regard to the processes of adoption of new technology (as well as regarding objectives and strategies), they are not completely open-ended choices. First of all, to make a choice you need to be involved, and we have seen plenty of instances throughout the book where many of the actors were not involved – employees and certain managers/staff specialists alike. Secondly, that choice is exercised in an existing intra- and inter-organizational context which can act as a constraint upon choice. To take just one example from the case studies, the Engineering Manager at Meadows & Butler felt compelled (as indeed he was!) to justify the CAD proposal in quantitative terms which achieved the required pay-back period stipulated by the company. Yet, like the Finance Director, he recognized that it was the qualitative (especially the strategic) benefits which were crucial, and many of these did not lend themselves to quantification. Political and social skills, including an understanding of the culture of the organization (for example, what can and cannot be done, how to 'dress' a proposal up) can be as significant to the outcome of the process as any intrinsic merits of the proposal itself.

We have also seen that there can be differences of view and emphasis about what is important and what should be done, not just between managers and employees/users but between managers and staff or technical specialists. These differences are resolved (if they are resolved at all) through the actors working within the organization's political system. But in order to exercise power you need either to have it in the first place (and to retain it) or to attain it. Bramley Building Society's Personnel Manager during the 1980s had been successful in building a power base, and we saw how the influence of personnel specialists upon the new technology adoption process increased over that time period. By 1993 he had moved into Operations, and the personnel specialist contribution to the new wave of technical change had waned.

The success (however it may be defined) of the new technology adoption process therefore depends upon the appropriateness and quality of the non-technological changes which go hand in hand with the technical changes, and upon the social, economic and organizational contexts into which that technology is in due course introduced. There is much to be said, then, not only for studying new technology adoption through an interdisciplinary perspective, but also for managing the process of its adoption in a way which is sensitive to, and knowledgeable about, the multi-faceted nature of new technology.

Notes

1 INTRODUCTION

1. A. Huczynski and D. Buchanan (1991) *Organizational Behaviour: an Introductory Text* (second edition), London: Prentice-Hall, p. 329.
2. For a detailed discussion of these issues see A. Friedman and D. Cornford (1989) *Computer Systems Development: History, Organization and Implementation*, Chichester: Wiley.
3. For a recent overview of the diffusion of new technology see I. McLoughlin and J. Clark (1994) *Technological Change at Work* (second edition), Buckingham: Open University Press.
4. Friedman and Cornford, *Computer Systems Development*.
5. J. Clark, I. McLoughlin, H. Rose and R. King (1988) *The Process of Technological Change: New Technology and Social Choice in the Workplace*, Cambridge: Cambridge University Press. Definition taken from J. Clark (1993) 'Personnel management, human resource management and technical change', in J. Clark (ed.), *Human Resource Management and Technical Change*, London: Sage, p. 13.
6. See D. Preece (1991) 'The whys and wherefores of new technology adoption', *Management Decision* 29 (1).
7. For an exposition and discussion of the change agent concept see D. Buchanan and D. Boddy (1992) *The Expertise of the Change Agent*, London: Prentice-Hall.
8. This issue has been discussed by myself and others in detail in Clark, *Human Resource Management*.
9. See, for example, J. Oakland (1993) *Total Quality Management: the Route to Improving Performance* (second edition), Oxford: Butterworth-Heinemann.
10. R. Whipp and P. Clark (1986) *Innovation and the Auto Industry*, London: Frances Pinter, p. 44.
11. A. M. Pettigrew (1985) *The Awakening Giant: Continuity and Change in ICI*, Oxford: Blackwell; A. M. Pettigrew and R. Whipp (1991) *Managing Change for Competitive Success*, Oxford: Blackwell; A. M. Pettigrew (ed.) (1988) *The Management of Strategic Change*, Oxford: Blackwell.

12 M. Marchington and R. Loveridge (1983) 'Management decision-making and shopfloor participation', in K. Thurley and S. Wood (eds), *Industrial Relations and Management Strategy*, Cambridge: Cambridge University Press, p. 78.

2 ADOPTING NEW TECHNOLOGY: MANAGERIAL STRATEGIES

1 This tripartite schema is, of course, only one of many which could be adopted. Davis, as another example, identifies four main types of strategy relevant to AMT: technology, manufacturing, marketing and human resource. See D. Davis (1986) 'Integrating technological, manufacturing, marketing, and human resource strategies', in D. Davis and associates (eds), *Managing Technological Innovation: Organizational Strategies for Implementing Advanced Manufacturing Technologies*, San Francisco: Jossey-Bass.
2 See, for example, M. E. Porter (1980) *Competitive Strategy*, New York: Free Press; M. E. Porter (1985) *Competitive Advantage: Creating and Sustaining Superior Performance*, New York: Free Press; G. S. Day (1986) *Analysis for Strategic Market Decisions*, St Paul, Minn.: West Publishing; R. Mansfield (1986) *Company Strategy and Organisational Design*, Beckenham: Croom Helm; H. F. Gospel and C. R. Littler (eds) (1983) *Managerial Strategies and Industrial Relations*, London: Heinemann; K. Ohmae (1982) *The Mind of the Strategist: the Art of Japanese Business*, London: McGraw-Hill; T. J. Peters and R. H. Waterman (1982) *In Search of Excellence: Lessons from America's Best Run Companies*, New York: Harper & Row; A. D. Chandler (1982) *Strategy and Structure*, Cambridge, Mass.: MIT Press.
3 K. Thurley and S. Wood (1983) 'Business strategy and industrial relations strategy', in K. Thurley and S. Wood (eds) *Industrial Relations and Management Strategy*, Cambridge: Cambridge University Press, p. 197.
4 J. Child, cited in W. Currie (1989) *Managerial Strategy for New Technology*, Aldershot: Avebury, p. 185. See also J. Child (1985) 'Managerial strategies, new technology and the labour process', in D. Knights, H. Willmott and D. Collinson (eds), *Job Redesign*, Aldershot: Gower.
5 M. J. Earl (1989) *mAnagement Strategies for Information Technology*, Hemel Hempstead: Prentice-Hall.
6 A. Jones and T. Webb (1987) 'Introducing computer integrated manufacturing', *Journal of General Management*, 12 (4): 60.
7 J. R. Kimberly (1986) 'The organizational context of technological innovation', in Davis *et al.* (eds), *Managing Technological Innovation*, pp. 39–40.
8 Currie, *Managerial Strategy*, p. 46.
9 Ibid., p. 3.
10 D. Boddy and D. Buchanan (1986) *Managing New Technology*, Oxford: Blackwell; D. J. Hickson, R. J. Butler, D. Cray, G. R. Mallory and

D. C. Wilson (1985) 'Comparing 150 decision processes', in J. M. Pennings (ed.), *Organization Strategy and Change*, San Francisco: Jossey-Bass; D. J. Hickson, D. Cray, G. R. Mallory and D. C. Wilson (1986) *Top Decisions: Strategic Decision Making in Organizations*, Oxford: Blackwell. Interestingly, out of the 150 strategic decisions taken by the top managers studied by Hickson *et al.* in their thirty UK organizations, twenty-three concerned process technology (for example, whether to invest in new assets and facilities to enhance competitiveness). This was the single most important category of decision. In addition, there were twenty-eight decisions to add to or modify the organization's products or services. Thus, clearly, technological innovation was a key aspect of strategic decision-making.
11 Currie, *Managerial Strategy*, p. 4.
12 Ibid., p. 199.
13 R. Coombs and A. Richards (1991) 'Technologies, products and firms' strategies, Part 1, A framework for analysis', *Technology Analysis and Strategic Management* 3 (1): 80.
14 'May' because even the best laid plans can come unstuck.
15 J. Kelly and S. Wood (1983) 'Taylorism and the recession', London School of Economics (mimeo).
16 S. G. Rothwell (1984) 'Company employment policies and new technology in manufacturing and service sectors', in M. Warner (ed.), *Microprocessors, Manpower and Society*, Aldershot: Gower, p. 119.
17 M. Rose and B. Jones (1985) 'Managerial strategy and trade union responses in work reorganization schemes at establishment level', in Knights *et al.*, *Job Redesign*, pp. 82–3, 91. They define strategy as 'a planned and co-ordinated plan [*sic*] of detailed objectives and implementation' (p. 90).
18 D. Marsden, T. Morris, P. Willman and S. Wood (1985) *The Car Industry: Labour Relations and Industrial Adjustment*, London: Tavistock, p. 35.
19 C. Clegg and N. Kemp (1986) 'Information technology: personnel, "where are you?"', *Personnel Review* 15 (1): 13.
20 J. H. Love and J. Walker (1986) 'Problems of new technology deployment in the mechanical engineering and printing industries: a case study', in C. A. Voss (ed.), *Managing Advanced Manufacturing Technology*, Bedford and Berlin: IFS and Springer-Verlag, p. 152.
21 W. N. Shaw *et al.* (1986) 'Implementing new technology in an engineering company – an ongoing saga?', in Voss, *Managing Advanced Manufacturing Technology*, p. 201.
22 Rothwell, 'Company employment policies', pp. 118–19.
23 J. Bessant (1983) 'Management and manufacturing innovation: the case of information technology', in G. Winch (ed.), *Information Technology in Manufacturing Processes: Case Studies in Technological Change*, London: Rossendale, p. 16.
24 See, for example, P. Thompson and E. Bannon (1985) *Working the System: the Shop Floor and New Technology*, London: Pluto Press; I. McLoughlin, H. Rose and J. Clark (1985) 'Managing the introduction of new technology', *Omega* 13 (4). See p. 78 of this volume for

an outline of McLoughlin *et al.*'s argument for sub-strategies. Storey has observed that problems still remain with the sub-strategy concept, in particular its ambiguity: J. Storey (1987) 'The management of new office technology: choice, control and social structure in the insurance industry', *Journal of Management Studies* 24 (1).
25 Thompson and Bannon, p. 3.
26 Ibid.
27 A. Friedman (1985) 'Managerial strategies, activities, techniques and technology: towards a complex theory of the labour process', paper presented to the Third Annual Conference, Organization and Control of the Labour Process, University of Manchester Institute of Science and Technology, April, p. 8. See also A. Friedman (1989) 'Management strategies, activities, techniques and technology: towards a complex theory of the labour process', in D. Knights and H. Willmott (eds), *Labour Process Theory*, London: Macmillan.
28 A. D. Chandler (1982) *Strategy and Structure*, Cambridge, Mass.: MIT Press.
29 R. Whipp and P. Clark (1986) *Innovation and the Auto Industry*, London: Frances Pinter, p. 7.
30 For an updating on Rover from one of the authors see P. Clark and C. De Bresson (1990) 'Innovation-design and innovation poles', in R. Loveridge and M. Pitt (eds), *The Strategic Management of Technological Innovation*, Chichester: Wiley.
31 H. Scarbrough (1986) 'The politics of technological change at BL', in O. Jacobi, R. Jessop, H. Kastendiek and M. Regini (eds), *Technological Change, Rationalisation and Industrial Relations*, Beckenham: Croom Helm, p. 95.
32 P. Willman and G. Winch (1985) *Innovation and Management Control: Labour Relations at BL Cars*, Cambridge: Cambridge University Press, p. 16.
33 Scarbrough, 'The politics of technological change', p. 114.
34 H. Scarbrough, R. Lannon and R. Hamilton (1986) 'Strategy for information technology: one step beyond', *Industrial Management and Data Systems*, January/February: 2–4.
35 J. E. Ettlie (1984) 'Implementation strategy for manufacturing innovations', in M. Warner (ed.), *Microprocessors, Manpower and Society*, Aldershot: Gower.
36 M. Earl (1987) 'Formulating information technology strategies', in N. Piercy (ed.), *Management Information Systems: the Technology Challenge*, Beckenham: Croom Helm.
37 M. Porter (1985) 'Technology and competitive advantage', *Journal of Business Strategy* 5 (3). See also P. Grindley (1991) 'Turning technology into competitive advantage', *Business Strategy Review* 2 (1); K. Pavitt (1990) 'What we know about the strategic management of technology', *California Management Review* 32 (3); G. R. Greenhalgh (1991) *Manufacturing Strategy: Formulation and Implementation*, Sydney: Addison-Wesley.
38 See K. Pavitt (1986) 'Technology, innovation and strategic management',

in J. McGee and H. Thomas (eds), *Strategic Management Research: a European Perspective*, Chichester: Wiley.
39 C. A. Voss (1986) 'Implementing manufacturing technology – a manufacturing strategy perspective', in Voss (ed.) *Managing Advanced Manufacturing Technology*, p. 95. On the role of manufacturing in organizational strategy see T. J. Hill (1985) *Manufacturing Strategy*, London: Macmillan; W. Skinner (1978) *Manufacturing in the Corporate Strategy*, Chichester: Wiley; E. S. Buffa (1984) *Meeting the Competitive Challenge*, Homewood, Ill.: Dow-Jones, Irwin; R. H. Hayes and S. C. Wheelwright (1984) *Restoring our Competitive Edge: Competing through Manufacturing*, Chichester: Wiley; R. J. Schonberger (1982) *Japanese Manufacturing Techniques: Nine Hidden Lessons in Simplicity*, New York: Free Press; R. J. Schonberger (1986) *World Class Manufacturing*, New York: Free Press.
40 W. Skinner (1984) 'Operations technology: blind spot in strategic management', *Interfaces* 14 (1): 117.
41 D. Buchanan and D. Boddy (1984) 'Information technology and productivity myths and realities', *Omega* 12 (3): 233–9. See also D. Buchanan and D. Boddy (1983) *Organisations in the Computer Age: Technological Imperatives and Strategic Choice*, Aldershot: Gower, p. 237.
42 Boddy and Buchanan, *Managing New Technology*, p. 6.
43 For example, Ettlie, 'Implementation strategy'; Voss, 'Implementing manufacturing technology'.
44 J. D. Goldhar and M. Jelinek (1985) 'Computer integrated flexible manufacturing: organisational, economic and strategic implications', *Interfaces* 15 (3): 101.
45 Ibid., p. 102.
46 ACARD (1983) *New Opportunities in Manufacturing: the Management of Technology*, London: HMSO.
47 D. Gerwin and J. C. Tarondeau, 'Uncertainty and the innovation process for computer-integrated manufacturing systems: four case studies', in E. Rhodes and D. Wield (eds) (1985) *Implementing New Technologies: Choice, Decision and Change in Manufacturing*, Oxford: Blackwell, p. 396.
48 Ibid., p. 395. See also L. Gunter (1990) 'Strategic options for CIM integration', in M. Warner, W. Wobbe and P. Brodner (eds), *New Technology and Manufacturing Management: Strategic Choices for Flexible Production Systems*, Chichester: Wiley.
49 B. Hochstreasser and C. Griffiths (1991) *Controlling IT Investment: Strategy and Management*, London: Chapman & Hall, p. 32.
50 Ibid., p. 150.
51 Ibid., pp. 150–1.
52 H. F. Gospel, 'Managerial structure and strategies: an introduction', in H. F. Gospel and C. R. Littler (eds) (1983) *Managerial Strategies and Industrial Relations*, London: Heinemann.
53 Ibid., pp. 12, 14, 17.
54 Ibid., p. 11.
55 See Friedman 'Managerial strategies', and A. Friedman (1977) *Industry*

and Labour: Class Struggle at Work and Monopoly Capitalism, London: Macmillan.
56 Friedman, 'Managerial strategies', p. 3.
57 Marsden *et al.*, *The Car Industry*, p. 75. Walton has illustrated the implications of control and commitment strategies for, *inter alia*, job design, organization structure and remuneration policies. He also draws on US case studies to support his argument for management moving from the former to the latter strategy. See R. E. Walton (1985) 'From control to commitment in the workplace', *Harvard Business Review* 63 (2).
58 G. Sewell and B. Wilkinson (1992) 'Someone to watch over me: surveillance, discipline and the just-in-time labour process' *Sociology* 26 (2): 271.
59 Marsden *et al.*, *The Car Industry*; Willman and Winch, *Innovation and Management Control*.
60 Marsden *et al.*, *The Car Industry*, p. 118. They go on to describe this strategy as a 'co-operative one, in a context of long-standing institutions and resistance from trade unions'.
61 Willman and Winch, *Innovation and Management Control*; Marsden *et al.*, *The Car Industry*.
62 Marsden *et al.*, *The Car Industry*, p. 179.
63 J. Northcott, M. Fogarty and M. Trevor (1985) *Chips and Jobs: Acceptance of New Technology at Work*, London: Policy Studies Institute, p. 29.
64 Ibid., p. 37.
65 Ibid., p. 36.
66 J. Storey, 'The phoney war? New office technology: organisation and control', in D. Knights and H. Willmott (eds), *Managing the Labour Process*, Aldershot: Gower, p. 61. See also Storey, 'The management of new office technology'.
67 Storey, 'The phoney war?', p. 64.
68 Loveridge and Pitt, *The Strategic Management*, p. 14. See also B. Jones, 'New production technology and work roles: a paradox of flexibility versus strategic control?', in Loveridge and Pitt, *Strategic Management*.

3 WHY IS NEW TECHNOLOGY INTRODUCED?

1 S. Hill (1981) *Competition and Control at Work*, London: Heinemann, p. 122.
2 H. Braverman (1974) *Labor and Monopoly Capital*, New York: Monthly Review Press.
3 A. Sorge, G. Hartman, M. Warner and I. Nicholas (1983) *Microelectronics and Manpower in Manufacturing*, Aldershot: Gower.
4 D. Buchanan and D. Boddy (1983) *Organisations in the Computer Age*, Aldershot: Gower, pp. 243, 47, 51.
5 D. Buchanan (1983) 'Using the new technology: management objectives and organisational choices', *European Management Journal* 1 (2): 71, 72. See also D. Buchanan (1986) 'Management objectives in technical change', in D. Knights and H. Willmott (eds), *Managing the Labour Process*, Aldershot: Gower.

6 A. S. Carrie and S. K. Banerjee (1984) 'Approaches to implementing manufacturing information systems', *Omega* 12 (3): 251.
7 E. Arnold and P. Senker (1982) *Designing the Future – the Implications of CAD Interactive Graphics for Employment and Skills in the British Engineering Industry*, EITB Occasional Paper, Watford: EITB, p. 6.
8 J. Bessant (1982) *Microprocessors in Production Processes*, London: Policy Studies Institute, pp. 20–4.
9 E. Arnold (1983) 'Information technology as a technological fix: computer aided design in the United Kingdom', in G. Winch (ed.), *Information Technology in Manufacturing Processes: Case Studies in Technological Change*, London: Rossendale.
10 B. Wilkinson (1983) *The Shopfloor Politics of New Technology*, London: Heinemann.
11 Bessant, *Microprocessors*.
12 Arnold and Senker, *Designing the Future*, p. 6.
13 J. E. Nahapiet (1984) 'Assessing costs and benefits in system design and selection', in H. J. Otway and M. Peltu (eds), *The Managerial Challenge of New Office Technology*, London: Butterworth, p. 187.
14 Ibid., pp. 191–2.
15 W. W. Daniel and N. Millward (1983) *Workplace Industrial Relations in Britain: the DE/PSI/ESRC Survey*, London: Heinemann; N. Millward and M. Stevens (1986) *British Workplace Insustrial Relations, 1980–84: the DE/ESRC/PSI/ACAS Surveys*, Aldershot: Gower; N. Millward, M. Stevens, D. Smart and W. R. Hawes (1992) *Workplace Industrial Relations in Transition: the ED/ESRC/PSI/ACAS Surveys*, Aldershot: Dartmouth.
16 W. W. Daniel (1987) *Workplace Industrial Relations and Technical Change*, London: Frances Pinter/Policy Studies Institute.
17 Ibid., p. 279.
18 Ibid., chapter VIII.
19 Ibid.; E. Batstone and S. Gourlay (1986) *Unions, Unemployment and Innovation*, Oxford: Blackwell; C. Gill (1985) *Work, Unemployment and New Technology*, Cambridge: Polity Press; W. W. Daniel and N. Millward (1993) 'Personnel management and technical change: the findings from the WIRS Series', in J. Clark (ed.), *Human Resource Management and Technical Change*, London: Sage.
20 J. Bessant, E. Braun and R. Moseley (1980) 'Microelectronics in manufacturing industry: the rate of diffusion', in T. Forester (ed.), *The Microelectronics Revolution*, Oxford: Blackwell.
21 G. Motteram and J. Sizer (1986) 'Costing of advanced manufacturing technology at Rolls-Royce, Derby manufacturing: a case study', in C. A. Voss (ed.), *Managing Advanced Manufacturing Technology*, Bedford: IFS, and Berlin: Springer.
22 Bessant, *Microprocessors*, p. 11.
23 Ibid., p. 20.
24 Ibid., p. 21.
25 A. Davies (1987) 'Organisational aspects of management information systems change', in N. Piercy (ed.) *Management Information Systems: the Technology Challenge*, Beckenham: Croom Helm, pp. 82–3.

26 W. Currie (1989) *Managerial Strategy for New Technology*, Aldershot: Avebury, p. xvi.
27 C. Smith (1985) 'Design Engineers and the Capitalist Firm', paper presented to the Third Annual Conference, Organization and Control of the Labour Process, University of Manchester Institute of Science and Technology, April.
28 Buchanan and Boddy, *Organisations in the Computer Age*, p. 46; G. C. White (1983) 'Technological changes and the content of jobs', *Employment Gazette*, August: 330; J. Fleck, 'Robotics in manufacturing organisations' in Winch, *Information Technology*, pp. 48–9.
29 J. Storey (1987) 'The management of new office technology: choice, control and social structure in the insurance industry', *Journal of Management Studies* 24 (1).
30 Arnold, 'Information technology', pp. 35–6.
31 Wilkinson, *Shopfloor Politics*.
32 Ibid., pp. 90–1.
33 National Computing Centre (1986) *The Impact of Office Technology*, Manchester: NCC.
34 J. Clark, A. Jacobs, R. King and H. Rose (1984) 'New technology, industrial relations and divisions within the workforce', *Industrial Relations Journal* 15 (3): 37.
35 Arnold and Senker, *Designing the Future*, pp. 5–6.
36 White, 'Technological changes'.
37 J. Bessant, 'Management and manufacturing innovation', in Winch, *Information Technology*, p. 17.
38 Buchanan and Boddy, *Organisations in the Computer Age*, p. 46. See also p. 243: machine monitoring and control of key process variables were objectives in two of their case study companies (United Biscuits and Ciba-Geigy).
39 Ibid., pp. 243–4.
40 D. A. Preece (1986) 'Organisations, flexibility and new technology' in Voss, *Managing Advanced Manufacturing Technology*.
41 For an overview of labour flexibility see Advisory, Conciliation and Arbitration Service (1988) *Labour Flexibility in Britain: the 1987 ACAS Survey*, Occasional Paper No. 41, London: ACAS; J. Atkinson (1985) *Flexibility, Uncertainty and Manpower Management*, Report No. 89, Brighton: University of Sussex, Institute of Manpower Studies; J. Atkinson (1987) 'Flexibility or fragmentation? The United Kingdom labour market in the eighties', *Labour and Society* 12, January; J. Atkinson and N. Meager (1986) 'Is flexibility just a flash in the pan?' *Personnel Management*, September; Incomes Data Services (1988) *Flexible Working*, IDS Study No. 407, London: IDS. For a critical treatment of the flexibility issue see P. Dawson and J. Webb (1989) 'New production arrangements: the totally flexible cage?' *Work, Employment and Society* 3 (2); A. Elger (1987) 'Flexible futures? New technology and the contemporary transformation of work', *Work, Employment and Society* 1 (4); J. MacInnes (1987) *Thatcherism at Work*, Milton Keynes: Open University Press; A. Pollert (ed.) (1991) *Farewell to Flexibility?* Oxford: Blackwell; A. Elger (1990) 'Technical innovation and work

reorganization in British manufacturing in the 1980s: continuity, intensification or transformation?' *Work, Employment and Society*, special issue, May.
42 For example, Atkinson, *Flexibility, Uncertainty and Manpower Management*; Atkinson and Meager, 'Is flexibility a flash in the pan?'
43 For example, MacInnes, *Thatcherism at Work*; Pollert, 'The orthodoxy of flexibility', in Pollert, 'Farewell to flexibility?'
44 For the amended IMS position see Atkinson and Meager, 'Is flexibility a flash in the pan?'
45 Sorge et al., *Microelectronics and Manpower*, p. 39.
46 Ibid., p. 155.
47 Bessant, *Microprocessors*, pp. 21–3. Other important objectives found by Bessant in his survey include: (1) improvements in process control and machine operation, (2) improvements in reliability and maintenance, (3) improvements in quality, (4) improved information systems. Examples of each of these improvements include working to finer tolerances, reduced cycle times and increased machine utilization for (1) above; modular design, permitting easier maintenance and replacement, longer intervals between failure of electronic elements, and self-diagnostic routines within the system for (2); monitoring raw materials input and computerized testing for materials input, and computerized testing, for (3); and direct display of information (for instance, on VDUs), analysis of data and transmission of monitored data to remote locations such as a central control room, for (4); Buchanan and Boddy, *Organisations in the Computer Age*, pp. 243–4; White, 'Technological changes', p. 330.
48 Policy Studies Institute (1982) *Microelectronics in Industry*, London: PSI.
49 R. G. Sell (1980) *Microelectronics and the Quality of Working Life*, Occasional Paper No. 17, London: Work Research Unit.
50 Arnold, 'Information technology', in Winch, *Information Technology*, pp. 35–6.
51 Fleck, 'Robotics in manufacturing organisations', in Winch, *Information Technology*, p. 48.
52 Buchanan and Boddy, *Organisations in the Computer Age*, p. 243.
53 Smith, 'Design engineers', pp. 19–20.
54 Wilkinson, *Shopfloor Politics*.
55 Ibid., p. 68.
56 Ibid., pp. 82–3.
57 Ibid., pp. 83–4.
58 Sorge et al., *Microelectronics and Manpower*, p. 78.
59 Ibid., p. 84.
60 Arnold, 'Information technology', in Winch, *Information Technology*, p. 39. See also R. S. Kaplan (1983) 'Measuring manufacturing performance: a new challenge for managerial accounting research', *Accounting Review* LVIII (4); R. S. Kaplan (1986) 'Must CIM be justified by faith alone?' *Harvard Business Review* 64 (2).
61 P. L. Primrose, G. Creamer and R. Leonard (1985) 'Identifying and quantifying the "company-wide" benefits of CAD within the structure of a comprehensive investment programme', in E. Rhodes and D. Wield

(eds), *Implementing New Technologies: Choice, Decision and Change in Manufacturing*, Oxford: Blackwell. See also Kaplan, 'Must CIM be justified?'; I. O. Angell and S. Smithson (1990) 'Managing information technology: a crisis of confidence?', *European Management Journal* 8 (1).
62 Cited in H. Downing (1983) 'On being automated', *ASLIB Proceedings* 35 (1): 40.
63 Ibid., pp. 38–51.
64 A. Davies (1986) *Industrial Relations and New Technology*, Beckenham: Croom Helm, pp. 193, 138.
65 D. Buchanan and J. Bessant (1985) 'Failure, uncertainty and control: the role of operators in a computer integrated production system', *Journal of Management Studies* 22 (3): 299.
66 Braverman, *Labor and Monopoly Capital*, p. 193.
67 Ibid., p. 195.
68 See, A. L. Friedman (1977) *Industry and Labour: Class Struggle at Work and Monopoly Capitalism*, London: Macmillan.
69 Some of the main post-Braverman texts are: Friedman, *Industry and Labour*; R. Edwards (1979) *Contested Terrain: the Transformation of the Workplace in the Twentieth Century*, London: Heinemann; A. Zimbalist (ed.) (1979) *Case Studies on the Labor Process*, New York: Monthly Review Press; S. Wood (ed.) (1982) *The Degradation of Work? Skill, Deskilling and the Labour Process*, London: Hutchinson; J. Storey (1983) *Managerial Prerogative and the Question of Control*, London: Routledge; Wilkinson, *Shopfloor Politics*; M. Burawoy (1979) *Manufacturing Consent: Changes in the Labour Process under Monopoly Capitalism*, London: University of Chicago Press; C. R. Littler (1982) *The Development of the Labour Process in Capitalist Societies: a Comparative Study of the Transformation of Work Organisation in Britain, Japan and the USA*, London: Heinemann; P. Thompson (1989) *The Nature of Work*, London: Macmillan; S. Wood (1989) *The Transformation of Work? Skill, Flexibility and the Labour Process*, London: Unwin Hyman. An exposition of the argument for the third position as it relates to technology can be found in J. Clark, I. McLoughlin, H. Rose and R. King (1988) *The Process of Technological Change: New Technology and Social Choice in the Workplace*, Cambridge: Cambridge University Press. Position 2 has been influentially argued by Buchanan: 'The implications of technical change depend on why and how new technology is applied – contingent on the objectives of managers in organizational positions from which they define why and how technologies are used.' See D. Buchanan (1986) 'Management objectives in technical change', in D. Knights and H. Willmott (eds), *Managing the Labour Process*, Aldershot: Gower.
70 H. H. Rosenbrock (1979) 'The re-direction of technology', research paper, London: Council for Science and Society; H. Shaiken (1979) 'Numerical control of work: workers and automation in the Computer Age', *Radical America* 13 (6). See also B. Burnes (1988) 'New technology and job design: the case of CNC', *New Technology, Work and Employment* 3 (2).

71 Thompson, *The Nature of Work*, p. 113.
72 Edwards, *Contested Terrain*, p. 112.
73 For a recent illustration of how new technology can be used to centralize and extend managerial control see G. Sewell and B. Wilkinson (1992) 'Someone to watch over me: surveillance, discipline and the just-in-time labour process', *Sociology* 26 (2). For a more general treatment of the new technology and control issue in organizations see J. Child (1987) 'Organizational design for advanced manufacturing technology', in T. Wall, C. Clegg and N. Kemp (eds) *The Human Side of Advanced Manufacturing Technology*, Chichester: Wiley, especially pp. 122–4.
74 Zimbalist, *Case Studies*, p. xiii.
75 Wilkinson, *Shopfloor Politics*, p. 85.
76 Ibid., p. 90.
77 Ibid., p. 89.
78 Ibid., p. 91.
79 Ibid.
80 Ibid.
81 Thompson, *The Nature of Work*, p. 110.
82 Ibid., p. 109.
83 Littler, *The Development of the Labour Process*, chapter 2, especially pp. 7–11.
84 A. Fox (1974) *Beyond Contract: Work, Power and Trust Relations*, London: Faber, pp. 16, 24–5.
85 Littler, *The Development of the Labour Process*, p. 9.
86 Ibid.
87 D. A. Preece (1984) 'Social aspects and effects of composing machine adoption in the British printing industry', *Journal of the Printing Historical Society* 18: 28. Along with social and political factors, technical developments in the industry, including photocomposition and direct-entry typesetting, have posed a much more serious challenge to the compositors' status, control and conception of skill. See, for example, A. Zimbalist, 'Technology and the labor process in the printing industry', in Zimbalist, *Case Studies*; D. A. Preece (1987) 'New technology and job design – lessons from the print industry?', *Employee Relations* 9 (2). Wilson has also provided a helpful analysis of the varieties of skill involved with CNC machine tools, and the implications for control. See F. Wilson (1988) 'CNC and constraint', in D. Knights and H. Willmott (eds) *New Technology and the Labour Process*, London: Macmillan.
88 C. Wright Mills (1951) *White Collar*, London: Oxford University Press, p. 220.
89 C. R. Littler, *The Development of the Labour Process*, p. 11.
90 D. Lee (1982) 'Beyond deskilling: skill, craft and class', in Wood, *The Degradation of Work?*, p. 148.
91 Littler, 'Deskilling and changing structures of control', in Wood, *The Degradation of Work?*, p. 122.
92 P. Senker (1984) 'Training for automation', in M. Warner (ed.), *Microprocessors, Manpower and Society: a Comparative, Cross-national Approach*, Aldershot: Gower, p. 139. See also P. Thompson

and E. Bannon (1985) *Working the System: the Shop Floor and New Technology*, London: Pluto Press.
93 B. Jones, 'Destruction or redistribution of engineering skills? The case of numerical control', in Wood, *The Degradation of Work?*, p. 179.
94 Ibid., pp. 198–200.
95 P. Kraft, 'The industrialization of computer programming: from programming to "software production"', in Zimbalist, *Case Studies*.
96 R. Crompton and G. Jones (1984) *White Collar Proletariat: Deskilling and Gender in Clerical Work*, London: Macmillan. On the issues of skill and de-skilling in non-manual work see also H. Rolfe (1986) 'Skill, deskilling and new technology in the non-manual labour process', *New Technology, Work and Employment* 1 (1), and S. Smith (1987) 'Information technology in banks: Taylorization or human-centred systems?', *Science and Public Policy* 14 (3).
97 Crompton and Jones, *White Collar Proletariat*, pp. 4, 6, 7.
98 Ibid., p. 48.
99 Ibid., p. 60.
100 Ibid., pp. 73, 77.
101 Ibid., p. 59.
102 Thompson, *The Nature of Work*, pp. 107–8.
103 Lee, 'Beyond de-skilling', in Wood, *The Degradation of Work?*, p. 160.
104 See, for example, Jones, 'Destruction or redistribution?'
105 T. Manwaring and S. Wood (1985) 'The ghost in the labour process', in D. Knights, H. Willmott and D. Collinson (eds), *Job Redesign*, Aldershot: Gower.
106 Wilkinson, *Shopfloor Politics*, pp. 45, 47.
107 Ibid., pp. 45–7.
108 D. F. Noble, 'Social choice in machine design: the case of automatically controlled machine tools', in Zimbalist, *Case Studies*, p. 38.
109 Ibid., p. 49.
110 T. Elger, 'Braverman, capital accumulation and deskilling', in Wood, *The Degradation of Work?*, p. 49.
111 D. Gallie (1978) *In Search of the New Working Class*, Cambridge: Cambridge University Press, p. 90.
112 Elger, 'Braverman', in wood, *The Degradation of Work?*, p. 50.
113 Sorge et al., *Microelectronics and Manpower*, p. 37.
114 See A. Friedman (1990) 'Managerial strategies, activities, techniques and technology: towards a complex theory of the labour process', in D. Knights and H. Willmott (eds), *Labour Process Theory*, London: Macmillan.
115 J. Child (1984) *Organisation: a Guide to Problems and Practice*, London: Harper & Row, chapter 9; Buchanan and Boddy, *Organisations in the Computer Age*; Bessant, 'Management and manufacturing innovation'. See also D. A. Preece (1991) 'The whys and wherefores of new technology adoption', *Management Decision* 29 (1).
116 R. I. Tricker (1980) 'Order or freedom – the ultimate isssue in information systems design', in N. Bjørn-Anderson, *The Human Side of Information Processing*, Amsterdam: North-Holland, p. 155.
117 Ibid., p. 156.
118 Ibid., p. 158.

119 Ibid. For a recent discussion of the centralization/decentralization of control potentiality of IT see B. P. Bloomfield and R. Coombs (1992) 'Information technology, control and power: the centralization and decentralization debate revisited', *Journal of Management Studies* 29 (4).
120 A. G. Hopwood (1983) 'Evaluating the real benefits', in H. J. Otway and M. Peltu (eds), *New Office Technology: Human and Organisational Aspects*, London: Frances Pinter, p. 49.
121 G. Symon and C. W. Clegg (1991) 'Technology-led change: a study of the implementation of CADCAM', *Journal of Occupational Psychology* 64 (4).
122 J. Child (1985) 'Managerial strategies, new technology and the labour process', in D. Knights, H. Willmott and D. Collinson (eds), *Job Redesign: Critical Pespectives on the Labour Process*, Aldershot: Gower.
123 Hopwood, 'Evaluating the real benefits', p. 46.
124 Child, 'Managerial strategies'.
125 Ibid.
126 Ibid.
127 Storey, *Managerial Prerogative*, p. 81.
128 A. Spencer (1981) 'What non-executive directors don't do', *Management Today*, May, p. 51.
129 I. McLoughlin, H. Rose and J. Clark (1984) 'Managing the Introduction of New Technology', paper presented to the annual conference of the British Universities Industrial Relations Association, Oxford University, July.
130 Ibid., p. 1.
131 P. Keen, 'Strategic planning for the new system', in Otway and Peltu, *New Office Technology*.
132 Sorge *et al.*, *Microelectronics and Manpower*, p. 42.
133 D. Buchanan, 'Technological imperatives and strategic choice', in Winch (ed.), *Information Technology*, p. 78.
134 Bessant, 'Management and manufacturing innovation', pp. 15–16.
135 Smith 'Design engineers', p. 21.
136 Buchanan and Boddy, *Organisations in the Computer Age*, p. 51.
137 Ibid., p. 242.
138 C. A. Voss (1984) 'Production/operations management – a key discipline and area for research', *Omega* 12 (3): 315.
139 Storey, 'The management of new office technology', p. 48. See also R. Barras and J. Swann (1984) *The Adoption and Impact of Information Technology in the UK Insurance Industry*, London: Technical Change Centre.
140 Arnold and Senker, *Designing the Future*, p. 7.
141 Ibid., p. 3.

4 ADOPTING NEW TECHNOLOGY: PROCESSES OF INVOLVEMENT

1 For an example of strong advocacy of a participative approach to new technology adoption and introduction see R. Hirscheim (1985) *Office*

Automation: Concepts, Technologies and Issues, London: Addison-Wesley. Some of the problems which can arise from a participative approach are discussed in K. D. Eason (1984) 'Managing technological change', in R. Paton (ed.) *Organizations: Cases, Issues, Concepts*, London: Harper & Row.
2. See, for example, B. C. Twiss (1985) *Non-MSC Research and Initiatives in the Field of Management Development for Technical Change*, Sheffield: Manpower Services Commission.
3. See, for example, S. Rothwell (1985) 'Supervisors and new technology', in E. Rhodes and D. Wield (eds), *Implementing New Technologies: Choice, Decision and Change in Manufacturing*, Oxford: Blackwell; C. Clegg and N. Kemp (1986) 'Information technology: Personnel, Where are you?', *Personnel Review* 15 (1).
4. See, for example, L. Willcocks and D. Mason (1988) 'New technology, human resources and workplace relations – the role of management', *Employee Relations* 10 (6).
5. F. Blackler and C. Brown (1985) 'Evaluation and the impact of information technologies on people in organisations', *Human Relations* 38 (3).
6. J. Child (1985) 'The introduction of new technologies: managerial initiative and union response in British banks', *Industrial Relations Journal* 16 (3): 23.
7. P. Cressey (1985) *The Role of the Parties concerned in the Introduction of New Technology*, Consolidated Report, Shankill, Co. Dublin: European Foundation for the Improvement of Living and Working Conditions, p. 67.
8. G. L. Lee (1986) 'The Adoption of Computer-based Systems in Engineering: managerial strategies and the role of professional engineers', paper presented to fourth annual conference, Organization and Control of the Labour Process, University of Aston, April, p. 16.
9. Ibid., p. 17.
10. P. Marginson, P. Edwards, R. Martin, J. Purcell and K. Sisson (1988) *Beyond the Workplace: Managing Industrial Relations in Multi-plant Enterprises*, Oxford: Blackwell.
11. R. Martin (1988) 'The management of industrial relations and new technology', in Marginson, *Beyond the Workplace*, p. 167.
12. Ibid., p. 168.
13. See D. Preece and M. Harrison (1988) 'The contribution of personnel specialists to technology-related organizational change', *Personnel Review* 17 (1).
14. N. Millward and M. Stevens (1986) *British Workplace Industrial Relations 1980–84: the DE/ESRC/PSI/ACAS Surveys*, Aldershot: Gower; N. Millward, M. Stevens, D. Smart and W. R. Hawes (1992) *Workplace Industrial Relations in Transition: the ED/ESRC/PSI/ACAS Surveys*, Aldershot: Dartmouth; W. W. Daniel (1987) *Workplace Industrial Relations and Technical Change*, London: Frances Pinter/Policy Studies Institute.
15. See Marginson, *Beyond the Workplace*.
16. K. Legge (1993) 'The role of personnel specialists: centrality or

marginalization?' in J. Clark (ed.), *Human Resource Management and Technical Change*, London: Sage.
17 Legge, 'The role of personnel specialists', p. 20.
18 See W. W. Daniel and N. Millward (1993) 'Findings from the Workplace Industrial Relations surveys', in Clark, *Human Resource Management*.
19 G. Sewell and B. Wilkinson (1993) 'Human resource management in "surveillance" companies', in Clark, *Human Resource Management*.
20 Legge, 'The role of personnel specialists', p. 34.
21 See C. Hendry (1993) 'Personnel leadership in technical and human resource change', in Clark, *Human Resource Management*; J. Storey (1992) *Developments in the Management of Human Resources*, Oxford: Blackwell.
22 Legge, 'The role of personnel specialists', p. 41.
23 Storey, *Developments in the Management of Human Resources*, as expressed in Legge, 'The role of personnel specialists', p. 41.
24 Preece and Harrison, 'The contribution of personnel specialists'.
25 D. Preece (1993) 'Human resource specialists and technical change at greenfield sites', in Clark, *Human Resource Management*; J. Clark (1993) 'Full flexibility and self-supervision in an automated factory', in Clark, *Human Resource Management*; Hendry, 'Personnel leadership'.
26 P. Garrahan and P. Stewart (1992) *The Nissan Enigma*, London: Mansell.
27 See Millward *et al.*, *Workplace Industrial Relations in Transition*.
28 For the first study see Cressey, *Role of the Parties*; for the second study see P. Cressey and R. Williams (1990) *Participation in Change: New Technology and the Role of Employee Involvement*, Dublin: European Foundation for the Improvement of Living and Working Conditions, and D. Frohlich, C. Gill and H. Krieger (1991) *Roads to Participation in the European Community? Increasing Prospects of Employee Representative Involvement in Technological Change*, Dublin: European Foundation for the Improvement of Living and Working Conditions. See also C. Gill (1993) 'Technological change and participation in work organization: recent results from a European Community Survey', *International Journal of Human Resource Management* 4 (2).
29 Cressey, *Role of the Parties*, p. 33.
30 Ibid., p. 68.
31 Ibid., p. 72.
32 Ibid., pp. 76–7.
33 C. Gill and H. Krieger (1992) 'The diffusion of participation in new information technology in Europe: survey results', *Economic and Industrial Democracy* 13 (3): 334.
34 Ibid., p. 348.
35 Ibid., pp. 348–50.
36 Ibid., p. 335.
37 Ibid., p. 338.
38 Ibid., p. 339.
39 Ibid., p. 341.
40 Ibid., p. 355.
41 D. Frohlich and H. Krieger (1990) 'Technological change and worker participation in Europe', *New Technology, Work and Employment* 5 (2).

42 Ibid., p. 102.
43 Daniel, *Workplace Industrial Relations and Technical Change*.
44 Millward and Stevens, *British Workplace Industrial Relations*.
45 W. W. Daniel and N. Millward, 'The WIRS surveys', in Clark, *Human Resource Management*, p. 57.
46 See W. W. Daniel and T. Hogarth (1990) 'Worker support for technical change', *New Technology, Work and Employment* 5 (2).
47 See Daniel and Millward, 'The WIRS surveys', pp. 69–74.
48 Ibid., p. 71.
49 Martin, 'The management of industrial relations', in Marginson *et al.*, *Beyond the Workplace*.
50 Daniel and Millward, 'The WIRS surveys', p. 74.
51 A. Davies (1986) *Industrial Relations and New Technology*, Beckenham: Croom Helm.
52 Trades Union Congress (1979) *Employment and Technology*, London: Trades Union Congress.
53 Davies, *Industrial Relations and New Technology*, pp. 97–8.
54 Ibid., p. 94.
55 Ibid., p. 168.
56 Ibid., p. 173.
57 Ibid., pp. 198–200.
58 P. Willman (1986) *New Technology and Industrial Relations: a Review of the Literature*, Research Paper No. 56, London: Department of Employment, p. 47.
59 Child, 'The introduction of new technologies', pp. 24–5.
60 Ibid., p. 26.
61 J. Clark, I. McLoughlin, H. Rose and R. King (1988) *The Process of Technological Change: New Technology and Social Choice in the Workplace*, Cambridge: Cambridge University Press, p. 207.
62 Ibid., p. 213.
63 Ibid.
64 See, for example, Cressey, *Role of the Parties*, pp. 12, 29.
65 Ibid., p. 69.
66 Ibid., p. 72.
67 Ibid., p. 65.
68 B. Wilkinson (1983) *The Shopfloor Politics of New Technology*, London: Heinemann, p. 85.
69 Ibid., p. 91.
70 Ibid., p. 81.
71 See J. Hillage, N. Meager and A. Rajan (1986) 'Technology agreements in practice: the experience so far', Report No. 113, Brighton: Institute of Manpower Studies.
72 J. Bessant (1986) 'Technology agreements head off resistance', *Works Management* 36 (5): 23.
73 Cressey, *Role of the Parties*, p. 11.
74 H. Rush and R. Williams (1984) 'Consultation and change: new technology and manpower in the electronics industry', in M. Warner (ed.), *Microprocessors, Manpower and Society*, Aldershot: Gower, p. 178. See also R. Williams and F. Steward (1985) 'Technology agreements in Great Britain: a survey, 1977–83', *Industrial Relations Journal* 16: 3.

75 *Labour Research* (1983) special issue on new technology, November.
76 R. Williams and R. Moseley (1983) 'Technology Agreements: Consensus, Control and Technical Change in the Workplace', paper presented to the EEC/FAST conference on 'The Transition to an Information Society', Selsdon Park, London.
77 J. Storey (n.d.) 'New Office Technology: Organisation and Response', Occasional Paper No. 4, Nottingham: Trent Business School, p. 36.
78 Ibid., p. 37.
79 Cressey, *Role of the Parties*, p. 70.
80 C. Gill (1985) *Work, Unemployment and the New Technology*, Cambridge: Polity Press, p. 167.
81 M. Dodgson and R. Martin (1987) 'Trade union policies on new technology: facing the challenges of the 1980s', *New Technology, Work and Employment* 2 (1).
82 See E. Batstone and S. Gourlay (1986) *Unions, Unemployment and Innovation*, Oxford: Blackwell; Clark *et al.*, *The Process of Technological Change*; B. Gustavsen (1985) 'Technology and collective agreements: some recent Scandinavian developments', *Industrial Relations Journal* 16 (4); Gill and Krieger, 'The diffusion of participation'.
83 J. Pugh (1983) 'A "culture of change" in the electronics industry', *Employment Gazette*, August, p. 360.
84 NEDO (1983) *The Introduction of New Technology*, London: NEDO. The Employment and Technology Task Force was established by the Electronics Economic Development Committee of the National Economic Development Office (NEDO).
85 Davies, *Industrial Relations and New Technology*; Rush and Williams, 'Consultation and change'; Cressey, *Role of the Parties*.
86 D. E. Guest (1986) 'Workers' participation and personnel policy in the United Kingdom: some case studies', *International Labour Review* 125 (6): see especially p. 690.
87 J. Child, R. Loveridge, J. Harvey and A. Spencer (1984) 'Microelectronics and the quality of employment in services', in P. Marstrand (ed.), *New Technology and the Future of Work and Skills*, London: Frances Pinter, pp. 174, 176.
88 See M. Rose and B. Jones (1985) 'Managerial strategy and trade union responses in work reorganization schemes at establishment level', in D. Knights and D. Collinson (eds) *Job Redesign: Organization and Control of the Labour Process*, Aldershot: Gower, especially p. 99.
89 C. R. Walker and R. H. Guest (1952) *The Man on the Assembly Line*, Cambridge, Mass.: Harvard University Press; C. R. Walker, R. H. Guest and A. N. Turner (1956) *The Foreman on the Assembly Line*, Cambridge, Mass.: Harvard University Press; E. L. Trist and K. W. Bamforth (1951) 'Some social and psychological consequences of the long-wall method of coal getting', *Human Relations* 4 (1).
90 See, for example, E. Mumford and D. Henshall (1979) *A Participative Approach to Computer Systems Design: a Case Study of the Introduction of a new Computer System*, London: Associated Business Press; E. Mumford and M. Weir (1979) *Computer Systems in Work Design – the ETHICS Method*, London: Associated Business Press.

91 See A. L. Friedman and D. S. Cornford (1989) *Computer Systems Development: History, Organization and Implementation*, Chichester: Wiley.
92 D. A. Preece (1985) 'The management of the adoption and introduction of new technology', in H. J. Bullinger (ed.), *Human Factors in Manufacturing: Proceedings of the Second International Conference*, Bedford: IFS.
93 M. Beirne and H. Ramsay (1986) 'Computer Redesign and "Labour Process" Theory: towards a critical appraisal', paper presented to the fourth annual conference, Organization and Control of the Labour Process, University of Aston, April; see also M. Beirne and H. Ramsay (1988) 'Computer redesign and labour process theory: towards a critical appraisal', in D. Knights and H. Willmott (eds), *New Technology and the Labour Process*, London: Macmillan; M. Beirne and H. Ramsay (eds) (1992) *Information Technology and Workplace Democracy*, London: Routledge.
94 Beirne and Ramsay, 'Computer redesign', p. 4.
95 Ibid., pp. 4–9.
96 D. A. Preece, 'Organisations, flexibility and new technology', in C. A. Voss (ed.), *Managing Advanced Manufacturing Technology*, Bedford: IFS, and Berlin: Springer.
97 D. A. Preece (1987) 'New technology and job design – lessons from the print industry?', *Employee Relations* 9 (2).
98 J. Wainwright and A. Francis (1984) *Office Automation, Organisation and the Nature of Work*, Aldershot: Gower.
99 Ibid., p. 202.
100 Ibid., pp. 62, 74.
101 Beirne and Ramsay, 'Computer redesign', p. 10.
102 Ibid., p. 16.
103 See, for example, P. Ehn and M. Kyng (1985) 'Trade Unions and Computers: the Scandinavian Collective Resource Research Approach', paper presented to the FAST conference 'The Press and the New Technologies – the challenge of a new knowledge', Brussels, November; S. Bødker, P. Ehn, J. Kammersgaard, M. Kyng and Y. Sundblad (1985) 'A UTOPIAN experience – on design of powerful computer-based tools for skilled graphic workers', in G. Bjerknes, P. Ehn and M. Kyng (eds), Proceedings of the Aarhus Conference on Development and Use of Computer-based Systems, Aarhus; P. Ehn (1988) *Work-oriented Design of Computer Artifacts*, Stockholm: Arbetslivscentrum.
104 See, for example, K. D. Eason (1982) 'The process of introducing information technology', *Behaviour and Information Technology* 1 (2); F. Blackler and C. Brown (1985) 'Evaluation and the impact of information technologies on people in organisations', *Human Relations* 38 (3); Davies, *Industrial Relations and New Technology*, p. 31.
105 Davies discusses this matter in rather more detail, as does Kelly. See Davies, *Industrial Relations and New Technology*; J. E. Kelly (1982) *Scientific Management, Job Redesign and Work Performance*, London: Academic Press.
106 B. Jones (1982) 'Destruction or redistribution of engineering skills?

The case of numerical control', in S. Wood (ed.), *The Degradation of Work? Skill, Deskilling and the Labour Process*, London: Hutchinson; Wilkinson, *Shopfloor Politics*. Gill also has a useful chapter on new technology on the shop floor which covers some of the issues discussed here: see C. Gill (1985) *Work, Unemployment and the New Technology*, Cambridge: Polity Press, chapter 3.

5 BRAMLEY BUILDING SOCIETY

1 See, for example, J. Purcell (1984) 'Industrial relations in building societies', *Employee Relations* 6 (1); A. I. R. Swabe and P. Price (1984) 'White-collar unionism in the building societies', *Employee Relations* 6 (3).
2 Purcell, 'Industrial relations in building societies'.
3 A. Rajan (1984) *New Technology and Employment in Insurance, Banking and Building Societies: Recent Experience and Future Impact*, Aldershot: Institute of Manpower Studies/Gower, p. 90.
4 Ibid., p. 90.
5 Ibid., p. 104.
6 Ibid., p. 108.
7 M. Boleat (1982) *The Building Society Industry*, London: Allen & Unwin, p. 210.
8 It can also be argued that the new technology led to reduced staffing levels, and hence labour cost savings, albeit this took place before the new technology was introduced. They remained the same or were reduced when cashiers left, in anticipation of the computerization of the branch office (subject to the maintenance of minimum staffing levels for security reasons). Had it not been for the impending introduction of new technology, these levels would have had to be increased more or less in line with any expansion in business volume. In the longer term the effect of this policy must, of course, be a decelerating (or no) increase in overall staff numbers in branch offices. Note that when labour savings are made in the way described here it is much more difficult to attribute them to the technology than if they had occured after the technology had been introduced.
9 The Computer Systems Manager's comment on this lack of communication was that the focus at the time was on getting the technical aspects right in the hope that management's claims for what the equipment would be able to do would turn out to be correct.
10 Report of the Chief Registrar of Friendly Societies (1991–2), London: Registry of Friendly Societies.
11 See, for example, J. M. Balmer and A. Wilkinson (1991) 'Building Societies: change, strategy and corporate identity', *Journal of General Management* 17 (2); R. Speed (1990) 'Building societies: new strategies for a competitive era', *Services Industries Journal* 10 (1).
12 D. Kerfoot and D. Knights (1993) 'Management, masculinity and manipulation: from paternalism to corporate strategy in financial services in Britain', *Journal of Management Studies* 30 (4): 659–60.

13 P. Cressey and P. Scott (1992) 'Employment, technology and industrial relations in the UK clearing banks: is the honeymoon over?' *New Technology, Work and Employment* 7 (2): 84.

6 PARK HILL BUILDING SOCIETY

1 R. Crompton and G. Jones (1984) *White-collar Proletariat: Deskilling and Gender in Clerical Work*, London: Macmillan.
2 L. Ashburner (1986) 'Technology, the Labour Process and Gender Differentiation in the Building Society Industry', paper presented at the fourth annual conference, Organization and Control of the Labour Process, University of Aston, April.
3 Ibid., p. 33.
4 John Child (1984) 'New technology and developments in management organisation', *Omega* 12 (3): 217.

7 DON LTD

1 For an overview of the nature and significance of green-field sites see D. A. Preece (1993) 'Human resource specialists and technical change at greenfield sites', in J. Clark (ed.), *Human Resource Management and Technical Change*, London: Sage.
2 If the language used by this manager echoes that used by labour process theorists, then it is probably not a coincidence: he had recently completed a part-time Master's degree in social science and industrial relations, which included the study of the labour process perspective.
3 D. A. Preece (1986) 'Organisations, flexibility and new technology', in C. A. Voss (ed.), *Managing Advanced Manufacturing Technology*, Bedford: IFS, and Berlin: Springer.
4 D. A. Preece (1985) 'The management of the adoption and introduction of new technology', in H. J. Bullinger (ed.), *Human Factors in Manufacturing: Proceedings of the Second International Conference*, Bedford: IFS, p. 237.
5 See, for example, B. Wilkinson (1983) *The Shopfloor Politics of New Technology*, London: Heinemann, chapter 7; D. Noble (1979) 'Social choice in machine design: the case of automatically controlled machine tools', in A. Zimbalist (ed.), *Case Studies on the Labour Process*, New York: Monthly Review Press; D. Buchanan and D. Boddy (1983) *Organisations in the Computer Age*, Aldershot: Gower; B. Jones (1982) 'Destruction or redistribution of engineering skills?', in S. Wood (ed.), *The Degradation of Work?*, London: Hutchinson; A Sorge, G. Hartman, M. Warner and I. Nicholas (1983) *Microelectronics and Manpower in Manufacturing*, Aldershot: Gower.
6 See Noble, 'Social choice'; Sorge et al., *Microelectronics and Manpower in Manufacturing*.
7 See, for example, chapter 3; Noble, 'Social choice'; H. Braverman (1974) *Labour and Monopoly Capital*, New York: Monthly Review Press; P. Thompson (1983) *The Nature of Work*, London: Macmillan.

8 In his machine tool manufacturer case study, Wilkinson documents how CNC machinists were correcting program faults and conducting a 'battle for control' with the programmers. One machinist had taught himself to program using an engineering drawing and the tape editing facility, and managers were turning a 'blind eye' to what was going on (*Shopfloor Politics*). Gill refers to a case study concerning the introduction of CNC into seven small metalworking shops where 'the day-to-day reality was filled with the unexpected: bugs in parts programs, unforeseen problems with the machines, off-standard castings, etc. Under these circumstances, operator intervention is critical, even though the need for many important skills is eliminated or reduced' (*Work, Unemployment and New Technology*, p. 85).

9 For a consideration of the part that personnel specialists have played in technological change see D. A. Preece and M. R. Harrison (1988) 'The contribution of personnel specialists to technology-related organizational change', *Personnel Review* 17 (1); K. Legge (1989) 'Information technology: personnel management's lost opportunity?', *Personnel Review Monograph* 18 (5); Clark, *Human Resource Management*.

10 Preece, 'The management of the adoption', p. 239.

8 MEADOWS & BUTLER

1 S. Tyson and A. Fell (1986) *Evaluating the Personnel Function*, London: Hutchinson, pp. 24–5.
2 Ibid., p. 25.
3 See D. A. Preece (1985) 'The management of the adoption and introduction of new technology', in H. J. Bullinger (ed.), *Human Factors in Manufacturing: Proceedings of the Second International Conference*, Bedford: IFS; D. A. Preece (1987) 'Case study', in M. J. Harrison (ed.), *Advanced Manufacturing Technology Implementation: Training and Management Development*, Sheffield: Manpower Services Commission.
4 P. L. Primrose, G. D. Creamer and R. Leonard (1985) 'Identifying and quantifying the "company-wide" benefits of CAD within the structure of a comprehensive investment programme', in E. Rhodes and D. Wield (eds), *Implementing New Technologies: Choice, Decision and Change in Manufacturing*. Oxford: Blackwell.
5 Ibid.

9 CONCLUSION

1 See, for example, P. Senker (1985) 'Implications of CAD/CAM for management', and R. H. Hayes and W. J. Abernathy, 'Managing our way to economic decline', both in E. Rhodes and D. Wield (eds), *Implementing New Technologies: Choice, Decision and Change in Manufacturing*, Oxford: Blackwell.
2 Rhodes and Wield, *Implementing New Technologies*, p. 221.
3 A. Friedman and D. Cornford (1989) *Computer Systems Development: History, Organization and Implementation*, Chichester: Wiley.

4 See, for example, P. Clark and N. Staunton (1989) *Innovation in Technology and Organization*, London: Routledge.
5 R. Martin (1988) 'The management of industrial relations and new technology', in P. Marginson, P. Edwards, R. Martin, J. Purcell and K. Sisson, *Beyond the Workplace: Managing Industrial Relations in Multiplant Enterprises*, Oxford: Blackwell.
6 For an overview of research findings and the debate in this area see P. Blyton and P. Turnbull (1994) *The Dynamics of Employee Relations*, Basingstoke: Macmillan, especially chapter 4.
7 J. Clark (1993) 'Full flexibility and self-supervision in an automated factory', in J. Clark (ed.), *Human Resource Management and Technical Change*, London: Sage.
8 For an overview of the debate about the nature of HRM see C. Hendry and A. Pettigrew (1990) 'Human resource management: an agenda for the 1990s', *International Journal of Human Resource Management* 1 (1).
9 D. Boddy and D. Buchanan (1986) *Managing New Technology*, Oxford: Blackwell.

Bibliography

Advisory Conciliation and Arbitration Service (1988) *Labour Flexibility in Britain: the 1987 ACAS Survey*, Occasional Paper No. 41, London: ACAS.

Advisory Council for Applied Research and Development (1983) *New Opportunities in Manufacturing: the Management of Technology*, London: HMSO.

Angell, I. O., and Smithson, S. (1990) 'Managing information technology: a crisis of confidence?', *European Management Journal* 8 (1).

Ansoff, H. I. (1969) *Business Strategy*, Harmondsworth: Penguin.

Arnold, E. (1983) 'Information technology as a technological fix: computer aided design in the United Kingdom', in G. Winch (ed.), *Information Technology in Manufacturing Processes*, London: Rossendale.

Arnold, E., and Senker, P. (1982) 'Designing the future – the implications of CAD interactive graphics for employment and skills in the British engineering industry', Occasional Paper, Watford: Engineering Industry Training Board.

Ashburner, L. (1986) 'Technology, the Labour Process and Gender Differentiation in the Building Society Industry', paper presented to the fourth annual confrence, Organization and Control of the Labour Process, University of Aston, April.

Atkinson, J. (1984) 'Flexibility, uncertainty and manpower management', Report No. 89, Brighton: Institute of Manpower Studies.

Atkinson, J. (1987) 'Flexibility or fragmentation? The United Kingdom labour market in the eighties', *Labour and Society* 12, January.

Atkinson, J., and Meager, N. (1986) 'Is flexibility just a flash in the pan?', *Personnel Management*, September.

Baldry, C., and Connolly, A. (1984) 'Drawing the Line: Computer-aided Design and the Organisation of the Drawing Office', paper presented to the second annual conference, Organization and Control of the Labour Process, University of Aston, April.

Balmer, J. M., and Wilkinson, A. (1991) 'Building societies: change, strategy and corporate identity', *Journal of General Management* 17 (2).

Barras, R., and Swann, J. (1984) *The Adoption and Impact of Information Technology in the UK Insurance Industry*, London: Technical Change Centre.

Barron, I., and Curnow, R. (1979) *The Future with Microelectronics*, London: Frances Pinter.
Batstone, E., and Gourlay, S. (1986) *Unions, Unemployment and Innovation*, Oxford: Blackwell.
Beirne, M., and Ramsay, H. (1986) 'Computer Redesign and "Labour Process" Theory: towards a critical appraisal', paper presented to the fourth annual conference, Organization and Control of the Labour Process, University of Aston, April.
Beirne, M., and Ramsay, H. (1988) 'Computer redesign and labour process theory: towards a critical appraisal', in D. Knights and H. Willmott (eds), *New Technology and the Labour Process*, Aldershot: Gower.
Beirne, M., and Ramsay, H. (eds) (1992) *Information Technology and Workplace Democracy*, London: Routledge.
Bessant, J. (1982) *Microprocessors in Production Processes*, London: Policy Studies Institute.
Bessant, J. (1983) 'Management and manufacturing innovation: the case of information technology', in G. Winch (ed.), *Information Technology in Manufacturing Processes*, London: Rossendale.
Bessant, J. (1986) 'Technology agreements head off resistance', *Works Management* 36 (5).
Bessant, J., and Grunt, M. (1985) *Management and Manufacturing Innovation in the United Kingdom and West Germany*, Aldershot: Gower.
Bessant, J., and Lamming, R. (1985) 'The technical and operational context', Units 2/3, PT 621, Implementation of New Technology, Open University – SERC Manufacturing Programme.
Bessant, J., Braun, E., and Moseley, R. (1980) 'Microelectronics in manufacturing industry: the rate of diffusion', in T. Forester (ed.), *The Microelectronics Revolution*, Oxford: Blackwell.
Bjerknes, G., Ehn, P., and Kyng, M. (eds) (1985) Proceedings of the Aarhus Conference on Development and Use of Computer Based Systems, University of Aarhus.
Bjorn-Anderson, N. (ed.) (1980) *The Human Side of Information Processing*, Amsterdam: North-Holland.
Blackler, F., and Brown, C. (1985) 'Evaluation and the impact of information technologies on people in organisations', *Human Relations* 38 (3).
Blau, P. M., and Schoenherr, R. A. (1971) *The Structure of Organizations*, New York: Basic Books.
Bloomfield, B. P., and Coombs, R. (1992) 'Information technology, control and power: the centralization and decentralization debate revisited', *Journal of Management Studies* 29 (4).
Blyton, P., and Turnbull, P. (1994) *The Dynamics of Employee Relations*, Basingstoke: Macmillan.
Boddy, D., and Buchanan, D. (1986) *Managing New Technology*, Oxford: Blackwell.
Bødker, S., Ehn, P., Kammersgaard, J., Kyng, M., and Sundblad, Y. (1985) 'A UTOPIAN experience: on design of powerful computer-based tools for skilled graphic workers', in G. Bjerknes, P. Ehn and M. Kyng (eds), Proceedings of the Aarhus Conference on Development and Use of Computer Based Systems.
Boleat, M. (1982) *The Building Society Industry*, London: Allen & Unwin.

Bower, J. L. (1985) 'Capital budgeting as a general management problem', in E. Rhodes and D. Wield (eds), *Implementing New Technologies*, Oxford: Blackwell.

Braun, E. (1978) 'The Dilemma of Automated Production', unpublished paper, Birmingham: Technology Policy Unit, University of Aston.

Braun, E., and MacDonald, S. (1978) *Revolution in Miniature*, Cambridge: Cambridge University Press.

Braverman, H. (1974) *Labor and Monopoly Capital: the Degradation of Work in the Twentieth Century*, New York: Monthly Review Press.

Brighton Labour Process Group (1977) 'The capitalist labour process', *Capital and Class* 1.

Buchanan, D. (1983) 'Using the new technology: management objectives and organisational choices', *European Management Journal* 1 (2).

Buchanan, D. (1986) 'Management objectives in technical change', in D. Knights and H. Willmott (eds), *Managing the Labour Process*, Aldershot: Gower.

Buchanan, D., and Bessant, J. (1985) 'Failure, uncertainty and control: the role of operators in a computer integrated production system', *Journal of Management Studies* 22 (3).

Buchanan, D., and Boddy, D. (1983) *Organisations in the Computer Age: Technological Imperatives and Strategic Choice*, Aldershot: Gower.

Buchanan, D., and Boddy, D. (1984) 'Information technology and productivity: myths and realities', *Omega* 12 (3).

Buchanan, D., and Boddy, D. (1992) *The Expertise of the Change Agent*, London: Prentice-Hall.

Buffa, E. S. (1984) *Meeting the Competitive Challenge*, Homewood, Ill.: Dow Jones, Irwin.

Bullinger, H. J. (ed.) (1985) *Human Factors in Manufacturing: Proceedings of the Second International Conference*, Bedford: IFS.

Burawoy, M. (1979) *Manufacturing Consent: Changes in the Labour Process under Monopoly Capitalism*, Chicago and London: University of Chicago Press.

Burnes, B. (1988) 'New technology and job design: the case of CNC', *New Technology, Work and Employment* 3 (2).

Carrie, A. S., and Banerjee, S. K. (1984) 'Approaches to implementing manufacturing information systems', *Omega* 12 (3).

Chandler, A. D. (1962) *Strategy and Structure*, Cambridge, Mass.: MIT Press.

Child, J. (1983) 'Managerial Strategies, New Technology and the Labour Process', Working Paper No. 1, Birmingham: Work Organisation Research Centre, University of Aston,

Child, J. (1984a) *Organisation: a Guide to Problems and Practice*, London: Harper & Row.

Child, J. (1984b) 'New technology and developments in management organisation', *Omega* 12 (3).

Child, J. (1985a) 'Management strategies: new technology and the labour process', in D. Knights and D. Collinson (eds), *Job Redesign*, Aldershot: Gower.

Child, J. (1985b) 'The introduction of new technologies: managerial initiative and union response in British banks', *Industrial Relations Journal* 16 (3).

Child, J. (1987) 'Organizational design for advanced manufacturing technology', in T. Wall, C. Clegg and N. Kemp (eds), *The Human Side of Advanced Manufacturing Technology*, Chichester: Wiley.

Child, J., Loveridge, R., Harvey, J., and Spencer, A. (1984) 'Microelectronics and the quality of employment in services', in P. Marstrand (ed.), *New Technology and the Future of Work and Skills*.

Clark, J. (1993a) 'Full flexibility and self-supervision in an automated factory', in J. Clark (ed.), *Human Resource Management and Technical Change*, London: Sage.

Clark, J. (ed.) (1993b) *Human Resource Management and Technical Change*, London: Sage.

Clark, J., Jacobs, A., King, R., and Rose, H. (1984) 'New technology, industrial relations and divisions within the workforce', *Industrial Relations Journal* 15 (3).

Clark, J., McLoughlin, I., Rose, H., and King, R. (1988) *The Process of Technological Change: New Technology and Social Choice in the Workplace*, Cambridge: Cambridge University Press.

Clark, P., and De Bresson, C. (1990) 'Innovation-design and innovation poles', in R. Loveridge and M. Pitt (eds), *The Strategic Management of Technological Innovation*, Chichester: Wiley.

Clark, P., and Staunton, N. (1989) *Innovation in Technology and Organization*, London: Routledge.

Clegg, C., and Kemp, N. (1986) 'Information technology: Personnel, where are you?' *Personnel Review* 15 (1).

Coombs, R., and Richards, A. (1991) 'Technologies, products and firms' strategies 1, A framework for analysis', *Technology Analysis & Strategic Management* 3 (1).

Cressey, P. (1985) *The Role of the Parties concerned in the Introduction of New Technology*, Consolidated Report, Shankill, Co. Dublin: European Foundation for the Improvement of Living and Working Conditions,

Cressey, P., and Scott, P. (1992) 'Employment, technology and industrial relations in the UK clearing banks: is the honeymoon over?', *New Technology, Work and Employment* 7 (2).

Cressey, P., and Williams, R. (1990) *Participation in Change: New Technology and the Role of Employee Involvement*, Shankill, Co. Dublin: European Foundation for the Improvement of Living and Working Conditions.

Crompton, R., and Jones, G. (1984) *White Collar Proletariat: Deskilling and Gender in Clerical Work*, London: Macmillan.

Currie, W. (1989) *Managerial Strategy for New Technology*, Aldershot: Avebury.

Daniel, W. W. (1987) *Workplace Industrial Relations and Technical Change*, London: Frances Pinter.

Daniel, W. W., and Hogarth, T. (1990) 'Worker support for technical change', *New Technology, Work and Employment* 5 (2).

Daniel, W. W., and Millward, N. (1983) *Workplace Industrial Relations in Britain: the DE/PSI/ESRC Survey*, London: Heinemann.

Daniel, W. W., and Millward, N. (1993) 'Personnel management and technical change: the findings from the WIRS series', in J. Clark (ed.), *Human Resource Management and Technical Change*, London: Sage.

Davies, A. (1984) 'Management–union participation during microtechnological change', in M. Warner (ed.), *Microprocessors, Manpower and Society*, Aldershot: Gower.

Davies, A. (1986) *Industrial Relations and New Technology*, Beckenham: Croom Helm.

Davies, A. (1987) 'Organisational aspects of management information systems change', in N. Piercy (ed.), *Management Information Systems*, Beckenham: Croom Helm.

Davis, D.D. and associates (1986) *Managing Technological Innovation*, San Francisco: Jossey-Bass.

Dawson, P., and Webb, J. (1989) 'New production arrangements: the totally flexible cage?' *Work, Employment and Society* 3 (2).

Day, G. S. (1986) *Analysis for Strategic Market Decisions*, St Paul, Minn.: West Publishing.

Dodgson, M., and Martin, R. (1987) 'Trade union policies on new technology: facing the challenges of the 1980s', *New Technology, Work and Employment* 2 (1).

Downing, H. (1983) 'On being automated', *ASLIB Proceedings* 35 (1).

Duncan, K. D., Gruneberg, M., and Wallis, D. (eds) (1980) *Changes in Working Life*, Chichester: Wiley.

Earl, M. (1984) 'Emerging trends in managing new information technologies', in N. Piercy (ed.), *The Management Implications of New Information Technology*, Beckenham: Croom Helm.

Earl, M. (1987) 'Formulating information technology strategies', in N. Piercy (ed.), *Management Information Systems*, Beckenham: Croom Helm.

Earl, M. (1989) *Management Strategies for Information Technology*, Hemel Hempstead: Prentice-Hall.

Eason, K. D. (1982) 'The process of introducing information technology', *Behaviour and Information Technology* 1 (2).

Eason, K. (1984) 'Managing technological change', in R. Paton (ed.), *Organizations: Cases, Issues, Concepts*, London: Harper & Row.

Edwards, R. (1979) *Contested Terrain: the Transformation of the Workplace in the Twentieth Century*, London: Heinemann.

Ehn, P. (1988) *Work Oriented Design of Computer Artifacts*, Stockholm: Arbetslivscentrum.

Ehn, P., and Kyng, M. (1985) 'Trade Unions and Computers: the Scandinavian Collective Resource Research Approach', paper presented to the FAST conference 'The Press and the New Technologies – the Challenge of a new Knowledge', Brussels, November.

Elger, A. (1982) 'Braverman, capital accumulation and deskilling', in S. Wood (ed.), *The Degradation of Work?* London: Hutchinson.

Elger, A. (1987) 'Flexible futures? New technology and the contemporary transformation of work', *Work, Employment and Society* 1 (4).

Elger, A. (1990) 'Technical innovation and work reorganization in British manufacturing in the 1980s: continuity, intensification or transformation?' *Work, Employment and Society*, special issue, May.

Ettlie, J. E. (1984) 'Implementation strategy for manufacturing inovations', in M. Warner (ed.), *Microprocessors, Manpower and Society*, Aldershot: Gower.

European Foundation for the Improvement of Living and Working Conditions (1986) 'How Modern Technology affects the Experienced Worker', Consolidated Report, Shankill, Co. Dublin.

Fleck, J. (1983) 'Robotics in manufacturing organisations', in G. Winch (ed.), *Information Technology*, London: Rossendale.

Forester, T. (ed.) (1980) *The Microelectronics Revolution*, Oxford: Blackwell.

Fox, A. (1974) *Beyond Contract: Work, Power and Trust Relations*, London: Faber.

Friedman, A. L. (1977) *Industry and Labour: Class Struggle at Work and Monopoly Capitalism*, London: Macmillan.

Friedman, A. L. (1985) 'Managerial Strategies, Activities, Techniques and Technology: towards a Complex Theory of the Labour Process', paper presented to the third annual conference, Organization and Control of the Labour Process, University of Manchester Institute of Science and Technology, April.

Friedman, A. L. (1990) 'Management strategies, activities, techniques and technology: towards a complex theory of the labour process', in D. Knights and H. Willmott (eds.), *Labour Process Theory*, London: Macmillan.

Friedman, A. L., and Cornford, D. (1989) *Computer Systems Development: History, Organization and Implementation*, Chichester: Wiley.

Frohlich, D., and Krieger, H. (1990) 'Technological change and worker participation in Europe', *New Technology, Work and Employment* 5 (2).

Frohlich, D., Gill, C., and Krieger, H. (1991) *Roads to Participation in the European Community? Increasing Prospects of Employee Representative Involement in Technological Change*, Shankill, Co. Dublin: European Foundation for the Improvement of Living and Working Conditions.

Gallie, D. (1978) *In Search of the New Working Class*, Cambridge: Cambridge University Press.

Garrahan, P., and Stewart, P. (1992) *The Nissan Enigma*, London: Mansell.

Gerwin, D., and Tarondeau, J. C. (1985) 'Uncertainty and the innovation process for computer-integrated manufacturing systems: four case studies', in E. Rhodes and D. Wield (eds), *Implementing New Technologies*, Oxford: Blackwell.

Gill, C. (1985) *Work, Unemployment and the New Technology*, Cambridge: Polity Press.

Gill, C. (1993) 'Technological change and participation in work organization: recent results from a European Community survey', *International Journal of Human Resource Management* 4 (2).

Gill, C., and Krieger, H. (1992) 'The diffusion of participation in new information technology in Europe: survey results', *Economic and Industrial Democracy* 13 (3).

Goldhar, J. D., and Jelinek, M. (1985) 'Computer integrated flexible manufacturing: organisational, economic and strategic implications', *Interfaces* 15 (3).

Gordon, D. M., Edwards, R., and Reich, M. (1982) *Segmented Work, Divided Workers: the Historical Transformation of Labor in the United States*, Cambridge: Cambridge University Press.

Gospel, H. F. (1983) 'Managerial structure and strategies: an introduction', in H. F. Gospel and C. R. Littler (eds), *Managerial Strategies and Industrial Relations*, London: Heinemann.

Gospel, H. F., and Littler, C. R. (eds) (1983) *Managerial Strategies and Industrial Relations*, London: Heinemann.

Greenhalgh, G. R. (1991) *Manufacturing Strategy: Formulation and Implementation*, Sydney: Addison-Wesley.

Grindley, P. (1991) 'Turning technology into competitive advantage', *Business Strategy Review* 2 (1).

Gunter, L. (1990) 'Strategic options for CIM integration', in M. Warner, W. Wobbe and P. Brodner (eds), *New Technology and Manufacturing Management*, Chichester: Wiley.

Gustavsen, B. (1985) 'Technology and collective agreements: some recent Scandinavian developments', *Industrial Relations Journal* 16 (4).

Hayes, R. H., and Abernathy, W. J. (1980) 'Managing our way to economic decline', *Harvard Business Review* 58 (4).

Hayes, R. H., and Wheelwright, S. C. (1984) *Restoring our Competitive Edge: Competing through Manufacturing*, Chichester: Wiley.

Hendry, C. (1993) 'Personnel leadership in technical and human resource change', in J. Clark (ed.), *Human Resource Management and Technical Change*, London: Sage.

Hendry, C., and Pettigrew, A. (1990) 'Human resource management: an agenda for the 1990s', *International Journal of Human Resource Management* 1 (1).

Hickson, D. J., Butler, R. J., Cray, D., Mallory, G. R., and Wilson, D. C. (1985) 'Comparing 150 decision processes', in J. M. Pennings (ed.), *Organization Strategy and Change*, San Francisco: Jossey-Bass.

Hickson, D. J., Cray, D., Mallory, G. R., and Wilson, D. C. (1986) *Top Decisions: Strategic Decision Making in Organizations*, Oxford: Blackwell.

Hill, S. (1981) *Competition and Control at Work*, London: Heinemann.

Hill, T. J. (1985) *Manufacturing Strategy*, London: Macmillan.

Hillage, J., Meager, N., and Rajan, A. (1986) 'Technology agreements in practice: the experience so far', Report No. 113, Brighton: Institute of Manpower Studies.

Hirscheim, R. (1985) *Office Automation: Concepts, Technologies and Issues*, London: Addison-Wesley.

Hochstrasser, B., and Griffiths, C. (1991) *Controlling IT Investment: Strategy and Management*, London: Chapman & Hall.

Hopwood, A. G. (1983) 'Evaluating the real benefits', in H. J. Otway and M. Peltu (eds), *New Office Technology*, London: Frances Pinter.

Huczynski, A., and Buchanan, D. (1991) *Organizational Behaviour: an Introductory Text* (second edition), London: Prentice-Hall.

Incomes Data Services (1982) *CAD Agreements and Pay*, 27 October, London: Incomes Data Services.

Incomes Data Services (1984) *Bending with the wind?*, IDS Study No. 322, London: Incomes Data Services.
Incomes Data Services (1988) *Flexible working*, IDS Study No. 407, London: Incomes Data Services.
Ingram, R. N. (1987) 'Recent developments in management information systems in the UK motor industry', in N. Piercy (ed.), *Management Information Systems*, Beckenham: Croom Helm.
Institute of Personnel Management (1980) *Personnel Policies and New Technology*, London: IPM.
Jacobi, O., Jessop, R., Kastendiek, H., and Regini, M. (eds) (1986) *Technological Change, Rationalisation and Industrial Relations*, Beckenham: Croom Helm.
Jenkins, C., and Sherman, B. (1979) *The Collapse of Work*, London: Eyre Methuen.
Jones, A., and Webb, T. (1987) 'Introducing computer integrated manufacturing', *Journal of General Management* 12 (4).
Jones, B. (1982) 'Destruction or redistribution of engineering skills? The case of numerical control', in S. Wood (ed.), *The Degradation of Work?* London: Hutchinson.
Jones, B. (1990) 'New production technology and work roles: a paradox of flexibility versus strategic control?', in R. Loveridge and M. Pitt (eds), *The Strategic Management of Technological Innovation*, Chichester: Wiley.
Jones, T. (ed.) (1980) *Microelectronics and Society*, Milton Keynes: Open University Press.
Kaplan, R. S. (1983) 'Measuring manufacturing performance: a new challenge for managerial accounting research', *Accounting Review* LVIII (4).
Kaplan, R. S. (1986) 'Must CIM be justified by faith alone?' *Harvard Business Review* 64 (2).
Keen, P. (1983) 'Strategic planning for the new system', in H. J. Otway and M. Peltu (eds), *New Office Technology*, London: Frances Pinter.
Kelly, J. E. (1982) *Scientific Management, Job Redesign and Work Performance*, London: Academic Press.
Kelly, J., and Wood, S. (1983) 'Taylorism and the Recession', mimeo, London School of Economics, January.
Kerfoot, D., and Knights, D. (1993) 'Management, masculinity and manipulation: from paternalism to corporate strategy in financial services in Britain', *Journal of Management Studies* 30 (4).
Kimberly, J. R. (1986) 'The organizational context of technological innovation', in D. D. Davis and associates, *Managing Technological Innovation*, San Francisco: Jossey-Bass.
Knights, D., and Collinson, D. (eds) (1985) *Job Redesign: Organisation and Control of the Labour Process*, Aldershot: Gower.
Knights, D., and Willmott, H. (eds) (1986) *Managing the Labour Process*, Aldershot: Gower.
Knights, D., and Willmott, H. (eds) (1988) *New Technology and the Labour Process*, London: Macmillan.
Knights, D., and Willmott, H. (eds) (1990) *Labour Process Theory*, London: Macmillan.

Kraft, P. (1979) 'The industrialisation of computer programming: from programming to "Software Production"', in A. Zimbalist (ed.), *Case Studies on the Labor Process*, New York: Monthly Review Press.

Labour Research (1983) Special issue on new technology, November.

Land, F. (1984) 'The impact of information technology on the work place', in N. Piercy (ed.), *The Management Implications of New Information Technology*, Beckenham: Croom Helm.

Land, F. (1987) 'Social aspects of information systems', in N. Piercy (ed.), *Management Information Systems*, Beckenham: Croom Helm.

Lee, D. (1982) 'Beyond deskilling: skill, craft and class', in S. Wood (ed.), *The Degradation of Work?* London: Hutchinson.

Lee, G. L. (1986) 'The Adoption of Computer-based Systems in Engineering: Managerial Strategies and the Role of Professional Engineers', paper presented to the fourth annual conference, Organization and Control of the Labour Process, University of Aston, April.

Legge, K. (1989) 'Information technology: personnel management's lost opportunity?', *Personnel Review Monograph* 18 (5).

Legge, K. (1993) 'The role of personnel specialists: centrality or marginalization?', in J. Clark (ed.), *Human Resource Management and Technical Change*, London: Sage.

Leonard-Barton, D., and Kraus, W. A. (1985) 'Implementing new technology', *Harvard Business Review* 63 (4).

Littler, C. R. (1982a) 'Deskilling and changing structures of control', in S. Wood (ed.), *The Degradation of Work?* London: Hutchinson.

Littler, C. R. (1982b) *The Development of the Labour Process in Capitalist Societies: a Comparative Study of the Transformation of Work Organisation in Britain, Japan and the USA*, London: Heinemann.

Love, J. H., and Walker, J. (1986) 'Problems of new technology deployment in the mechanical engineering and printing industries', in C. A. Voss (ed.), *Managing Advanced Manufacturing Technology*, Bedford: IFS, and Berlin: Springer.

Loveridge, R., and Pitt, M. (eds.) (1990) *The Strategic Management of Technological Innovation*, Chichester: Wiley.

Lupton, T., and Tanner, I. (1980) 'Work organisation design in Europe', in K. D. Duncan, M. Gruneberg and D. Wallis (eds), *Changes in Working Life*, Chichester: Wiley.

McGee, J., and Thomas H. (eds) (1986) *Strategic Management Research: a European Perspective*, Chichester: Wiley.

MacInnes, J. (1987) *Thatcherism at Work*, Milton Keynes: Open University Press.

McLoughlin, I., and Clark, J. (1994) *Technological Change at Work* (second edition), Buckingham: Open University Press.

McLoughlin, I., Rose, H., and Clark, J. (1984) 'Managing the Introduction of new Technology', paper presented to the annual conference of the British Universities Industrial Relations Association.

McLoughlin, I., Rose, H., and Clark J. (1985) 'Managing the introduction of new technology', *Omega* 13 (4).

Mansfield, R. (1986) *Company Strategy and Organisational Design*, Beckenham: Croom Helm.

Manwaring, T., and Wood, S. (1985) 'The ghost in the labour process', in D. Knights and D. Collinson (eds), *Job Redesign*, Aldershot: Gower.

Marchington, M., and Loveridge, R. (1983) 'Management decision-making and shopfloor participation', in K. Thurley and S. Wood (eds), *Industrial Relations and Management Strategy*, Cambridge: Cambridge University Press.

Marginson, P., Edwards, P., Martin, R., Purcell, J., and Sisson, K. (1988) *Beyond the Workplace: Managing Industrial Relations in Multi-plant Enterprises*, Oxford: Blackwell.

Marsden, D., Morris, T., Willman, P., and Wood, S. (1985) *The Car Industry: Labour Relations and Industrial Adjustment*, London: Tavistock.

Marstrand, P. (ed.) (1984) *New Technology and the Future of Work and Skills*, London: Frances Pinter.

Martin, R. (1988) 'The management of industrial relations and new technology', in P. Marginson, P. Edwards, R. Martin, J. Purcell and K. Sisson, *Beyond the Workplace*, Oxford: Blackwell.

Mills, C. Wright (1951) *White Collar*, Oxford: Oxford University Press.

Millward, N., and Stevens, M. (1986) *British Workplace Industrial Relations, 1980–84: the DE/ESRC/PSI/ACAS Surveys*, Aldershot: Gower.

Millward, N., Stevens, M., Smart, D., and Hawes, W. R. (1992) *Workplace Industrial Relations in Transition: the ED/ESRC/PSI/ACAS Surveys*, Aldershot: Dartmouth.

Motteram, G., and Sizer, J. (1986) 'Costing of advanced manufacturing technology at Rolls-Royce, Derby manufacturing: a case study', in C. A. Voss (ed.), *Managing Advanced Manufacturing Technology*, Bedford: IFS, and Berlin: Springer.

Mumford, E., and Henshall, D. (1979) *A Participative Approach to Computer Systems Design: a Case Study of the Introduction of a New Computer System*, London: Associated Business Press.

Mumford, E., and Weir, M. (1979) *Computer Systems in Work Design: the ETHICS Method*, London: Associated Business Press.

Nagy, K. (1985) 'New technology and the work organisation/acceptance of the change', in H. J. Bullinger (ed.), *Human Factors in Manufacturing*, Bedford: IFS.

Nahapiet, J. E. (1984) 'Assessing costs and benefits in system design and selection', in H. J. Otway and M. Peltu (eds), *The Managerial Challenge of New Office Technology*, London: Butterworth.

National Computing Centre (1986) *The Impact of Office Technology*, Manchester: NCC.

National Economic Development Office (1983) *The Introduction of New Technology*, London: NEDO.

Nicholas, I., Wather, M., Hartmann, G. and Sorge, A. (1983) 'Automating the shopfloor: applications of CNC in manufacturing in Great Britain and West Germany', *Journal of General Management* 8 (3).

Nichols, T. (1986) *The British Worker Question: a New Look at Workers and Productivity in Manufacturing*, London: Routledge.

Nichols, T., and Armstrong, P. (1976) *Workers Divided*, Glasgow: Fontana.

Nichols, T., and Beynon, H. (1977) *Living with Capitalism*, London: Routledge.

Noble, D. (1979) 'Social choice in machine design: the case of automatically controlled machine tools', in A. Zimbalist (ed.), *Case Studies on the Labour Process*, New York: Monthly Review Press.

Northcott, J., and Rogers, P. (1982) *Microelectronics in Industry: Survey Statistics*, London: Policy Studies Institute.

Northcott, J., Fogarty, M., and Trevor, M. (1985) *Chips and Jobs: Acceptance of New Technology at Work*, London: Policy Studies Institute.

Oakland, J. (1993) *Total Quality Management: the Route to Improving Performance* (second edition), Oxford: Butterworth-Heinemann.

Ohmae, K. (1982) *The Mind of the Strategist: the Art of Japanese Business*, London: McGraw-Hill.

Otway, H. J., and Peltu, M. (eds) (1983) *New Office Technology: Human and Organisational Aspects*, London: Frances Pinter.

Otway, H. J., and Peltu, M. (eds) (1984) *The Managerial Challenge of New Office Technology*, London: Butterworth.

Paton, R. (ed.) (1984) *Organizations: Cases, Issues, Concepts*, London: Harper & Row.

Pavitt, K. (1986) 'Technology, innovation and strategic management', in J. McGee and H. Thomas (eds), *Strategic Management Research: a European Perspective*.

Pavitt, K. (1990) 'What we know about the strategic management of technology', *California Management Review*, spring.

Pennings, J. M. (ed.) (1990) *Organization Strategy and Change*, San Francisco: Jossey-Bass.

Peters, T. J., and Waterman, R. H. (1982) *In Search of Excellence: Lessons from America's Best Run Companies*, New York: Harper & Row.

Pettigrew, A. M. (1973) *The Politics of Organisational Decision-making*, London: Tavistock.

Pettigrew, A. (1985) *The Awakening Giant: Continuity and Change in ICI*, Oxford: Blackwell.

Pettigrew, A. (ed.) (1988) *The Management of Strategic Change*, Oxford: Blackwell.

Pettigrew, A., and Whipp, R. (1991) *Managing Change for Competitive Success*, Oxford: Blackwell.

Piercy, N. (ed.) (1984) *The Management Implications of New Information Technology*, Beckenham: Croom Helm.

Piercy, N. (ed.) (1987) *Management Information Systems: the Technology Challenge*, Beckenham: Croom Helm.

Policy Studies Institute (1982) *Microelectronics in Industry*, London: Policy Studies Institute.

Pollert, A. (ed.) (1991) *Farewell to Flexibility?* Oxford: Blackwell.

Porter, M. E. (1980) *Competitive Strategy*, New York: Free Press.

Porter, M. E. (1985a) *Competitive Advantage: Creating and Sustaining Superior Performance*, New York: Free Press.

Porter, M. E. (1985b) 'Technology and competitive advantage', *Journal of Business Studies*, winter.

Preece, D. A. (1984) 'Social aspects and effects of composing machine adoption in the British printing industry', *Journal of the Printing Historical Society* 18.

Preece, D. A. (1985) 'The management of the adoption and introduction of new technology', in H. J. Bullinger (ed.), *Human Factors in Manufacturing*, Bedford: IFS.

Preece, D. A. (1986) 'Organisations, flexibility and new technology', in C. A. Voss (ed.), *Managing Advanced Manufacturing Technology*, Bedford: IFS, and Berlin: Springer.

Preece, D. A. (1987) 'New technology and job design – lessons from the print industry?' *Employee Relations* 9 (2).

Preece, D. A. (1989) *Managing the Adoption of New Technology*, London: Routledge.

Preece, D. A. (1991) 'The whys and wherefores of new technology adoption', *Management Decision* 29 (1).

Preece, D. A. (1993) 'Human resource specialists and technical change at greenfield sites', in J. Clark (ed.), *Human Resource Management and Technical Change*, London: Sage.

Preece, D. A., and Harrison, M. J. (1988) 'The contribution of personnel specialists to technology-related organisational change', *Personnel Review* 17 (1).

Primrose, P. L., Creamer, J., and Leonard, R. (1985) 'Identifying and quantifying the "company-wide" benefits of CAD within the structure of a comprehensive investment programme', in E. Rhodes and D. Wield (eds), *Implementing New Technologies*, Oxford: Blackwell.

Pugh, J. (1983) 'A "culture of change" in the electronics industry', *Employment Gazette*, August.

Purcell, J. (1984) 'Industrial relations in building societies', *Employee Relations* 6 (1).

Rajan, A. (1984) *New Technology and Employment in Insurance, Banking and Building Societies: Recent Experience and Future Impact*, Special Report, Institute for Manpower Studies, Aldershot: Gower.

Rhodes, E., and Wield, D. (eds) (1985) *Implementing New Technologies: Choice, Decision and Change in Manufacturing*, Oxford: Blackwell.

Rockart, J. F., and Scott Morton, M. S. (1984) 'Implications of changes in information technology for corporate strategy', *Interfaces* 14 (1).

Rolfe, H. (1986) 'Skill, deskilling and new technology in the non-manual labour process', *New Technology, Work and Employment* 1 (1).

Rose, M., and Jones, B. (1985) 'Managerial strategy and trade union responses in work reorganisation schemes at establishment level', in D. Knights and D. Collinson (eds), *Job Redesign: Organisation and Control of the Labour Process*, Aldershot: Gower.

Rosenbrock, H. H. (1979) 'The Re-direction of Technology', Research Paper, London: Council for Science and Society.

Rosenbrock, H. H. (1981) 'Engineers and the Work that People do', Work Research Unit, Occasional Paper No. 21.

Rosenbrock, H. H. (1983) 'Technology, control, information and work organisation: what are the options?' *Work and People* 9 (2).

Rothwell, S. (1984) 'Company employment policies and new technology in the manufacturing and service sectors', in M. Warner (ed.), *Microprocessors, Manpower and Society*, Aldershot: Gower.

Rothwell, S. (1985) 'Supervisors and new technology', in E. Rhodes and D. Wield (eds), *Implementing New Technologies*, Oxford: Blackwell.
Rothwell, S., and Davidson, D. (1984) 'Technological Change, Company Personnel Policies and Skill Deployment', Sheffield: MSC.
Rush, H., and Williams, R. (1984) 'Consultation and change: new technology and manpower in the electronics industry', in M. Warner (ed.), *Microprocessors, Manpower and Society*, Aldershot: Gower.
Scarbrough, H. (1986) 'The politics of technological change at BL', in O. Jacobi, R. Jessop, H. Kastendiek and M. Regini (eds), *Technological Change, Rationalisation and Industrial Relations*, Beckenham: Croom Helm.
Scarbrough, H., Lannon, R., and Hamilton, R. (1986) 'Strategy for information technology: one step beyond', *Industrial Management and Data Systems*, January/February.
Schendel, D. E., and Hofer, C. W. (eds) (1979) *Strategic Management: a New View of Business Policy and Planning*, Boston, Mass.: Little Brown.
Schonberger, R. J. (1982) *Japanese Manufacturing Techniques: Nine Hidden Lessons in Simplicity*, New York: Free Press.
Schonberger, R. J. (1986) *World Class Manufacturing*, New York: Free Press.
Sell, R. G. (1980) 'Microelectronics and the quality of working life', Occasional Paper No. 17, London: Work Research Unit.
Senker, P. (1983) 'Some Problems in justifying CAD/CAM', paper presented at AUTOMAN conference, Birmingham.
Senker, P. (1984) 'Training for automation', in M. Warner (ed.), *Microprocessors, Manpower and Society*, Aldershot: Gower.
Senker, P. (1985) 'Implications of CAD/CAM for management', in E. Rhodes and D. Wield (eds), *Implementing New Technologies*, Oxford: Blackwell.
Sewell, G., and Wilkinson, B. (1992) 'Someone to watch over me: surveillance, discipline and the just-in-time labour process', *Sociology* 26 (2).
Sewell, G., and Wilkinson, B. (1993) 'Human resource management in "surveillance" companies', in J. Clark (ed.) *Human Resource Management and Technical Change*, London: Sage.
Shaiken, H. (1979) 'Numerical control of work: workers and automation in the Computer Age', *Radical America* 13 (6).
Shaw, W. N., Patrick, K., and Alexander, K. (1986) 'Implementing new technology in an engineering company: an ongoing saga?' in C. A. Voss (ed.), *Managing Advanced Manufacturing Technology*, Bedford: IFS, and Berlin: Springer.
Simon, H. A. (1957) *Administrative Behavior*, New York: Macmillan.
Skinner, W. (1978) *Manufacturing in the Corporate Strategy*, Chichester: Wiley.
Skinner, W. (1984) 'Operations technology: blind spot in strategic management', *Interfaces* 14 (1).
Smith, C. (1985) 'Design Engineers and the Capitalist Firm', paper presented to the third annual conference, Organization and Control of the Labour

Process, University of Manchester Institute of Science and Technology, April.
Smith, S. (1987) 'Information technology in banks: Taylorization or human-centred systems?', *Science and Public Policy* 14 (3).
Sorge, A., Hartman, G., Warner, M., and Nicholas, I. (1983) *Microelectronics and Manpower in Manufacturing*, Aldershot: Gower.
Speed, R. (1990) 'Building societies: new strategies for a competitive era', *Services Industries Journal* 10 (1).
Spencer, A. (1981) 'What non-executive directors don't do', *Management Today*, May.
Storey, J. (1983) *Managerial Prerogative and the Question of Control*, London: Routledge.
Storey, J. (1985a) 'The means of management control', *Sociology* 19 (2).
Storey, J. (1985b) 'The phoney war? New office technology: organisation and control', in D. Knights and H. Willmott (eds), *Managing the Labour Process*, Aldershot: Gower.
Storey, J. (1987) 'The management of new office technology: choice, control and social structure in the insurance industry', *Journal of Management Studies* 24 (1).
Storey, J. (1992) *Developments in the Management of Human Resources*, Oxford: Blackwell.
Storey, J. (n.d.) 'New Office Technology: Organisation and Response', Occasional Paper No. 4, Nottingham: Trent Business School.
Swabe, A. I. R., and Price, P. (1984) 'White-collar unionism in the building societies', *Employee Relations* 6 (3).
Swords-Isherwood, N., and Senker, P. (1978) 'Technological and Organisational Change in Machine Shops', report prepared for the Engineering Industry Training Board (Science Policy Research Unit), mimeo, May.
Swords-Isherwood, N., and Senker, P. (eds) (1980) *Microelectronics and the Engineering Industry: the Need for Skills*, London: Frances Pinter.
Symon, G., and Clegg, C. (1991) 'Technology-led change: a study of the implementation of CADCAM', *Journal of Occupational Psychology* 64 (4).
Thompson, P. (1989) *The Nature of Work*, London: Macmillan.
Thompson, P., and Bannon, E. (1985) *Working the System: the Shop Floor and New Technology*, London: Pluto Press.
Thurley, K., and Wood, S. (1983a) 'Business strategy and industrial relations strategy', in K. Thurley and S. Wood (eds), *Industrial Relations and Management Strategy*, Cambridge: Cambridge University Press.
Thurley, K., and Wood, S. (eds) (1983b) *Industrial Relations and Management Strategy*, Cambridge: Cambridge University Press.
Trades Union Congress (1979) *Employment and Technology*, London: Trades Union Congress.
Tricker, R. I. (1980) 'Order or freedom – the ultimate issue in information systems design', in N. Bjorn-Anderson (ed.), *The Human Side of Information Processing*, Amsterdam: North-Holland.
Trist, E. L., and Bamforth, K. (1951) 'Some social and psychological consequences of the long wall method of coal getting', *Human Relations* 4 (1).

Twiss, B. C. (1985) *Non-MSC Research and Initiatives in the Field of Management Development for Technical Change*, Sheffield: Manpower Services Commission.

Voss, C. A. (1984) 'Production/operations management – a key discipline and area for research', *Omega* 12 (3).

Voss, C. A. (1986a) 'Implementing manufacturing technology: a manufacturing strategy perspective', in C. A. Voss (ed.), *Managing Advanced Manufacturing Technology*, Bedford: IFS, and Berlin: Springer.

Voss, C. A. (ed.) (1986b) *Managing Advanced Manufacturing Technology*, Bedford: IFS, and Berlin: Springer.

Wainwright, J., and Francis, A. (1984) *Office Automation, Organisation and the Nature of Work*, Aldershot: Gower.

Walker, C. R., and Guest, R. H. (1952) *The Man on the Assembly Line*, Cambridge, Mass.: Harvard University Press.

Walker, C. R., Guest, R. H., and Turner, A. N. (1956) *The Foreman on the Assembly Line*, Cambridge, Mass.: Harvard University Press.

Wall, T. D., Burnes, B., Clegg, C.W. and Kemp, N.J. (1984) 'New technology, old jobs', *Work and People* 10 (2).

Wall, T., Clegg, C., and Kemp, N. (eds) (1987) *The Human Side of Advanced Manufacturing Technology*, Chichester: Wiley.

Walton, R. E. (1985) 'From control to commitment in the workplace', *Harvard Business Review* 63 (2).

Warner, M. (ed.) (1984) *Microprocessors, Manpower and Society: a Comparative, Cross-national Approach*, Aldershot: Gower.

Warner, M., Wobbe, W., and Brodner, P. (1990) (eds.) *New Technology and Manufacturing Management: Strategic Choices for Flexible Production Systems*, Chichester: Wiley.

Watson, T. J. (1986) *Management, Organisation and Employment Strategy*, London: Routledge.

Whipp, R., and Clark, P. (1986) *Innovation and the Auto Industry*, London: Frances Pinter.

White, G. C. (1983) 'Technological changes and the content of jobs', *Employment Gazette*, August.

Wield, D. (1985) 'The introduction of new manufacturing technologies into Babcock Power Ltd', in E. Rhodes and D. Wield (eds), *Implementing New Technologies*, Oxford: Blackwell.

Wilkinson, B. (1983) *The Shopfloor Politics of New Technology*, London: Heinemann.

Wilkinson, F. (ed.) (1981) *The Dynamics of Labour Market Segmentation*, London: Academic Press.

Willcocks, L., and Mason, D. (1988) 'New technology, human resources and workplace relations – the role of management', *Employee Relations* 10 (6).

Williams, R., and Moseley, R. (1983) 'Technology Agreements: Consensus, Control and Technical Change in the Workplace', paper presented to the EEC/FAST conference 'The Transition to an Information Society', Selsdon Park, London.

Williams, R., and Steward, F. (1985) 'Technology agreements in Great Britain: a survey, 1977–83', *Industrial Relations Journal* 16 (3).

Willman, P., and Winch, G. (1985) *Innovation and Management Control: Labour Relations at BL Cars*, Cambridge: Cambridge University Press.

Willmott, H. (1984) 'Images and ideals of managerial work', *Journal of Management Studies* 21 (3).

Wilson, F. (1988) 'CNC and constraint', in D. Knights and H. Willmott (eds) *New Technology and the Labour Process*, London: Macmillan.

Winch, G. (ed.) (1983) *Information Technology in Manufacturing Processes: Case Studies in Technological Change*, London: Rossendale.

Winterton, J. and R. (1985) *New Technology: the Bargaining Issues*, Occasional Papers in Industrial Relations, Universities of Leeds and Nottingham/Institute of Personnel Management.

Wood, S. (ed.) (1982) *The Degradation of Work? Skill, Deskilling and the Labour Process*, London: Hutchinson.

Wood, S. (ed.) (1989) *The Transformation of Work? Skill, Flexibility and the Labour Process*, London: Unwin Hyman.

Wynne, B. (1984) 'Management autonomy in bargaining and negotiation', in H. J. Otway and M. Peltu (eds), *The Managerial Challenge*, London: Butterworth.

Zimbalist, A. (1979a) 'Technology and the labor process in the printing industry', in A. Zimbalist (ed.), *Case Studies on the Labor Process*, New York: Monthly Review Press.

Zimbalist, A. (ed.) (1979b) *Case Studies on the Labor Process*, New York: Monthly Review Press.

Index

Abbey National 126, 127, 141
Abernathy, W.J. 257
ACARD 241
accountants 86
acquisitions *see* mergers and acquisitions
administrative managers 224–5
adoption content 233–4
adoption phase 1, 4; stages 6–9
adoption processes 234–5; Bramley Building Society 133–6; Don Ltd 182–6; Meadows and Butler 203–8; Park Hill Building Society 164–6
advanced manufacturing technology (AMT) 2, 3, 53; *see also* computer-aided design/drafting (CAD), computer-integrated manufacturing (CIM), computer numerical control (CNC), flexible manufacturing systems, materials requirements planning, robotics
Advisory Conciliation and Arbitration Service (ACAS) 155, 243
AEEU 193
aerospace industry 51, 57
AEU 176, 184, 189, 198, 213
Alliance and Leicester Building Society 128
Angell, I.O. 245
area managers 156, 157
Arnold, E. 242, 243, 244, 248; business and technical objectives 53, 56; competition 43; cost justification 44, 44–5, 48; DCF and investment decisions 59; labour productivity 52; suppliers 82–3
Ashburner, L. 155, 255
Atkinson, J. 54, 243, 244
automated teller machines (ATMs) 3, 128, 130
autonomy: responsible and direct control 34–6; skill and new technology 65, 73

Balmer, J.M. 254
Bamforth, K.W. 252
Banerjee, S.K. 43, 242
banks/banking: competition with building societies 128; culture 141–2; service improvements 57; terms and conditions of employment 104–5; *see also* financial services sector
Bannon, E. 25, 67, 238, 239, 247
bargaining power: de-skilling and 70; international comparison 97–9
Barras, R. 82, 248
Batstone, E. 242, 252
Beirne, M. 112–16, 117–18, 253
Benedetti, C. de 60
Bessant, J. 238, 242, 243, 245, 247, 248, 251; business and technical objectives 53, 55; 'design space' 74–5; labour cost savings 48–9, 49; managerial control 60–1; savings on non-labour costs 43–4; tactical

Index 275

decision making 25, 79–80
BIFU 125–6, 136, 144–5
Birmingham Midshires Building Society 128
Blackler, F. 87, 249, 253
Bloomfield, B.P. 248
Blyton, P. 257
Boddy, D. 236, 237, 240, 241, 243, 247, 248, 255, 257; business and technical objectives 55; differing attitudes to change 80–1; enabling characteristics of new technology 74; financial and economic objectives 42–3; labour cost savings 51; managerial strategies 21; strategic choices 30–1, 234; strategic, operating and control objectives 43, 79
Bødker, S. 253
Boleat, M. 127, 254
Bramley Building Society 123–49, 235; adoption process 134–6; branch office numbers 124; employee involvement 148–9, 225; external context 126–30, 140–3, 227, 228; internal context 123–6, 143–7, 231, 232, 232–3; key developments since 1986/7 140–9; labour reduction 222; objectives 131–3; social and organizational aspects 136–40, 148–9; staff numbers 124; strategy 222–3, 223; technological changes 130–1, 147–8, 229
branch managers: Bramley Building Society 125, 137–8; Park Hill Building Society 156–7
branch on-line terminal systems: Bramley Building Society 123, 130–1; Park Hill Building Society 160–1, 163, 164–6
Braun, E. 242
Braverman, H. 41, 241, 245, 255; control 61; skill 66, 67, 71
British Aerospace 51
British Leyland 28
Brown, C. 87, 249, 253
Buchanan, D. 236, 237, 241, 243, 245, 247, 248, 255, 257; business

and technical objectives 55; competition 42–3; control 60–1; differing attitudes to change 80–1; enabling characteristics of new technology 74; labour cost savings 51; managerial strategies 21; strategic choices 30–1, 234; strategic, operating and control objectives 43, 79
Buffa, E.S. 241
building societies 227; financial services industry environment 126–30, 140–3; *see also* Bramley Building Society, Park Hill Building Society
Building Societies Act 128–9
Building Societies Association 127
Building Societies Commission 129
Building Societies Ombudsman 129
Burawoy, M. 245
Burnes, B. 245
business development managers 146
business objectives 39, 52–60
business strategies *see* corporate/business strategies
Butler, R.J. 237–8

capital saving 43–4
capitalism 61–2
Carrie, A.S. 43, 242
Caterpillar Tractor 42–3, 80–1
Chandler, A.D. 26, 237, 239
'change agents' 7–8
Child, J. 237, 246, 247, 248, 249, 251, 252, 255; consultation 111; manager/staff specialist involvement 87; managerial strategies 77–8; objectives 74, 76; project teams 167; unions 105
choice: 'managerial choice' perspective 62; selection stage 94–5, 106; social 5–6; strategic choices 30–1, 234
Ciba-Geigy 53
Clark, J. 236, 238–9, 243, 245, 248, 250, 251, 252, 256, 257; engineering system 5–6; news-gathering 53; unions 105–6

Clark, P. 9, 26–7, 236, 239, 257
Clegg, C. 24, 76, 238, 248, 249
clerical work 68–70
CoBRA project 147, 148
collective bargaining 103–6, 108, 144–5; *see also* staff associations, trade unions
commitment 34–6
communication: lack of in Bramley Building Society 139–40, 254; Park Hill Building Society 166
Community Charge 211
competition: engineering sector 173; financial services sector 127–8, 140; learning from competitors' mistakes 183; as objective 42–3
compulsory competitive tendering (CCT) 210–11
computer-aided design/drafting (CAD) 3; business and technical objectives 53, 56; cost justification 44–5; Don Ltd 181, 182, 185–6, 193, 229–30; integrative potential 20; labour cost savings 51, 52; Meadows and Butler 199, 201–3, 209–10, 215–16, 216, 230, 234 (adoption process 204–8; financial appraisal 205–6, 209, 218–19); possible benefits 209–10; suppliers 82–3
computer-aided manufacturing (CAM) 20, 203, 215
computer department staff 137, 224–5
computer-integrated manufacturing (CIM) 3, 20, 31, 32, 60–1
computer numerical control (CNC) 3, 53; Don Ltd 176, 181, 181–2, 193, 221, 223 (adoption process 182–5; social and organizational aspects 186–90); flexibility 55; investment appraisal 58–9, 79; managerial control 62–3, 72, 186–90, 256
computer redesign 112–17
consistency 56
consultants, external 78, 125, 153–4, 155

consultation 102–3, 104, 110–11; *see also* employee involvement, staff associations, trade unions
contexts of technology adoption *see* external contexts, internal contexts
control 37; budgetary 50; direct and responsible autonomy 34–6; job redesign and 119; objectives 42, 43, 52, 56, 79 (managerial control 60–4); remote 44; skills and 69–70, 72–3, 74, 221–2
control systems engineers (CSEs) 184
Coombs, R. 238, 248
Cornford, D. 4, 228, 236, 253, 256
corporate/business strategy 21, 22–3, 222–4; Bramley Building Society 148; labour strategy and 36, 144; *see also* managerial strategies
corporate-level decision making 88: Don Ltd 182, 185–6, 219, 229–30; Meadows and Butler 199, 205–8, 230
cost justification 43–52; labour costs 46–52; Meadows and Butler 205–6, 209; non-labour costs 43–6; *see also* financial and economic objectives, investment appraisal
craftsmanship 66
Cray, D. 237–8
Creamer, G. 244–5, 256
Cressey, P. 106, 111, 250, 251, 252, 256; banks/ banking 141–3
Crompton, R. 68–70, 248, 256
culture: banks/banking 141–2; organizational 143–4, 231
Currie, W. 237, 238, 243; budgetary control 50; organizational strategy 21, 21–2
customer orientation 129, 133, 153, 168, 227
customer services managers 146

Daniel, W.W. 89, 101, 242, 249, 250, 251; employee involvement 101–3; employment effects 47

Davies, A. 242, 245, 251, 252, 253; collective bargaining 103–5; objectives 50, 60
Davis, D. 237
Dawson, P. 243
Day, G.S. 237
De Bresson, C. 239
decision making: levels of 88–9, 219–20, 229–30; tactical and strategic 25, 79–80; *see also* corporate-level decision making
design engineers 80
'design in use' 119; *see also* job redesign
de-skilling 63–4, 64–5, 67–8, 70, 71–2; *see also* skills
Devine system 160–1, 163, 164–6
direct control 34–6; *see also* control
direct numerical control (DNC) 53, 62–3
direct sales consultants 146
discounted cash flow (DCF) 59
distributive bargaining 104–5
diversification 128–9
divisional managers 88, 229–30
Dodgson, M. 109, 252
Don Ltd 172–94, 228; adoption process 183–6; control and skill 222; corporate-level decision making 182, 185–6, 219, 229–30; customer orientation 227; employee involvement 225; external context 173, 190–2; grading structure 174–6, 177, 180, 184, 186; internal context 173–81, 192; key developments since 1986/7 190–4; labour flexibility 173–4, 176, 231–2; objectives 181–3, 193; organizational restructuring 177–80; personnel specialists 190, 224, 233; social and organizational aspects 186–91, 193–4; strategy and tactics 222, 223, 223–4; technological changes 180–1, 192, 229
Downing, H. 60, 245

Earl, M. 19–20, 28, 237, 239

Eason, K.D. 249, 253
economic objectives *see* financial and economic objectives
editing CNC machines 176, 186–90
Edwards, P. 249
Edwards, R. 63, 245, 246
efficiency 58–9
Ehn, P. 253
Elger, A. 73, 243, 243–4, 247
emission standards 191
employee involvement 11, 85, 91–120, 224–6; Bramley Building Society 148–9, 225; consultation 110–11; job redesign 111–19; organizational strategy 28–9; unions 92–109
employee representation 232; *see also* staff associations, trade unions
employment: effects of new technology 47; financial services sector 142–3; terms and conditions 105, 176–7
employment relations 33; *see also* industrial relations, labour strategy
energy saving 44
engineering companies: industrial environment 173, 191–2, 210–12; *see also* Don Ltd, Meadows and Butler
engineering specialists: involvement 86, 87–8, 224–5; Meadows and Butler 203, 205–8, 209, 224
engineering system 5–6
enterprise/establishment level management decision making 88–9
ergonomic systems design 113, 114–15
Ettlie, J.E. 28, 239, 240
European Foundation for the Improvement of Living and Working Conditions (EFILWC) 94–100, 106
European legislation 212
evaluation 95, 106–7

external consultants 78, 125, 153–4, 155
external contexts 10–11, 226–30; building societies 126–30, 140–3, 163, 227, 228; corporate/divisional group as context of plant-level operations 229–30; customers 227; Don Ltd 173, 191–2; Meadows and Butler 210–12, 230; suppliers 228–9; technology 229

feasibility/progression stage 7, 8
Fell, A. 198, 256
financial and economic objectives 39, 40–52, 219–21; Don Ltd 182, 220; *see also* cost justification, investment appraisal
financial flexibility 54
financial services sector 126–30, 140–3, 163; *see also* Bramley Building Society, Park Hill Building Society
Fleck, J. 51, 56, 243, 245
flexibility 4–5, 53–6, 74, 194; *see also* labour flexibility
flexible manufacturing systems (FMS) 3; Don Ltd 181, 182, 193, 220, 230
Fogarty, M. 242
Fox, A. 65, 247
Francis, A. 116–17, 254
Friedman, A. 236, 239, 240–2, 245, 247, 253, 256; development of computer systems 4, 228; managerial strategy 26
Frohlich, D. 100, 250, 250–1
fuel-efficiency 191
functional labour flexibility 54, 71, 232; Don Ltd 173–4, 176, 194; Meadows and Butler 214; *see also* skills

Gallie, D. 73, 248
Garrahan, P. 93, 251
Germany, West 42
Gerwin, D. 32, 241
Gill, C. 242, 250, 252, 254; control 256; employee involvement 97–9, 108

GKN Hardy Spicer 91
Goldhar, J.D. 31, 240
Gospel, H.F. 33–4, 237, 240
Gourlay, S. 242, 252
grading structure (Don Ltd) 174–6, 177, 180, 184, 186
Greenhalgh, G.R. 239
Griffiths, C. 32–3, 240
Grindley, P. 239
Guest, D.E. 111, 252
Guest, R.H. 252
Gunter, L. 240
Gustavsen, B. 252

Halifax Building Society 132, 133
Hamilton, R. 239
Harrison, M. 249, 256
Hartman, G. 241, 255
Harvey, J. 252
Hawes, W.R. 242, 249
Hayes, R.H. 240, 256
Hendry, C. 91, 250, 257
Henshall, D. 252
Hickson, D.J. 21, 237–8
Hill, S. 40, 42, 241
Hill, T.J. 29, 30, 240
Hillage, J. 251
Hirscheim, R. 248–9
Hochstrasser, B. 32–3, 240
Hogarth, T. 251
home ownership 127
Hong Kong and Shanghai Bank 141
Hopwood, A.G. 76, 76–7, 248
Huczynski, A. 236
human resource management (HRM) 144, 194, 233

implementation: employee involvement and 94–5, 97, 106–7, 111; of objectives and strategies 79–83
Incomes Data Services (IDS) 243
incremental innovation 182–3
industrial relations 33; international comparison of systems 97–9; *see also* labour strategies
information technology (IT) 2, 3; Bramley Building Society 123,

Index 279

130–1, 147–8; business and technical objectives 53; Don Ltd 193; economic and financial objectives 46; levels in design of information systems 75; managerial strategies 19–20, 32–3, 37; Meadows and Butler 199, 199–201, 203–4, 216–17; Park Hill Building Society 159–62, 163, 164–6, 170–1; social and organizational objectives 60; *see also* branch on-line terminal systems, mainframes, microcomputers, minicomputers, personal computers
initiation stage 7, 7–8
Institute of Manpower Studies 77, 107
insurance companies 51–2, 82, 128; *see also* financial services sector
integrative bargaining 104–5
integrative potential 20, 31, 43
internal contexts 10–11, 231–4; Bramley Building Society 123–6, 143–7, 231, 232, 232–3; Don Ltd 173- 81, 192–3; labour flexibility 232–3; managerial style and employee representation 23; Meadows and Butler 195–8, 212–15, 231, 232, 233; Park Hill Building Society 150–8, 168–9, 231, 232; personnel management 232–3
introduction phase 6–7
inventory and production control system (IPCS) 199, 199–201, 203–4, 216–17
investment appraisal 58–60, 218–20; Don Ltd 181–2, 219; Meadows and Butler 205–8, 218–19; *see also* cost justification, financial and economic objectives
investment decision 7, 8
investments department, merger with mortgages department 151–3
investment proposals 214–15
involvement *see* employee involvement, managers' involvement, staff specialists

Jacobs, A. 243
Jelinek, M. 31, 240
job redesign 111–19
Jones, A. 20, 237
Jones, B. 37, 238, 241, 247, 252, 253–4, 256; de-skilling 67–8; managerial strategies 23
Jones, G. 68–70, 247, 255

Kammersgaard, J. 253
Kaplan, R.S. 244, 245
Keen, P. 78, 248
Kelly, J. 23, 238, 253
Kemp, N. 24, 238, 249
Kerfoot, D. 141, 254
Kimberly, J.R. 20, 237
King, R. 6, 236, 243, 245, 251
Knights, D. 141, 255
Kraft, P. 68, 248
Krieger, H. 97–9, 100, 250, 250–1, 252
Kyng, M. 252

labour cost savings 44, 45, 46–52, 220–1; Bramley Building Society 138, 254; Meadows and Butler 213, 254; Park Hill Building Society 154
labour flexibility 54, 231–2; control and skill 74; Don Ltd 173–4, 176, 232–3; Meadows and Butler 214, 232
labour productivity 52
Labour Research Department 107
labour strategies 23–4, 33–7, 116, 222–4; Bramley Building Society 138–40; Don Ltd 173–7; Meadows and Butler 212–14; Park Hill Building Society 153–5; rationality 77–8
Lannon, R. 239
learning, organizational 183, 185–6
Lee, D. 66, 71, 246, 247
Lee, G.L. 87–8, 249
Legge, K. 89–91, 249–50, 256
Leonard, R. 244–5, 256
Littler, C.R. 65, 66, 237, 245, 246

local authorities (LAs) 210–11
Love, J.H. 24, 238
Loveridge, R. 11, 37, 238, 241, 252

MacInnes, J. 243, 244
mainframe computers: Bramley Building Society 130; Park Hill Building Society 159–60
maintenance staff 183–4
Mallory, G.R. 237–8
management consultants 78
management information systems 75
management levels: decision making 88–9, 220–1, 229–30; differing attitudes to change 80–1
management style 232; international comparison 97–9
'managerial choice' perspective 62
managerial control 60–4; *see also* control
managerial processes 226–35; adoption content 233–4; adoption processes 234–5; external contexts 226–31; internal contexts 231–4
managerial strategies 17–38, 222–4; Don Ltd 189–91; evidence for 23–5; labour *see* labour strategies; organizational level 26–9; rationality 77–9; reasons for 19–23; technology level 29–33
manufacturing strategy 29–32,
managers' involvement 85, 86–91, 164–6; *see also* engineering specialists, personnel specialists, staff specialists, training specialists
Mansfield, R. 237
manufacturing flexibility 55
manufacturing strategy 29–32, 222–4; *see also* Don Ltd, Meadows and Butler
Manwaring, T. 71, 248
Marchington, M. 11, 238
Marginson, P. 250
marketing/selling 129, 133, 168, 227
Marsden, D. 23–4, 34–5, 35–6, 238, 241

Martin, R. 109, 249, 251, 252, 257; levels of decision making 88
Marxist tradition 41
Mason, D. 250
material saving 44
materials requirements planning (MRP) 3, 200; *see also* inventory and production control system
McLoughlin, I. 237, 238–9, 245, 248, 251; engineering system 6; managerial strategy 78
Meadows and Butler 195–217, 227, 228; adoption process 203–8; CAD *see* computer-aided design; control and skill 221; corporate-level influence 230; employee involvement 224, 225–6; external context 210–12, 230; internal context 195–8, 212–15, 231, 232, 233; investment climate 220–1; IPCS 199, 199–201, 203–4, 216–17; key developments since 1986/7 210–17; objectives 199–203; social and organizational aspects 209–10, 216–17; strategy 225; technological changes 198–9, 215–16, 230
Meager, N. 243, 244, 251
mergers and acquisitions: building societies 127, 128, 140–1; engineering industry 191–2
microcomputers 3, 130–1, 160; 'one per desk' (OPD) 161–2; *see also* branch on-line terminal systems
Midland Bank 141
Millward, N. 101–3, 243, 250, 251, 252
minicomputers 3, 160; *see also* branch on-line terminal systems
Morris, T. 239
mortgages 127, 127–8, 133, 151–3
Moseley, R. 107–8, 243, 253
motor industry 34–5, 35–6
Motteram, G. 49, 243
MSF 193

Index 281

multi-skilling *see* functional labour flexibility
Mumford, E. 112, 117, 253

Nahapiet, J.E. 46, 243
National Computing Centre 244
National Economic Development Office (NEDO) 110–11, 252
National Union of Banking Employees (NUBE) 125, 155
negotiation 96–7; *see also* consultation, employee involvement
network committee 164–5
new technology agreements (NTAs) 107–8, 135
news-gathering 53
Nicholas, I. 241, 255
Nissan 93
Noble, D.F. 71–3, 247, 255
Northcott, J. 36, 241
numerical control (NC) 51; differing attitudes to 80–1; Don Ltd 176, 181, 186–8; skill and control 67–8, 71–2; *see also* computer numerical control, direct numerical control
numerical labour flexibility 54, 232

Oakland, J. 237
objectives 31–2, 39–84, 218–22; Bramley Building Society 131–3; business and technical 39, 52–60; Don Ltd 181–3, 193; employee involvement 97–9; financial and economic *see* financial and economic objectives; implementing 79–83; Meadows and Butler 199–203; Park Hill Building Society 162–4, 220; in practice 75–6; rationality 76–9; social and organizational 39, 60–74, 220–2; variety of 74–5
occupational groups 50–1, 77, 80–1
Ohmae, K. 238

on-line branch terminal systems *see* branch on-line terminal systems
'one per desk' microcomputers (OPD) 161–2
open systems environment 147–8, 169, 170, 225
operating objectives 43, 79
operator programming 71–2, 187–90, 256
organization and methods (O&M) function 153–4
organizational aspects *see* social and organizational aspects
organizational change 101–2, 111
organizational design 113, 114–15
organizational learning 183, 185–6
organizational politics 113–16; *see also* politics, internal
organizational strategy 18–19, 26–9, 222–4; *see also* managerial strategies
organizational structure: Bramley Building Society 145–6; Don Ltd 177–80; Meadows and Butler 197; Park Hill Building Society 151–3, 169
output 173, 184, 192

Park Hill Building Society 150–71; adoption process 164–6; branch managers' changing role 156–7; branch office numbers 150–1; branch office terminal system 160–1, 163, 164–6; employee involvement 225; external context 163, 227, 228; internal context 150–8, 168–9, 231, 232; key developments since 1986/7 168–71; labour utilization/composition 153–5; mainframe computer 159–60; objectives 162–4, 220; 'one per desk' microcomputers 161–2; project teams 153–4, 157–8, 165–6, 167–8, 170; social and organizational aspects 166–8, 170–1; staff association 155–6,

166–7, 169, 231; staff numbers 150–1, 152, 154; strategy 222–3; technological changes 158–62, 169–70, 229
passive user involvement 113, 114–15
Pavitt, K. 239, 239–40
pay-back method 205–6
personal computers (PCs) 3; Bramley Building Society 148; Meadows and Butler 215, 216; Park Hill Building Society 169–70
personnel specialists 89–91, 224–5, 232–3; Bramley Building Society 135–6, 144, 233–4; Don Ltd 190, 224, 233; Park Hill Building Society 165–6, 223, 232
Peters, T.J. 237
Pettigrew, A. 10, 91, 236, 257
Pirelli Cables 91
Pitt, M. 37, 241
planning: employee involvement 94–5, 97, 106; and systems design 7, 8–9
Plessey 25–6
Policy Studies Institute 56, 244
politics, internal 22–3, 113–16, 229–30, 234–5; objectives 219–20; organizational strategy 27–8; savings on costs 46; *see also* employee involvement, industrial relations, labour strategies
Pollert, A. 243, 244
Porter, M.E. 29, 237, 239
Preece, D.A. 236, 243, 246, 247, 249, 250, 253, 255, 256; personnel specialists 91
Price, P. 254
Primrose, P.L. 60, 209–10, 244–5, 256
process engineers 183, 185, 187–90
product improvements 56–7, 211–12
productivity, labour 52
products, as new technology 2, 3

profitability 40–2
programming CNC machines 176, 186–90, 256
progression/feasibility stage 7, 8
project teams 153–4, 157–8, 165–6, 167–8, 170
public limited company (PLC) status 129
Pugh, J. 252
Purcell, J. 249, 254

quality 56–8, 194

Rajan, A. 127, 251, 254
Ramsay, H. 112–16, 117–18, 253
rationality 46, 76–9
redundancy 47
refuse disposal market 210–12
regional managers 156
regulation 97–9, 212
remote control 44
resistance 64, 100; consultation and 111; control and skills 70–1; managers 86–7
re-skilling 73; *see also* skills
responsible autonomy 34–6
Rhodes, E. 256
Richards, A. 238
robotics 3, 51, 56
Rolfe, H. 247
Rose, H. 236, 238–9, 243, 245, 248, 251; engineering system 6
Rose, M. 23, 238, 252
Rosenbrock, H.H. 245
Rothwell, S. 23, 24, 238, 249
Rush, H. 107, 251
Russia 192

savings: labour 46–52; non-labour 43–6
savings rates 127–8
Scandinavia 118
Scarbrough, H. 27–8, 239
Schonberger, R.J. 240
Scott, P. 142–3, 255
selection stage 94–5, 106
Sell, R.G. 56, 245
selling/marketing 129, 133, 168, 227

Senker, P. 242, 243, 246, 248, 256; business and technical objectives 53, 56; competition 43; cost justification 44–5, 48; skills 67; suppliers 82–3
service improvements 57–8, 132–3, 163
service provision 2, 3
Sewell, G. 35, 90, 241, 246, 250
Shaiken, H. 245
Shaw, W.N. 24, 238
short-term contracts 174
'single-entry' key stroking 131, 160
single-union agreements 92, 93
Sisson, K. 250
Sizer, J. 49, 243
skills 52, 64–74; Bramley Building Society 146; control and 69–70, 72–3, 74, 221–2; Don Ltd 185, 187; Meadows and Butler 203; Park Hill Building Society 170; polarization 68–9
Skinner, W. 29–30, 240
Smart, D. 242, 249
Smith, C. 243, 244, 248; aerospace industry 51, 57, 80
Smith, S. 247
Smithson, S. 245
social choice 5–6
social and organizational aspects 20–2, 226–35; adoption content 233–4; adoption processes 234–5; Bramley Building Society 136–40, 148–9; Don Ltd 186–91, 194; external contexts 227–31; internal contexts 231–4; Meadows and Butler 209–10, 216–17; objectives 39, 60–74, 220–2 (*see also* control, skills); Park Hill Building Society 166–8, 170–1
social status 65–6
socio-technical design 113, 114–15
Sorge, A. 241, 244, 247, 248, 255; autonomy 73; flexibility 55; justification of CNC 59; managerial strategies 78–9; training 42
space saving 44
Speed, R. 254

Spencer, A. 78, 248, 252
staff associations 226; Bramley Building Society 124–6, 135, 136, 136–7, 138, 139, 144; Park Hill Building Society 155–6, 166–7, 169, 231; *see also* trade unions
staff specialists 85, 86–91; Park Hill Building Society 164–6; *see also* computer department staff, engineering specialists, personnel specialists, training specialists
status, social 65–6
Staunton, N. 257
Stevens, M. 242, 249, 251
Steward, F. 252
Stewart, P. 93, 250
Storey, J. 239, 241, 243, 245, 248, 250, 252; 'locking into' technology 82; managerial strategy 36, 78; objectives 51–2; personnel specialists 91
strategic alliances 128
strategic choices 30–1, 234
strategic innovation 26–7
strategic objectives 31, 43, 79
strategy *see* corporate/business strategy, labour strategies, managerial strategies, organizational strategies
structural flexibility 54–5
subcontracting 174, 193
sub-strategies 25–6, 78, 239
Sundblad, Y. 253
suppliers 82–3, 228–9
Swabe, A.I.R. 254
Swann, J. 82, 248
Symon, G. 76, 248
systems design, planning and 7, 8–9
systems rationalization 112–17

tactical decision making 25, 79–80
tape production/editing, CNC 186–90
Tarondeau, J.C. 32, 240
task range 65
TASS 176, 186, 194
Taylorism 86, 116, 187
teams, project 153–4, 157–8,

165–6, 167–8, 170
technical control 63
technical flexibility 55
technical objectives 39, 52–60
technocentric design 113, 114–15
technological changes: Bramley Building Society 130–1, 147–8, 229; Don Ltd 181, 193, 229; Meadows and Butler 198–9, 215–16, 229; Park Hill Building Society 158–62, 169–70, 229
technological trajectories 29
technology level strategies 29–33
terms and conditions of employment 105, 176–7
Thompson, P. 238, 239, 245, 246, 246–7, 247, 255; managerial strategies 25; skills 64–5, 67, 70
Thurley, K. 18, 25, 237
time flexibility 54
trade unions 111; Bramley Building Society 125–6; Don Ltd 176–7, 194; employee involvement 92–109; job redesign 117, 119; Meadows and Butler 198, 213–14; *see also* staff associations
Trades Union Congress (TUC) 104, 105, 251
training 129–30, 165, 194; West German and British compared 42
training specialists: Bramley Building Society 135–6, 140; Don Ltd 180, 225
Trevor, M. 241
Tricker, R.I. 75, 247–8
Trist, E.L. 252
Turnbull, P. 257
Turner, A.N. 252
Twiss, B.C. 249
Tyson, S. 198, 256

unions *see* trade unions
United Biscuits 53
UTOPIA project 118

vehicle market 210–12

Venture Pressings 91
Voss, C.A. 81, 240, 248

Wainwright, J. 116–17, 253
Walker, C.R. 252
Walker, J. 24, 238
Walton, R.E. 241
Warner, M. 241, 255
Waterman, R.H. 237
Webb, J. 243
Webb, T. 20, 237
Weir, M. 252
Wheelwright, S.C. 240
Whipp, R. 9, 26–7, 236, 239
White, G.C. 51, 53, 56, 243, 244
Wield, D. 256
Wilkinson, A. 254
Wilkinson, B. 241, 242, 243, 244, 246, 247, 250, 251, 254, 255; CNC programming 256; control 35, 44, 52, 63–4; employee involvement 106–7; justification of CNC 58–9; personnel specialists 90; skills 71
Willcocks, L. 249
Williams, R. 107, 107–8, 250, 251, 252
Willman, P. 238, 239, 241, 251; collective bargaining 105; managerial strategy 28, 35–6
Wilson, D.C. 238
Wilson, F. 247
Winch, G. 28, 35–6, 239, 241
women 154–5
Wood, S. 237, 238, 245, 247; managerial strategy 18, 23, 25; skills 71
work relations 33; *see also* industrial relations, labour strategies
worker resistance *see* resistance
Workplace Industrial Relations Surveys (WIRS) 47, 89, 90, 100, 102, 223
works committee 198
Wright Mills, C. 66, 246

Zimbalist, A. 246, 246, 255